WINDOWS® 7
FOR SENIORS
QuickSteps™

About the Author

Marty Matthews has used computers for over 40 years, from some of the early mainframe computers to recent personal computers. He has done this as a programmer, systems analyst, manager, vice president, and president of a software firm. As a result, he has firsthand knowledge of not only how to program and use a computer, but also how to make the best use of all that can be done with a computer.

Thirty years ago, Marty wrote his first computer book on how to buy minicomputers. Twenty-seven years ago, Marty and his wife Carole began writing books as a major part of their occupation. In the intervening years, they have written more than 70 books, including ones on desktop publishing, web publishing, Microsoft Office, and Microsoft operating systems—from MS-DOS through Windows 7. Recent books published by McGraw-Hill include *Computing for Seniors QuickSteps, Windows 7 QuickSteps,* and *Microsoft Office 2010 QuickSteps.*

Marty and Carole live on an island in Puget Sound in Washington State.

About the Technical Editor

John Cronan has over 30 years of computer experience and has been writing and editing computer-related books for 20 years. His recent books include *eBay QuickSteps, Second Edition, Microsoft Office Excel 2010 QuickSteps,* and *Microsoft Office Access 2010 QuickSteps.* John and Faye (and cat Little Buddy) reside in Everett, Washington.

WINDOWS® 7 FOR SENIORS

QuickSteps™

MARTY MATTHEWS

New York Chicago San Francisco
Lisbon London Madrid Mexico City
Milan New Delhi San Juan
Seoul Singapore Sydney Toronto

The McGraw·Hill Companies

Cataloging-in-Publication Data is on file with the Library of Congress

McGraw-Hill books are available at special quantity discounts to use as premiums and sales promotions, or for use in corporate training programs. To contact a representative, please e-mail us at bulksales@mcgraw-hill.com.

Trademarks: McGraw-Hill, the McGraw-Hill Publishing logo, QuickSteps™, and related trade dress are trademarks or registered trademarks of The McGraw-Hill Companies and/or its affiliates in the United States and other countries and may not be used without written permission. All other trademarks are the property of their respective owners. The McGraw-Hill Companies is not associated with any product or vendor mentioned in this book.

Information has been obtained by McGraw-Hill from sources believed to be reliable. However, because of the possibility of human or mechanical error by our sources, McGraw-Hill, or others, McGraw-Hill does not guarantee the accuracy, adequacy, or completeness of any information and is not responsible for any errors or omissions or the results obtained from the use of such information.

WINDOWS® 7 FOR SENIORS QUICKSTEPS™

1234567890   QDB QDB   10987654321

ISBN   978-0-07-176805-4
MHID   0-07-176805-X

SPONSORING EDITOR / Roger Stewart

EDITORIAL SUPERVISOR / Patty Mon

PROJECT MANAGER / Vasundhara Sawhney, Glyph International

ACQUISITIONS COORDINATOR / Joya Anthony

TECHNICAL EDITOR / John Cronan

COPY EDITOR / Lisa McCoy

PROOFREADER / Susie Elkind

INDEXER / Valerie Perry

PRODUCTION SUPERVISOR / Jean Bodeaux

COMPOSITION / Glyph International

ILLUSTRATION / Glyph International

ART DIRECTOR, COVER / Jeff Weeks

COVER DESIGNER / Pattie Lee

SERIES CREATORS / Marty and Carole Matthews

SERIES DESIGN / Bailey Cunningham

**Page Gilbert-Baennen
and Tom Baennen**

Long-time close friends
who have been both an inspiration
and a great help in creating this book.
Thanks, Page and Tom, for all you do for us!

Contents at a Glance

Contents

1

2

5

6

7

Chapter 8 **Creating Documents and Pictures** 191

Chapter 9 **Using Applications** 219

10

Acknowledgments

This book is a team effort of truly talented people. Among them are:

John Cronan, technical editor, corrected many errors, added many tips and notes, and greatly improved the book. John is also a good friend and an author in his own right. Thanks, John!

Lisa McCoy, copy editor, added to the readability and understandability of the book while always being a joy to work with. Thanks, Lisa!

Valerie Perry, indexer, who adds so much to the usability of the book, and does so quickly and with much thought. Thanks, Valerie!

Patty Mon and **Vasundhara Sawhney**, editorial supervisor and project manager, greased the wheels and straightened the track to make a smooth production process. Thanks, Patty and Vas!

Roger Stewart, sponsoring editor, believed in us enough to sell the series and continues to stand behind us as we add more books. Thanks, Roger!

Carole Matthews, partner in life, partner in work, partner in our parenting adventure. Thank you for sharing all this with me. I love you, Carole!

Introduction

Most of my friends and acquaintances are seniors, as I am, and I have spent a fair amount of time helping them get comfortable with computers in general and Windows 7 in particular. This book is written for them in a voice without jargon using relevant examples in clear, step-by-step instructions. This book zeroes in on only the most important topics and uses brief instructions in plain language with many color visuals to clearly lead the reader through the steps necessary to perform a task. In addition, a group of fellow seniors have added their comments in "QuickQuotes" about what is being discussed to provide personalized input on a topic.

QuickSteps™ books are recipe books for computer users. They answer the question "how do I..." by providing a quick set of steps to accomplish the most common tasks with a particular operating system or application.

The sets of steps are the central focus of the book. QuickSteps sidebars show how to quickly perform many small functions or tasks that support the primary functions. Notes, Tips, and Cautions augment the steps, and are presented in a separate column so as not to interrupt the flow of the steps. The introductions are minimal, and other narrative is kept brief. Numerous full-color illustrations and figures, many with callouts, support the steps.

QuickSteps™ books are organized by function and the tasks needed to perform that function. Each function is a chapter. Each task, or "How To," contains the steps needed for accomplishing the function, along with the relevant Notes, Tips, Cautions, and screenshots. You can easily find the tasks you want to perform through:

- The table of contents, which lists the functional areas (chapters) and tasks in the order they are presented

- A How To list of tasks on the opening page of each chapter

- The index, which provides an alphabetical list of the terms that are used to describe the functions and tasks

- Color-coded tabs for each chapter or functional area, with an index to the tabs in the Contents at a Glance (just before the table of contents)

Conventions Used
in This Book

Windows 7 for Seniors QuickSteps uses several conventions designed to make the book easier for you to follow. Among these are:

- A 🔍 or a 🪐 in the table of contents or the How To list in each chapter references a QuickSteps or QuickFacts sidebar in a chapter.

- **Bold type** is used for words on the screen that you are to do something with, like "…click the **File** menu, and click **Save As**."

- *Italic type* is used for a word or phrase that deserves special emphasis.

- ***Italic bold type*** is used for a word or phrase that is being defined.

- <u>Underlined type</u> is used for text that you are to type from the keyboard.

- SMALL CAPITAL LETTERS are used for keys on the keyboard, such as ENTER and SHIFT.

- When you are expected to enter a command, you are told to press the key(s). If you are to enter text or numbers, you are told to type them.

How to...

Chapter 1

Getting Started with Windows 7

Most of us seniors cannot imagine life without a phone. How do you summon aid or keep in contact with your family without it? Our children, and especially grandchildren, can't imagine life without a computer, and even that is being supplemented or replaced with a smart phone, really just a computer in a very small package. Today, a computer is highly desirable for a large number of functions, especially communications, but including shopping, banking, investing, photography, music, research, genealogy, and game playing, to name just a few. The majority of computers are controlled by the Microsoft Windows operating system, of which its latest version is Windows 7. This book is dedicated to helping you, a senior, get the most out of Windows 7 and your computer.

If you are just starting out with Windows 7, it is likely that you also have a new computer, so we want to begin by looking at your computer and seeing what you have available to you and how to use it. Then we'll start your computer and look at Windows 7, explore what it is and does, and how you use it. The purpose of this chapter is to help you understand what it is that you have in your computer and how to get started using it. Many of the subjects in the chapter will be expanded upon in future chapters.

Look at Your Computer

A *computer* is any device that can store and then execute a series of instructions, called a *program*, to produce some useful result. There are many different types of computers, from devices in your car, cell phones, and music players to the mainframe and supercomputers that fill a room. In this book, when we say "computer" we are talking about personal computers or *PCs* that generally one person uses at a time, and in particular, PCs that run Windows 7.

Review the Types of Personal Computers

There are a variety of Windows 7 computers, all with pretty much the same components, which have the ability to perform the same functions and run the same programs. These generally fall into three types (see Figure 1-1):

- **Portable computers**, such as netbook, notebook, and laptop computers, in which all the components of the computer are in a single case that can be closed and, more or less, easily carried around.

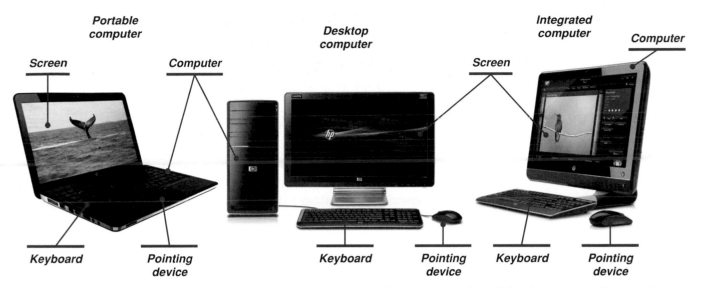

Portable computer

Screen   Computer

Desktop computer

Integrated computer   Computer

Screen

Keyboard   Pointing device

Keyboard   Pointing device

Keyboard   Pointing device

Figure 1-1: All personal computers have the same components. Here are examples of the three types of computers from Hewlett-Packard (HP), their Pavilion DV5 notebook, Pavilion 600 desktop, and All-in-One (AiO) 200 integrated computers. (Images courtesy of HP ©1994–2010 Hewlett-Packard Company. All Rights Reserved.)

- **Desktop computers** in which the keyboard, mouse, and screen are separate from the rest of the computer. Desktop computers are generally larger and heavier, and with the separate components, they are not very portable. They can be, but aren't always, faster and more powerful than the other types of computers.

- **Integrated computers** in which the screen and the rest of the computer are in a single case, but the keyboard and mouse are still separate, making the computer not very portable.

Identify the Parts of Your Computer

Independent of the type computer, all have the same set of six primary external components, four of which are shown in Figure 1-1:

- The **computer** itself processes what is entered on the keyboard, pointed to by the mouse, read from a disc, or received from the Internet, and then displayed on the screen.
- The **screen** displays information from the computer.
- The **keyboard** transmits typed information from you to the computer.
- A **pointing device**, such as a mouse, allows you to point to and select objects on the screen.
- An **optical disc** drive reads information, music, or videos contained on either a CD (compact disc) or a DVD (digital video disc) into the computer.
- **Connecting receptacles** allow you to connect other devices to a computer, such as a printer, a camera, an external hard drive, a sound system, or a TV.

In addition, all computers have four or five major internal components and many other minor components.

- The **central processing unit**, or CPU, does all the real work of the computer, and the technology behind its intelligence is the reason that the huge computers we knew "back in the day," which took up the square footage of half a football field, now can fit in a small space on your desk.
- **Memory** is used to temporarily store information that the computer is using while it is turned on. When you turn the computer off, the contents of the memory disappear.
- The **hard disk** is a rotating magnetic disk within your computer that is used to store both programs and information on your computer that you want stored for longer periods. The information on a hard disk remains intact when you turn your computer off.

TIP

You don't need to know much about the internal components, just that they are there performing their stated functions.

The hard disk is used to store information you write, pictures you take, your email address list, your financial records, and many other pieces of information you don't want to lose.

- **Flash memory** is solid-state memory like regular memory, but it retains its contents when the power is turned off. Flash memory is common in small, chewing-gum-package-size "sticks" that plug into a USB (Universal Serial Bus) receptacle and are called USB flash drives. Increasingly, you can buy larger amounts of flash memory that are permanently mounted in the computer to supplement or even replace the hard disk.

- The **motherboard** is used to plug in the CPU and memory and to connect to the hard disk and various external components. It is the central connecting device joining all of the computer's components.

Use Your Computer

The exact way that a computer is used depends on the computer. Determining this requires that you refer to the information that came with the computer. Here are some general rules of thumb for using a computer:

- **Start the computer** by quickly pressing and releasing a power button, one of which is shown in Figure 1-2, and most of which have a symbol similar to the one shown.

- **Stop the computer** by indicating to the operating system that you want to do so, as explained in the next section. In a real emergency you often can stop the computer by pressing and holding down the power button. This can be dangerous, however, since if you have not saved the information that is in memory, you will lose it. If you use the operating system to shut down, you will be reminded to save information in memory.

- **Insert a disc in an optical drive** by opening the drive. There is normally a button or area that you press to do this. The button is often located on the drive, to its right, or below the drive. When the drive

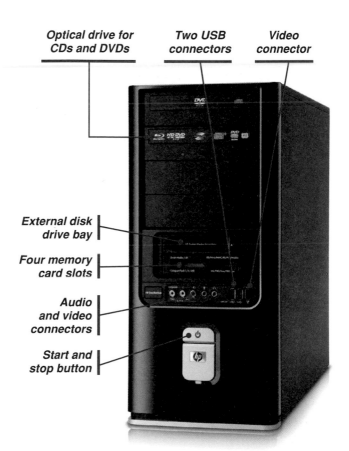

Optical drive for CDs and DVDs　**Two USB connectors**　**Video connector**

External disk drive bay

Four memory card slots

Audio and video connectors

Start and stop button

Figure 1-2: *A computer may have a few or many connectors into which you can plug external devices such as printers, cameras, and other devices. (Image courtesy of HP ©1994–2010 Hewlett-Packard Company. All Rights Reserved.)*

is open, handle a disc only by its edges or center and place it in the tray that has opened. Then press the button again or gently press the front of the open tray to close it. After a minute or two you should see some instructions appear on the screen telling you what to do next, as described in the following section.

- **Connect a printer** or other device to the computer. Most printers and many other devices connect to a computer using a USB connector, shown in Figure 1-2, into which a cable from the printer or other device is inserted. In addition to USB connectors, your computer may have slots for memory cards used in cameras and other devices, as well as connectors for audio, video, and external hard disks. These connecting receptacles can be on the front, back, and/or sides of a computer. Your computer instructions will describe these to you.

Explore Windows 7

We said that a computer is a device that stores and executes a set of instructions. Windows 7 is the foundation set of instructions, the main program that is executed on your computer. The Windows 7 program is called an *operating system*, and performs *the* central role in managing what a computer does and how it is done. An operating system provides the interface between you and the computer hardware: it facilitates your running other programs, such as Microsoft Word, storing a file, printing a document, connecting to the Internet, or retrieving information from a CD without you knowing anything about how the hardware works.

Start and Use Windows 7

To start Windows, you need only to turn on the computer. When you do, you'll see a screen with features similar to Figure 1-3.

NOTE

The desktop image on your screen can be virtually any image you want it to be. Computer manufacturers generally ship a computer with an image of their own, but you can select a different one for yourself. The background image in Figure 1-3 is a favorite photo of mine looking west across Admiralty Inlet toward the Olympic Peninsula from Whidbey Island in Washington State.

The desktop is used for windows, dialog boxes, and icons

The Recycle Bin icon opens a folder of deleted files

Desktop icon for a program you can run, or a file or folder you can open

The Start button opens the Start menu

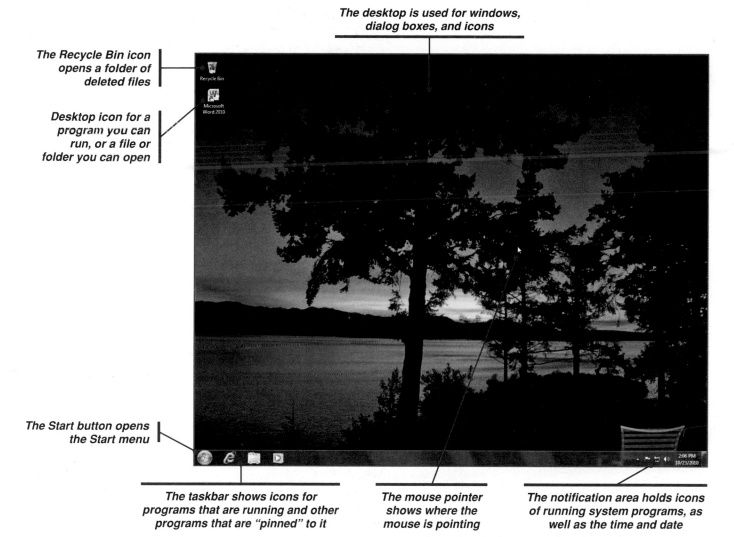

The taskbar shows icons for programs that are running and other programs that are "pinned" to it

The mouse pointer shows where the mouse is pointing

The notification area holds icons of running system programs, as well as the time and date

Figure 1-3: When you have started Windows 7, your screen should have the main features shown here, but with a different background image.

QUICK**FACTS**

UNDERSTANDING THE MOUSE

- **Highlight an** *object* (a button, an icon, a border, etc.) on the screen by pointing to it. *Point* at an object on the screen by moving the mouse until the tip of the pointer is on top of the object.

- **Select an object on the screen** by clicking it. *Click* means to point at an object you want to select and quickly press and release the left mouse button.

- **Open an object or start a program** by double-clicking it. *Double-click* means to point at an object you want to select and press and release the mouse button twice in rapid succession.

- **Open a context menu**, which allows you to do things specific to an object, by right-clicking it. *Right-click* means to point at an object and quickly press and release the right mouse button.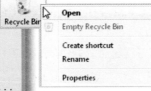

Continued . . .

USE THE MOUSE

In this book, for simplicity, we'll call any pointing device—including a touch pad, trackballs, pointing sticks, and graphic tablets—with two or more buttons a *mouse*. (We also assume you are using a two-button mouse.) Moving the mouse moves the pointer on the screen. You *select* an object on the screen by moving the pointer so that it is on top of the object and then pressing the left button on the mouse.

You can control the mouse with either your left or right hand; therefore, the buttons may be switched. This book assumes you are using your right hand to control the mouse and that the left mouse button is "the mouse button." The right button is always called the "right mouse button." If you switch the buttons, you must change your interpretation of these phrases.

I have found that many left-handed people, including myself, use the mouse with their right hand. It saves having to change the mouse buttons, and some mice are designed exclusively for the right hand.

USE THE SCREEN

The Windows 7 screen can hold windows and other objects. In its simplest form, shown in Figure 1-3, you see a background scene, a bar at the bottom with a button on the left and the time and date on the right, and some icons in the upper left.

The parts of a screen are

- The **desktop**, which takes up most of the screen.

- The **Start button** in the lower-left area, which opens the Start menu.

- The **taskbar** across the bottom, which identifies programs that are running or "pinned" to it.

- The **notification area** in the lower-right area, which holds icons of running system programs.

UNDERSTANDING THE MOUSE
(Continued)

- **Move an object on the screen** by dragging it. *Drag* means to point at an object you want to move, then press and hold the mouse button while moving the mouse. You will drag the object as you move the mouse. When the object is where you want it, release the mouse button.

UNDERSTANDING THE NOTIFICATION AREA

The *notification area* on the right of the taskbar contains the icons of special programs and system features, as well as the time and date.

- **Show hidden icons** by clicking the up arrow to see the icons of hidden programs and then click any you wish to open.

- **Open a system feature** by clicking one of the icons in the middle (between the Show Hidden Icons arrow and the Time/Date icon) to open a system feature.

- Set the time and date by clicking the time and date area to see a calendar and an analog clock, then click **Change Date And Time Settings** (see related Note on the next page).

Continued . . .

- **Desktop icons**, which can be in any number and anywhere on the desktop, are in the upper-left area of Figure 1-3. Desktop icons are used to start programs or open files or folders.

- The **mouse pointer**, which can be anywhere on the screen.

USE THE DESKTOP

The *desktop* is the entire screen, except for the bar at the bottom. Windows, dialog boxes, and icons, such as the Recycle Bin, are displayed on the desktop. You can store *shortcuts*, which are icons to load your favorite programs, on the desktop. You can drag windows, dialog boxes, files, and icons around the desktop. Double-click an icon on the desktop to open it.

USE A DESKTOP ICON

A *desktop icon* represents a program or folder that can be started or opened and moved about the screen. For example, the Recycle Bin is a desktop icon for a folder that contains all of the files that have been deleted since the Recycle Bin was last emptied. Double-click a desktop icon to open or start what it refers to.

USE THE MOUSE POINTER

The *mouse pointer*, or simply the *pointer* or *mouse*, shows where the mouse is pointing. Move the mouse to move the pointer.

USE THE TASKBAR

The *taskbar* at the bottom of the screen contains the active *tasks*, which are icons and titles of the programs that are available or running on the computer or folders that are open. The taskbar also holds the Start button on the left and the notification area on the right. Click a program on the taskbar to open it.

Open the Start Menu

The *Start button*, on the left of the taskbar, or just "Start," opens the Start menu when clicked. This provides you with primary access to

UNDERSTANDING THE NOTIFICATION AREA *(Continued)*

- **Show the desktop** by clicking the far right of the taskbar in an unmarked rectangular area, which, if you click in it, will minimize all open windows and dialog boxes and display the desktop (click it again to have the objects reappear on the desktop).

NOTE

If you are connected to the Internet, you should never need to set your time and date, even when changing to or from Daylight Saving Time, because Windows automatically synchronizes your computer's time with a local time server.

NOTE

The icons you have in the notification area will depend on the programs and processes you have running and the system features you have available. The icons shown here include system messages, which opens the Action Center, ![icon], Network, which opens the Network And Sharing Center ![icon], and Speakers, which allows you to control the sound from your computer ![icon]. In a laptop or notebook computer you probably have two additional icons: Power ![icon] and Wireless ![icon].

the programs, utilities, and settings that are available in Windows. To open the Start menu:

1. Point at the Start button by moving the pointer so that it is over the Start button. You will see that the button changes color. When this happens, the button is said to be highlighted.

2. Press and release the left mouse button (given that your mouse buttons have not been switched to accommodate left-handers) while the pointer is on the Start button. The Start menu will open, as you can see in Figure 1-4.

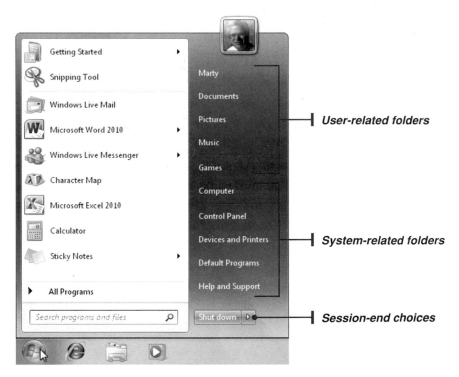

Figure 1-4: The Start menu provides access to the programs, utilities, and settings in Windows.

NOTE

Your taskbar may have more or fewer objects than those shown here:

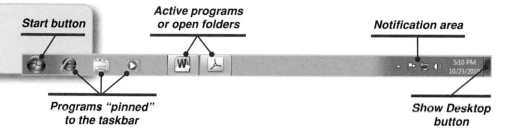

Start button

Active programs or open folders

Notification area

5:10 PM
10/23/2010

Programs "pinned" to the taskbar

Show Desktop button

NOTE

The two steps describing how to open the Start menu can be replaced with the two words "click **Start**." You can also open the Start menu by pressing the **Windows Flag** key on your keyboard, if you have that key, or by pressing both the **CTRL** and **ESC** keys together (**CTRL+ESC**). In the rest of this book, you will see the phrase "click **Start**." This means open the Start menu using any technique you wish.

NOTE

If you are looking on the Start menu for programs to access the Internet, you'll see how to add them in Chapter 2.

EXPLORE THE START MENU

The left column of the Start menu contains named icons for programs and folders, as well as access to control functions and other menus, as shown in Figure 1-4. The most important menu item is All Programs, which opens a submenu within the Start menu of all your programs. The buttons in the lower-right area—Shut Down and session-ending choices, also called "power buttons"—are important control functions discussed later in this chapter. The Search text box in the lower-left area allows you to enter criteria and search the files and folders on the computer or sites on the Internet for those that contain a match. All other options on the menu open folders or start programs, or both. The seven lower icons on the left change to reflect the programs you have used most recently (which are probably different from those shown here). In most cases, these are the programs that Windows 7 initially displays.

The remaining items in the right column of the Start menu fall into two categories: user-related folders and system-related folders, programs, and options.

OPEN USER-RELATED FOLDERS

The top five options on the right in Figure 1-4 (including the user's name at the top) are used to access folders related to the user who is logged on. These options start the Windows Explorer program and display the folder identified. Clicking the user's name opens a folder

NOTE

Depending on the programs you have run and the edition of Windows 7 you have (Starter, Home Basic, Home Premium, Professional, Enterprise, or Ultimate), your Start menu may be different from the one shown here for Windows 7 Ultimate edition.

containing the user's set of folders, as shown next. Windows Explorer will be discussed later in this chapter and again in Chapter 3.

OPEN SYSTEM-RELATED FOLDERS

The remaining five icons in the bottom-right area of the Start menu (see Figure 1-4) help you manage your computer and its resources or get help. The function of each is as follows:

- **Computer** starts the Windows Explorer program and displays disk storage devices on the computer. From this point you can open any disk, folder, and file that is available to you on your computer and the network to which you are connected by double-clicking the object you want to open.

- **Control Panel** provides access to many of the settings that govern how Windows and the computer operate. This allows you to customize much of Windows and to locate and solve problems.

STARTING A PROGRAM

The method for starting a program depends on where the program icon is located. Here are the alternatives:

- **On the desktop** Double-click the program icon, or "shortcut," on the desktop.

- **On the Start menu** Click the program icon on the Start menu.

- **On the taskbar or notification area** Click the program icon in the notification area.

- **On the All Programs menu:**

  1. Click **Start**.

  2. Click **All Programs**.

  3. Click the relevant folder or folders.

  4. Click the program icon, as shown in Figure 1-5.

TIP

When you move the pointer to an option on the Start menu, the option takes on a colored background and becomes selected, as shown in Figure 1-5. If you don't immediately click the item, a little message box, or *screen tip*, will appear. It gives you information about the option you selected.

- **Default Programs** allows you to associate a program with a file type and automatically start that program when you double-click that type of file.

- **Devices And Printers** allows you to check the status of and change the settings on the hardware devices and printers in or connected to your computer.

- **Help And Support** opens a window from which you can search for information on how to use Windows 7. It includes a tutorial and a troubleshooting guide. Help is discussed in more detail later in this chapter.

Your computer's manufacturer may have added an icon that connects you to the manufacturer's Internet Help center.

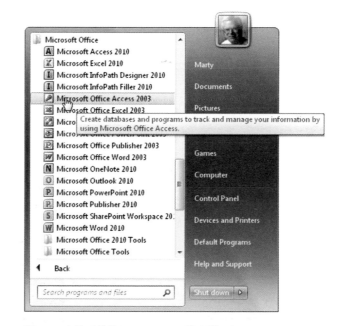

Figure 1-5: All Programs on the Start menu may lead you through one or more folders before you find the program you want.

Use a Window

When you start a program or open a folder, the program or folder appears in a "window" on your screen, as shown with the Windows Explorer window in Figure 1-6.

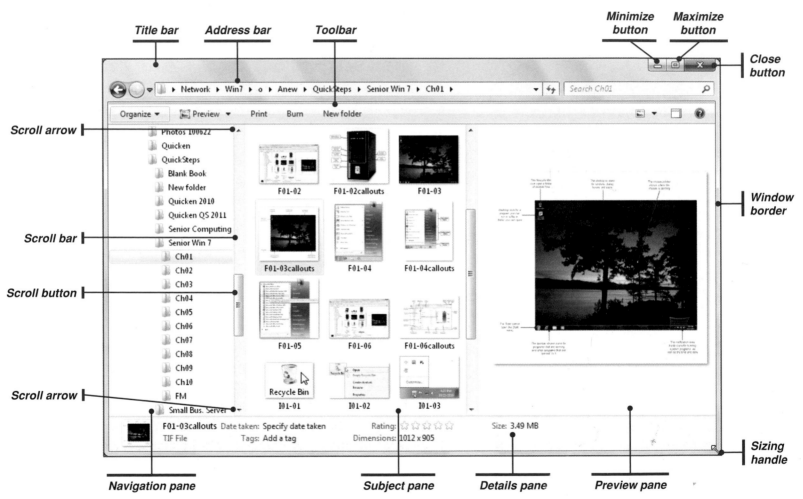

Figure 1-6: The Windows Explorer window has a number of different features that allow you to perform many tasks.

The window in Figure 1-6 has a number of features that are referred to in the remainder of this book. Not all windows have all of the features shown in the figure, and some windows have features unique to them.

- The **title bar** is used to drag the window around the screen, and may contain the name of the program or folder in the window (the Windows Explorer window in Windows 7 does not contain a name in the title bar).

- The **address bar** displays the complete address (minus the file name) of what is being displayed in the subject pane. In Figure 1-6, this is (from right to left) the Ch01 folder, in the Senior Win 7, QuickSteps, Anew folders, on drive O of the Win7 computer in the local network.

- The **toolbar** contains tools related to the contents of the window. Click a tool to use it. The toolbar is always displayed.

- The **Minimize button** decreases the size of the window so that you see it only as a task on the taskbar.

- The **Maximize button** increases the size of the window so that it fills the screen. When the window is maximized, this button becomes the **Restore button**, which, when clicked, returns the screen to its previous size.

- The **Close button** shuts down and closes the program, folder, or file in the window.

- The **window border** separates the window from the desktop, and can be used to size the window horizontally or vertically by dragging the horizontal or vertical border, respectively.

- The **sizing handle** in each corner of the window allows the window to be sized diagonally by dragging with the mouse, increasing or decreasing the window's height and width.

QUICKSTEPS

CHANGING WINDOWS EXPLORER

The window shown in Figure 1-6 has all of its panes turned on. By default, the preview pane is not visible. You can turn these panes on and turn other panes off.

- **Turn on panes** Click **Organize** on the toolbar, click **Layout**, and click **Preview Pane** (see Figure 1-7).

- **Turn off panes** Click **Organize** on the toolbar, click **Layout**, and click **Details Pane** or **Navigation Pane**.

- **Turn on Classic menus** Click **Organize** on the toolbar, click **Layout**, and click **Menu Bar** if you miss the menus that were in Windows Explorer in earlier versions of Windows.

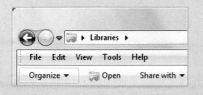

TIP

Double-clicking a window's title bar toggles between maximizing and restoring a window to its previous size. This may be easier than clicking the Maximize and Restore buttons.

NOTE

All windows have a title bar with the Minimize, Maximize, and Close buttons. The title bars of many program windows also have a control menu icon on the left of the title bar and the program name in the middle of the title bar. All windows have a border and sizing handle, both of which can be used to change the size of the window. Many windows also have a menu bar. Other features are optional.

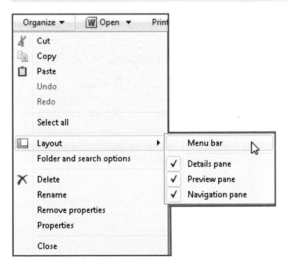

Figure 1-7: By default, menus are not available in Windows Explorer, but you can turn them on if you wish.

- The **preview pane** displays the object selected in the subject pane. For example, in Figure 1-6, the navigation pane points to a particular folder whose files of screenshots are shown in the subject pane, where one particular file is selected and displayed in the preview pane. By default, the preview pane is turned off.

- The **details pane** displays detailed information about the object that is selected in the subject pane. The preview pane is turned on by default.

- The **subject pane** displays the principal subject of the window, such as files, folders, programs, documents, or images. The subject pane is always on.

- The **navigation pane** provides links to the most commonly used folders related to the user who is logged on, as well as an optional hierarchical list of disks and folders on the computer. The navigation pane is turned on by default.

- **Scroll arrows** move the window contents in small increments in the direction of the arrow.

- The **scroll button** can be dragged in either direction to move the contents accordingly.

- The **scroll bar** contains the scroll arrows and scroll button and allows you to move the contents of the pane within the window so that you can see information that wasn't displayed. Clicking the scroll bar itself moves the contents in larger increments.

Use a Menu

A *menu* provides a way of selecting an action, such as turning on the preview pane, as shown in Figure 1-7. To use a menu in an open window:

1. Click the menu name.

2. Move the pointer to the option you want.

3. Click the option you want.

TIP

There are several ways to distinguish a dialog box from a window. The purpose of a window is to display information, while the purpose of a dialog box is to gather information. Dialog boxes cannot be sized and do not have a control menu icon, a menu bar, or Minimize and Maximize buttons.

Use a Dialog Box

Dialog boxes gather information. A *dialog box* uses a common set of controls to accomplish its purpose. Figures 1-8 and 1-9 show two frequently used dialog boxes with many of the controls often seen.

The common controls in dialog boxes are used in these ways:

- The **title bar** contains the name of the dialog box and is used to drag the box around the desktop.
- **Tabs** let you select from among several pages in a dialog box.
- A **drop-down list box** displays a list from which you can choose one item that will be displayed when the list is closed.

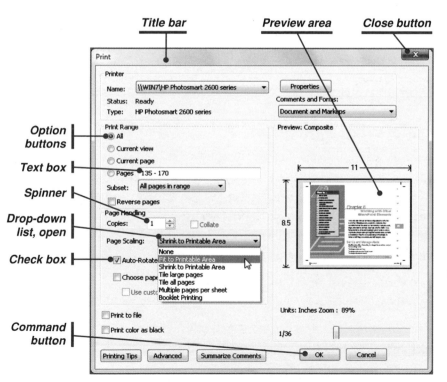

Figure 1-8: This dialog box demonstrates some of the standard controls you'll find in dialog boxes.

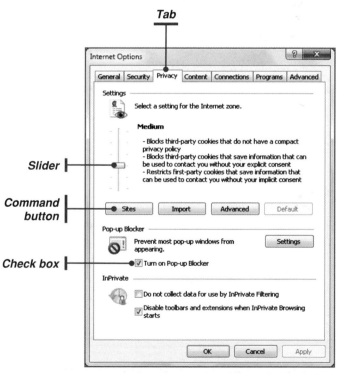

Figure 1-9: Dialog boxes come in many different sizes and with different controls.

- A **list box** (not shown) lets you select one or more items from a list; it may include a scroll bar.
- **Option buttons**, also called radio buttons, let you select one among mutually exclusive options.
- **Check boxes** let you turn features on or off.
- A **preview area** shows you the effect of the changes you make.
- A **text box** lets you enter and edit text.
- **Command buttons** perform functions such as closing the dialog box and accepting any changes (the OK button), or closing the dialog box and ignoring the changes (the Cancel button).
- A **spinner** lets you select from a sequential series of numbers.
- A **slider** lets you select from several values.

You will have a great many opportunities to use dialog boxes. For the most part, you can try dialog boxes and see what happens; if you don't like the outcome, you can come back and reverse the setting.

Navigate with Windows 7

When multiple windows are open, and possibly a dialog box or two, navigating among them and displaying the one(s) you want could be difficult. Figure 1-10, for example, shows such a situation. Earlier versions of Windows tried to address this, but Windows 7 has added a number of features to handle it elegantly, including (see the following sections on how to find and use these features):

- **Aero Peek** shows what's hidden on the desktop.
- **Aero Shake** minimizes other open windows.
- **Aero Snap** resizes and positions windows.
- **Jump Lists** display recent files and program options.
- **Taskbar Previews** show what is open in a program.

TIP

Figures 1-10 and 1-11 show you an example of personalizing the desktop and, with it, the taskbar and windows borders. To do this, right-click the desktop, click **Personalize**, click a new theme, and click **Close**.

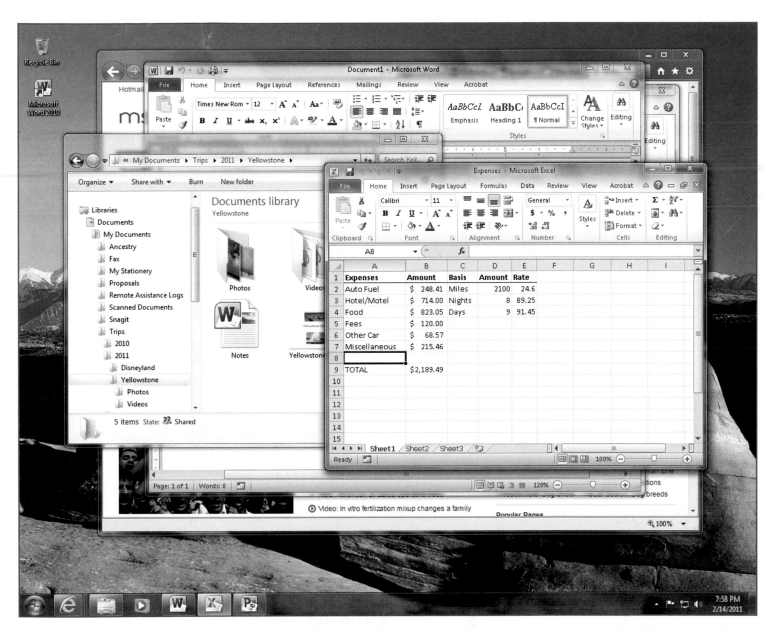

Figure 1-10: A screen can become cluttered with windows and dialog boxes, making it difficult to find what you want.

BOBBI FINDS PROGRAMS AND FOLDERS

I often have several programs and folders open on my computer, and until Windows 7 I would have difficulty finding something that I was working on or getting to an icon on my desktop. Now with Aero Peek I can immediately see what's on my desktop, and using taskbar previews I can easily see and choose from among the several documents I might have open in Word or several Internet sites I have open in Internet Explorer. I think these new features are a real asset.

Bobbi S., 69, Washington

USE AERO PEEK

Aero Peek allows you to see what's hidden on the desktop behind all the open windows. You can do this on a temporary (or "peek") basis or a more long-lasting one.

- **Temporarily peek** at the desktop (this only applies if you are using Aero themes):

  When you have a screen full of windows, like Figure 1-10, move the mouse pointer to ("mouse over") the **Show Desktop** area in the lower-right corner of the taskbar. All the open windows will become transparent ("glass") frames and you can see what was hidden on the desktop, such as the files, folders, and email shown in Figure 1-11.

- **Return** to the original desktop after a temporary peek:

  Move the mouse pointer away from the **Show Desktop** area. All the open windows will reappear, as shown in Figure 1-10.

- **Hide** all open windows so you can see and work on the desktop:

  Click the **Show Desktop** area on the far right of the taskbar. All the open windows will be hidden, and you can move the mouse around the entire desktop.

- **Unhide** all open windows and return to the original desktop:

  Click the **Show Desktop** area on the far right of the taskbar. All the open windows will be returned to their original position.

USE AERO SHAKE

Aero Shake allows you to minimize all open windows except for the one you are "shaking." To "shake" a window:

Point to the title bar of the window you want to remain open. Press and hold the mouse button while moving the mouse rapidly to the left and then to the right, as if you were shaking it.

–Or–

Select the window you want to keep displayed. Press and hold the **Windows Flag** key while pressing **HOME**.

To return the minimized windows to their original size and position, repeat the same steps.

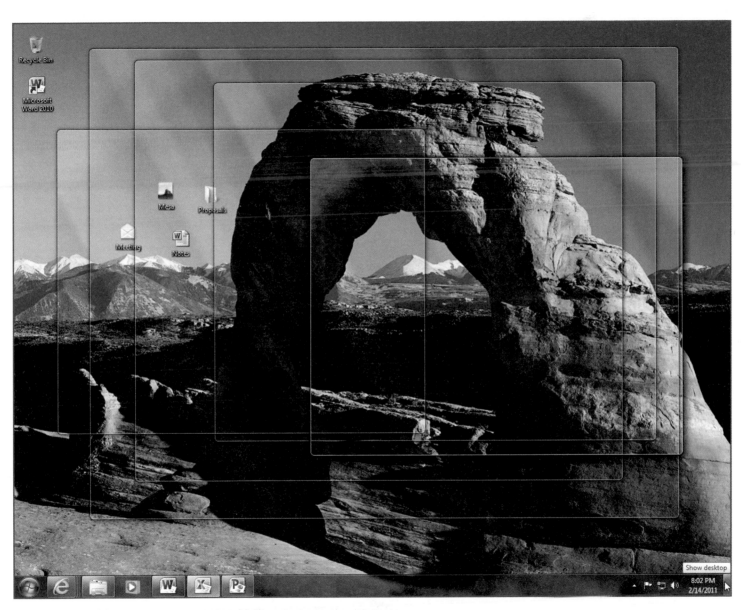

Figure 1-11: With Aero Peek, all open windows become transparent.

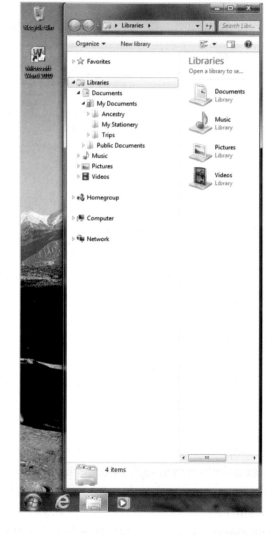

USE AERO SNAP

Aero Snap "snaps" a window to various parts of the screen, a function similar to the Maximize/Restore button (which can still be used) on the title bar of a selected, floating (not already maximized) window, with some useful additions.

- **Maximize** a floating window:

  Point within the title bar or the window, not on its edge, and drag it to the top of the screen. The window will be maximized to fill the screen.

  –Or–

  Double-click the title bar.

  –Or–

  Select the window you want to be maximized. Press and hold the **Windows Flag** key while pressing **UP ARROW**.

- **Restore** a maximized window (independent of how it was maximized):

  Point within the title bar or the window and drag it away from the top of the screen.

  –Or–

  Double-click the title bar.

  –Or–

  Select the window you want to be restored. Press and hold the **Windows Flag** key while pressing **DOWN ARROW**.

- **Vertically maximize** a floating window while not spreading it out horizontally:

  Point to the top or bottom edge of a window, and when the pointer turns into a double-headed arrow, drag it to the corresponding edge of the screen. The window will be vertically maximized.

  –Or–

- Select the window you want to be maximized. Press and hold the **Windows Flag** key while pressing **SHIFT+UP ARROW**.

- **Left-align** a floating window and have it occupy 50 percent of the screen:

  Point to the title bar of a window and drag it to the corresponding edge of the screen. When the mouse pointer (not the edge of the window) reaches the edge of the screen, the window will fill the left 50 percent of the screen.

  –Or–

  Select the window you want to be left-aligned. Press and hold the **Windows Flag** key while pressing **LEFT ARROW**.

- **Right-align** a floating window and have it occupy 50 percent of the screen:

  Point at the title bar of a window and drag it to the corresponding edge of the screen. When the mouse pointer (not the edge of the window) reaches the edge of the screen, the window will fill the right 50 percent of the screen.

  –Or–

  Select the window you want to be right-aligned. Press and hold the **Windows Flag** key while pressing **RIGHT ARROW**.

- **Restore a window that is filling 50 percent of the screen**:

  Point at the title bar of a window and drag it down and away from the window edge it was aligned to.

  –Or–

  Double-click the title bar twice.

  –Or–

  Select the window you want to be restored. Press and hold the **Windows Flag** key while pressing the key opposite the one used to enlarge it.

USE JUMP LISTS

Jump lists are a context or pop-up menu for application icons on the taskbar or the Start menu. When you right-click a program icon on either the Start menu or taskbar, or click the right arrow to the right of a program on the start menu, a menu will appear containing a list of recent files or webpages, as well as options to close the

Frequent
- CNN.com - Breaking News, U.S., ...
- The Seattle Times | Seattle Times ...
- MSN.com
- Google
- Technology News - CNET News

Tasks
- Start InPrivate Browsing
- Open new tab

- Internet Explorer
- Unpin this program from taskbar
- Close window

application, pin or unpin it from the Start menu or taskbar, and open the application with a blank file or webpage. (This is different than simply pointing at an open taskbar program, which shows the taskbar previews; see the next section.)

USE TASKBAR PREVIEWS

Taskbar previews are a miniature image, or thumbnail, of an open window attached to a taskbar icon. When you mouse over, or point at, an icon on the taskbar, a thumbnail of the open window or windows related to that icon will temporarily appear, as shown next. If you then move the mouse to the thumbnail, a temporary full-sized image will appear (see Figure 1-12). When you move the mouse off the thumbnail or the icon, the corresponding image will disappear. Open a window by clicking its thumbnail (or by clicking the task on the taskbar). Close a window by clicking the **Close** button on the thumbnail (the Close button appears when the mouse pointer is placed on the thumbnail).

End Your Windows Session

You have several ways you can end your Windows session, depending on what you want to do. All of these can be found on the Start menu.

1. Click **Start**. Note in the lower right of the Start menu there is a button marked Shut Down and a right-pointing arrow to open several options (these are also called the "power" buttons), which are in addition to Shut Down.

2. Click either **Shut Down** or the right arrow, and then click the option you want.

TIP

Look at the icons on the taskbar in Figure 1-12. It is obvious by its bright highlight that the Windows Explorer icon is selected and the one displaying the thumbnails. You can also tell that the Windows Media Player icon (the one following Windows Explorer), by its lack of any highlight and border, doesn't have an open window. The Excel icon shows it has open windows by its unhighlighted icon but defined border.

NOTE

If you see in an exclamation mark in a shield on the Shut Down button, you are being told that when you click Shut Down, updates will be installed and then the computer will be shut down.

Default Programs
Help and Support

Switch user
Log off
Lock

Restart

Shut down
Sleep

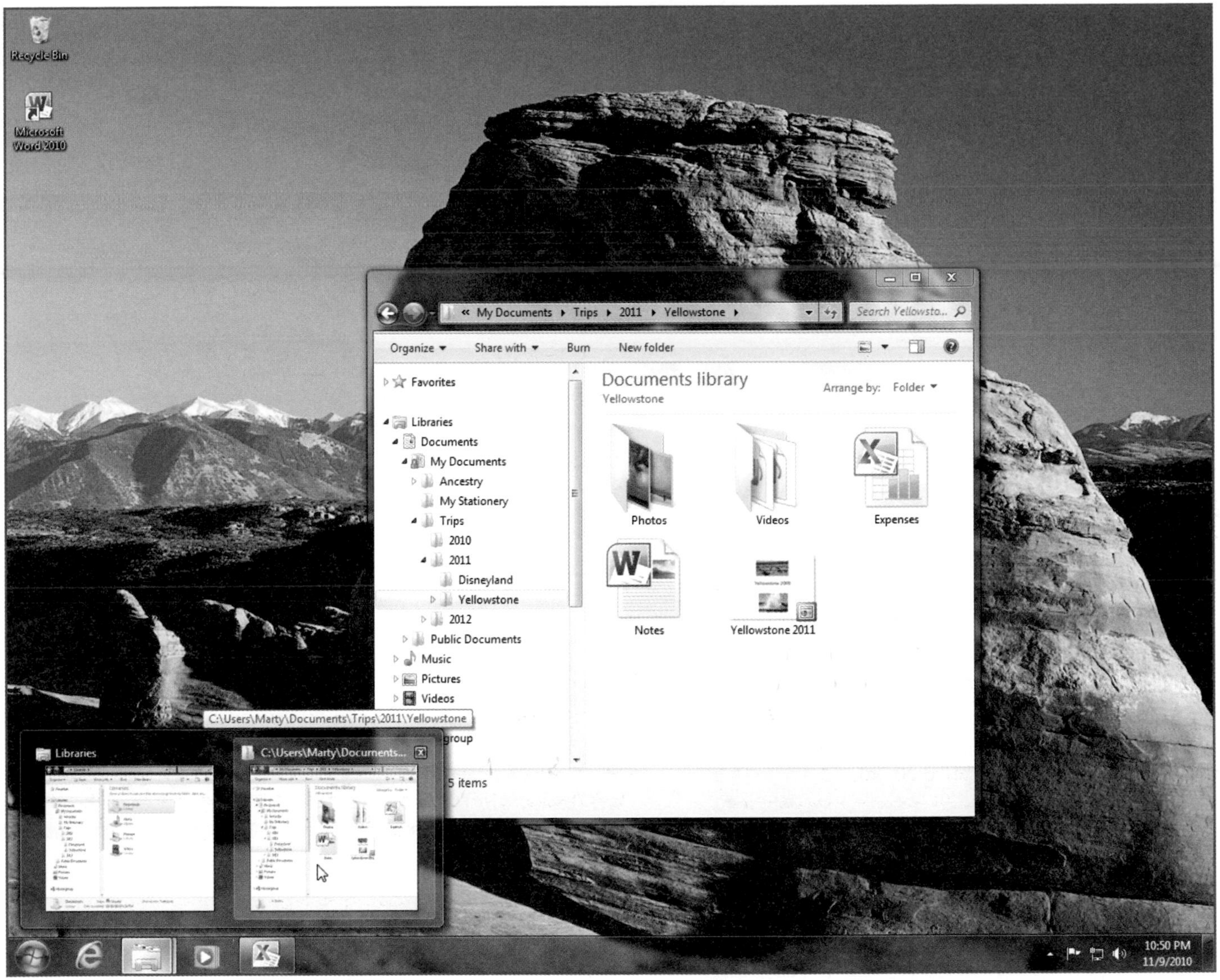

Figure 1-12: The natural instinct is to move the mouse from the thumbnail to the temporary larger window to open it, but that causes both images to disappear. You must click the thumbnail.

The meaning of the various options are

- **Shut Down** closes all active programs and network connections and logs off all users so that no information is lost, and then turns off the computer (if it is done automatically) or tells you when it is safe for you to turn it off. When you start up the computer, you must reload your programs and data and reestablish your network connection to get back to where you were when you shut down.
- **Switch User** leaves all active programs, network connections, and your user account active but hidden while you let another person use the computer.
- **Log Off** closes all active programs, network connections, and your user account but leaves Windows 7 and the computer running so another person can log on.
- **Lock** leaves all active programs, network connections, and your user account active but displays the Welcome screen, where you must click your user icon and potentially enter a password, if you have established one, to resume using the computer.
- **Restart** closes all active programs and network connections and logs off all users so that no information is lost. Windows is then shut down and restarted. This is usually done when there is a problem that restarting Windows will fix or to complete setting up some programs.
- **Sleep** leaves all active programs, network connections, and your user account active and in memory, but also saves the state of everything on disk. Your computer is then put into a low-power state that allows you to quickly resume working exactly where you were when you left. In a desktop computer, it is left running in this low-power state for as long as you wish. In a mobile computer (laptops, notebooks, netbooks, and tablet PCs), after three hours or if the battery is low, your session is again saved to disk and the computer is turned off.

TIP

There are two distinct schools of thought on whether you use Sleep or Shut Down when you leave the computer for any length of time. There are two primary considerations: security and power usage. Older computers used less power running in Sleep mode than the power consumed during shutting down and starting up. New computers have reduced the power consumed during these events, so it is now a toss-up. From the security standpoint, there is no security like having your computer completely turned off. A computer is also pretty secure in Sleep mode, but it is theoretically possible for a hacker to awaken it. The choice becomes a matter of preference. I turn my computers off; my wife leaves hers on.

Figure 1-13: *The Windows 7 Help And Support window provides you with several options for getting help.*

Often, some of the best help with a computer can come from your children and grandchildren!

RESUME FROM SLEEP

There are several ways to resume operation after a computer has been put into Sleep mode, which depend on your type of computer, how it was put to sleep, and how long it has been sleeping. A computer can be put into Sleep mode by your action on the Start menu, by shutting the cover of a laptop, or as the result of the computer not being used for a time. The ways to resume include the following:

- Press any key on your keyboard. This works with most desktop computers and mobile computers that have only been asleep a short time.

- Quickly press the power button on your computer. This works with most recent computers of all types. Holding down the computer's power button will, in most cases, either fully turn off the computer or cause it to restart (shut fully down and then restart).

- Open the top. This works with most laptop computers.

Find Help

Windows 7 Help provides both built-in documentation and online assistance that you can use to learn how to work with Windows 7. For example, to use Help to start a program:

1. Click **Start** and click **Help And Support**. The Windows Help And Support window, like the one shown in Figure 1-13, opens.

2. In the Search Help text box, type <u>start a program</u>. A number of options related to starting a program will be displayed.

3. Click the **Close** button to close the Help And Support window.

Chapter 2

Making the Computer Yours

It is important to you to have your computer work the way you do. You will be able to do things easier and reduce your level of frustration. Microsoft realizes this and has built into Windows 7 many features that can be customized. You can keep the default Windows 7 setup if you wish, or you can change the display, Start menu, taskbar, and sounds. You can also rearrange the desktop and enable accessibility options.

Change the Screen

An important aspect of Windows that leads to your enjoyment and efficient use of it is how it looks. Windows 7 provides significant flexibility in this area. You can change how the screen looks, including the desktop, the Start menu, and the taskbar.

TIP

Themes allow you to control many facets of Windows 7 just by changing the theme.

Personalize Windows

Much of what you see on the Windows 7 screen is controlled by the Personalization window. Open it to make many of the changes in this chapter. (Several of the features controlled in the Personalization window, such as sounds and the mouse pointer, are discussed on their own later in this chapter.)

1. With Windows 7 running and displayed on your computer, right-click a blank area of the desktop. The desktop *context menu* is displayed.

2. Click **Personalize**. The Personalization window opens, as shown in Figure 2-1.

CHANGE THE DESKTOP THEMES AND COLORS

You can use any picture, color, or pattern you want for your desktop background. Windows 7 comes with a number of alternatives. From the Personalization window:

1. Drag the scroll button on the right, and review the themes that are available with Windows 7 (or click **Get More Themes Online** to view Microsoft's online library). Click the theme you want to use. With each theme you can select a desktop background and a window color, as well as the sounds used and a screen saver.

2. Click **Desktop Background**. Click the **Picture Location** down arrow, and select a source of pictures; or click **Browse** and navigate to a location on your computer where you have a picture you want to use (Chapter 3 explains how to navigate on your computer).

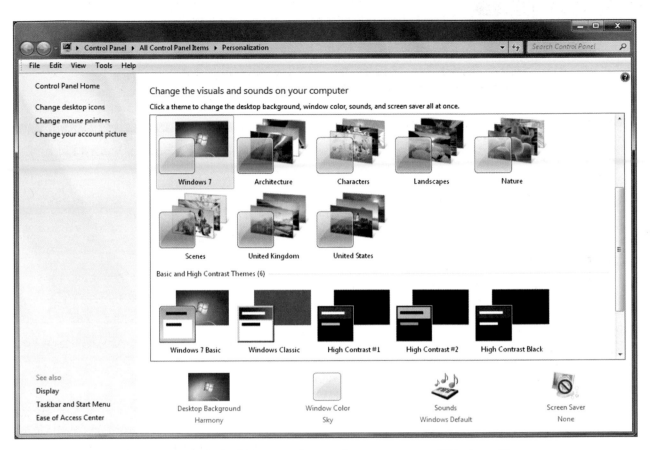

Figure 2-1: The Personalization window lets you change the appearance of Windows 7.

NOTE

You can select a new theme and almost immediately see the changes on the desktop. If you don't like the changes, select a different theme.

Click **OK**, and click the picture or pictures desired, shown in Figure 2-2 (if you select more than one picture, each picture will appear as the background, similar to a slide show, changing each background every 30 minutes by default).

3. Click **Save Changes** to close the Desktop Background window.

4. At the top of the themes list, click **Save Theme** to save any changes to a previous theme or to save a new theme.

5. In the Save Theme As dialog box, name the theme, and click **Save**.

Figure 2-2: Selecting a background picture causes it to be instantly displayed as your background.

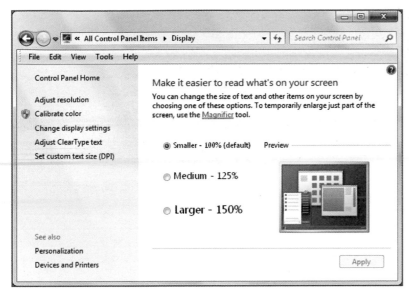

Figure 2-3: *Increasing the text and object size lets you see less of what's on the screen, but what you see is larger and possibly easier to read.*

CHANGE THE RESOLUTION AND TEXT SIZE

Depending on your computer and monitor, you can display Windows 7 with various resolutions and text sizes. You can select the text and object size in the Display window and then go on to adjust the resolution. From the Personalization window:

1. Click **Display** in the lower left. The Display window will appear, as shown in Figure 2-3.

2. Click the text and object size you want to use, and click **Apply**.

3. Click **Adjust Resolution**. If you have more than one display device, click **Identify**. The display's number appears on each screen. In the Display drop-down list, click the display whose resolution you want to change.

4. Click the **Resolution** drop-down arrow. Drag the slider up or down to adjust the resolution. (You can try this and if you don't like it, come back and change it.)

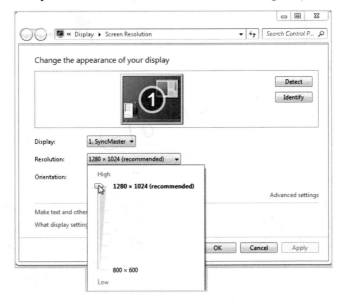

NOTE

The Advanced Settings link in the lower-right corner of the Screen Resolution window provides access to settings that are specific to your display hardware.

Window Color and Appearance

Window Color and Appearance

Inactive Window

Active Window

Normal   Disabled   Selected

Window Text

Message Box

Message Text

OK

To turn on Windows Aero, select a Windows theme. Colors and sizes selected here apply only if you have selected the Windows 7 Basic theme or an Ease of Access theme.

Item: Size: Color 1:   Color 2:

Desktop

Font: Size: Color:

                                    B i

OK   Cancel   Apply

5. Click **Apply** to save the settings, and then click the **Back** arrow in the upper-left area until you are back to the Personalization window.

ALTER THE APPEARANCE OF OBJECTS

You can alter the appearance of windows, icons, and dialog boxes, changing their shapes and colors, as well as the font used in those objects. From the Personalization window:

1. Click **Window Color** at the bottom of the window. The Window Color And Appearance window will open.

2. Click a different color scheme, if desired; scroll down and turn off transparency if you don't like looking through window borders; or change the color intensity.

3. Click **Advanced Appearance Settings** to open the old-style (circa Windows XP) Window Color And Appearance dialog box, as shown on the left. Select an object whose color and/or font you want to change, make those changes. All settings made here will provide a Windows Classic look or style.

4. When you are ready, click **OK** to close the Window Color And Appearance dialog box. Then click **Save Changes** to return to the Personalization window.

SELECT THE SOUNDS WINDOWS 7 PLAYS

You can select the sounds that are played when various events occur, such as a critical stop or Windows shutdown, in the Sound dialog box. Make sure your speakers are plugged in and turned on. Then from the Personalization window:

1. Click **Sounds** at the bottom. The Sound dialog box will appear, displaying the Sounds tab, as shown in Figure 2-4.

2. Click the **Sound Scheme** down arrow, and select one of the options.

3. Double-click a **Program Events** option to hear its current sound played.

4. Click the **Sounds** down arrow to select a different sound for the event. Click **Test** to hear the sound.

Figure 2-4: Sounds can be associated with various events.

5. When you have made all the changes you want to the association of sounds and events, click **Save As** to save your changes as a new scheme. Type a name for the new scheme, and click **OK**.

6. When you are ready, click **OK** to close the Sound dialog box.

PICK A NEW SCREEN SAVER

When the computer is left on but not in use, the unchanging image on the screen can be burned into the face of a cathode-ray tube (CRT) monitor. The newer, thin, flat-screen liquid crystal display (LCD) monitors are not as affected by this, but plasma displays can be. To prevent this damage, you can choose to use a *screen saver*, which constantly changes the image on the screen when the computer is not in use. Windows 7 provides a number of alternative screen savers you can use. From the Personalization window:

1. Click **Screen Saver** in the lower-right corner. The Screen Saver Settings dialog box appears.

2. Click the **Screen Saver** down arrow, and review the options in the drop-down list.

3. Click a screen saver option to see it previewed in the dialog box (see Figure 2-5).

4. Click **Preview** to see the screen saver on your full screen. Press ESC to return to the dialog box.

5. Click the up or down arrow on the **Wait** spinner to set the time to wait before enabling the screen saver.

6. When you have the screen saver you want, click **Settings**, if it is enabled, to see what settings are available for your screen saver. With the Photos option, you can select the folder, such as Pictures, from which to display photos.

7. When you are ready, click **OK** to close the dialog box.

Figure 2-5: *You can use your own photos with the Photos screen saver option.*

NOTE

By default, Windows smoothes the edges of screen fonts using ClearType. You can adjust how ClearType works from the Personalization window by clicking **Display**, and then in the Display window clicking **Adjust ClearType Text**. In the ClearType Text Tuner, you can turn ClearType on or off; by clicking **Next**, you can fine-tune how ClearType operates. ClearType is only effective if you are using a notebook computer or a flat-panel display.

USE A DIFFERENT MOUSE POINTER

If it is difficult for you to see the mouse pointer, you can change how it looks and behaves in the Mouse Properties dialog box. From the Personalization window:

1. Click **Change Mouse Pointers** in the upper-left area. The Mouse Properties dialog box will appear with the Pointers tab displayed, as shown in Figure 2-6.

2. Click the **Scheme** down arrow, and choose the scheme you want to use.

3. If you want to customize a particular mouse pointer, select that pointer, click **Browse**, locate and select the pointer you want to use, and click **Open**.

4. Click **OK** to close the Mouse Properties dialog box.

Figure 2-6: *The mouse pointer should be easily seen and instantly informative for you.*

While you can make a lot of changes to the screen and its contents, the first step is to get comfortable with the default screen and content, and only then look at what changes might be beneficial to you.

Figure 2-7: Add the icons to the desktop for the programs you use most often.

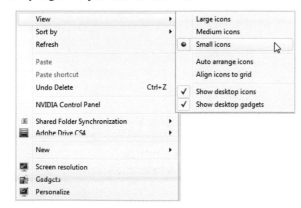

Add Windows Program Icons

When you first install and start up Windows 7, you will only have a couple icons on the desktop, including the Recycle Bin, which is the only one Windows has by default. Some computer manufacturers may include additional icons. The purpose of having program icons on the desktop, called *shortcuts,* is to be able to easily start the programs by double-clicking their icons. To add Windows program icons, such as Windows Explorer and Control Panel, to the desktop and customize them:

1. Right-click a blank area of the desktop, and click **Personalize** to open the Personalization window.

2. Click **Change Desktop Icons** on the left to open the Desktop Icon Settings dialog box, shown in Figure 2-7.

3. In the Desktop Icons area, click one to five icons that you want to have on the desktop. For example, you might want icons for Computer and Control Panel. You might use the others less often, and they can be quickly accessed from the Start menu.

4. To customize a Windows program icon, click the icon and click **Change Icon**. A dialog box will appear displaying alternate icons.

5. Select the alternative you want, and click **OK**.

6. When you are satisfied with the Windows program icons you have selected and/or changed, click **OK**.

7. Click the **Close** button to close the Personalization window.

Change Desktop Icons

When you have the icons that you want on the desktop, you can change the size of the icons, their order, and their alignment through the desktop context menu.

Right-click a blank area of the desktop to open the context menu, and click **View** to open the View submenu.

RESIZE ICONS

Windows 7 gives you the choice of three different sizes of icons. The size you choose is a function of both the resolution you are using on your display and your personal preference. By default (the way Windows is set up when you first install and/or start it), your icons will be medium size. From the **View** submenu:

Recycle Bin   Recycle Bin   Recycle Bin
Large   *Medium*   *Small*

Click each of the sizes to see which is best for you.

ALIGN ICONS

You can drag desktop icons where you want them; by default, Windows 7 will align your icons to an invisible grid. If you don't like that, from the **View** submenu:

Click **Align Icons To Grid** to clear the check mark and allow any arrangement on the desktop that you want.

If you should move your icons around and then change your mind, reopen the **View** submenu and:

Click **Align Icons To Grid** to reselect it. Your icons will jump to the invisible grid and be aligned.

ARRANGE ICONS

By default, there is no particular order to the icons on the desktop, so you can drag them into the order that suits you. However, you can have Windows arrange and sort the icons in several ways. From the **View** submenu:

Click **Auto Arrange Icons**. By default, the icons will be placed in a column alphabetically by name, except that the *system* icons (Computer, Recycle Bin, Internet Explorer, User's Files, Control Panel, and Network) will be at the top.

ADDING OTHER PROGRAM ICONS TO THE DESKTOP

The method for adding other program icons, or shortcuts, to the desktop depends on where the icons are.

ADD ICONS FROM THE START MENU

Click **Start** to open the menu, and drag the icon from the menu to the desktop.

ADD ICONS FROM THE ALL PROGRAMS MENU

1. Click **Start**, and click **All Programs**.

2. Locate and point to the icon, hold down the right mouse button, and drag the icon to the desktop. (This is called *right-drag*.)

3. Click **Copy Here**.

ADD ICONS FROM OTHER MENUS

1. Click **Start**, click **All Programs**, and open additional folders as needed.

2. Point to the icon, and right-drag the icon to desktop.

3. Click **Copy Here**.

ADD ICONS NOT ON A MENU

1. Click **Start**, and click **Computer**.

2. In the Computer window, open the drive and folder(s) needed to locate the program (most programs are stored in their own folder within the Program Files folder on the C: drive).

3. Drag the program icon to the desktop.

If you want to change the order in which Windows 7 arranges desktop icons:

1. Right-click a blank area of the desktop to open the context menu, and click **Sort By** to open that submenu.

2. Click one of the options to have the icons sorted in that manner.

RENAME DESKTOP ICONS

When you add program icons to the desktop, they may have the word "Shortcut" in their names, or they may have names that are not meaningful to you. To rename desktop icons:

1. Right-click an icon name you want to change, and click **Rename**.

2. Type the new name that you want to use, and press **ENTER**.

Change the Start Menu

The Start menu has several areas you can customize, including the size of the icons, the number of programs on it, the programs to use for the Internet and for email, and how the Start menu operates.

CHANGE WHAT IS DISPLAYED ON THE START MENU

Windows 7 gives you considerable flexibility as to what is displayed on the Start menu and how those items work.

1. Right-click **Start** and click **Properties** to open the Taskbar And Start Menu Properties dialog box.

2. With the Start Menu tab selected, click **Customize**. The Customize Start Menu dialog box will appear (see Figure 2-8).

3. Scroll through the list of links, icons, and submenus. Select the ones you want included on the Start menu, and indicate how they should operate. Toward the end of the list there is an option that lets you change the size of the icons on the Start menu.

4. Use the **Number Of Recent Programs To Display** spinner to select the number displayed in the lower-left corner of the Start menu.

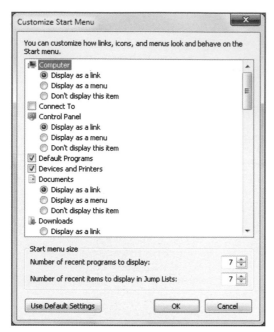

Figure 2-8: You can customize what is
displayed on the Start menu and how
those items work.

NOTE

Changing the size of icons only affects the icons
on the left of the Start menu. The purpose of
smaller icons is to list more programs.

5. Use the **Number Of Recent Items To Display In Jump Lists** spinner
   to select the number displayed in jump lists (see Chapter 5).

6. To return to the original default settings, click **Use Default Settings**.

7. When you have made the changes you want, click **OK** twice.

ADD PROGRAMS TO THE START MENU

You can add programs to the upper-left corner of the Start menu
(where they will remain unless you remove them).

1. Click **Start**, click **All Programs**, and open the appropriate folders to
   display the program you want on the Start menu.

2. Right-click the program, and click **Pin To Start Menu**. The program
   will appear on the Start menu. For example, if you want to add
   Internet Explorer, click **Start**, click **All Programs**, right-click **Internet
   Explorer**, and click **Pin To Start Menu**.

3. Click outside the Start menu to close it.

TIP

TIP

To remove a program on the Start menu, click **Start**, right-click the program, and if it is one you added in the upper-left corner of the menu (semi-permanent area), click **Unpin From Start Menu**. If the program you want to remove is in the lower-left corner (recently used program area), click **Remove From This List**. Then click outside the Start menu to close it.

NOTE

The picture that is displayed on the Start menu comes from your user account, as described in Chapter 6. To change this picture, right-click the desktop, click **Personalize**, click **Change Your Account Picture** on the left, click one of the pictures shown, click **Change Picture**, and click **Close** to close the Personalization window; or click **Browse For More Pictures**, navigate to the drive and folder with the picture you want (see Chapter 3), click that picture, and click **Open**. Click **Close** to close the User Accounts dialog box.

Figure 2-9 shows a changed Start menu, which you can compare with Figure 1-4 in Chapter 1.

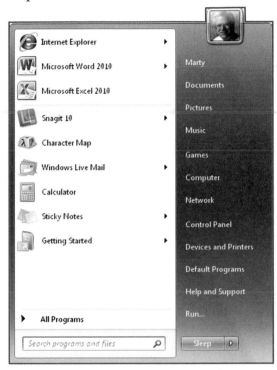

Figure 2-9: A Start menu with changes described in this chapter.

Change the Taskbar

The taskbar at the bottom of the Windows 7 screen has four standard areas: the Start button on the left, the task list in the middle, and the notification area and the Show Desktop button on the right. In addition, there is an optional "pin-to" area next to the Start button. You can change the taskbar by moving and sizing it and by changing its properties.

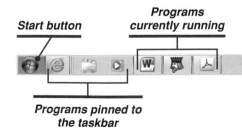

Start button

Programs currently running

Notification area, date and time

Programs pinned to the taskbar

Show Desktop button

NOTE

You can turn on a second optional area on the taskbar next to the notification area that lets you open the Tablet PC Input Panel to enter text on the screen without a keyboard. Instead, you write with a mouse or stylus, or click a keyboard layout on the screen. Right-click the **Start** button, click **Properties**, click the **Toolbars** tab, click **Tablet PC Input Panel**, and click **OK**.

QUICK QUOTES

PAGE PICKS WHAT SHE NEEDS TO LEARN

In truth, there is far more about my computer that I don't know than what I know, but I get along pretty well and can do what I want to do. I started out with the idea that I had to learn all about my computer, but quickly found that was a tall order, and so changed my objective to learning just what I needed to know to do writing, emailing, online banking, a small amount of shopping, surfing the Internet, and managing my pictures. It works well and is a great asset . . . and I'm always curious about what I don't know and want to know more.

Page G. B., 68, Washington

MOVE AND SIZE THE TASKBAR

You can move the taskbar to any of the four sides of the screen. Do this by dragging any empty area of the taskbar to another edge. For example, Figure 2-10 shows the taskbar moved to the right edge of the screen.

You can size the taskbar by dragging the inner edge (top edge when the taskbar is on the bottom) in or out. Here is a taskbar at double its normal size.

In either case, you must first unlock the taskbar. See the "Changing Taskbar Properties" QuickSteps to do this.

Permanently Pin Icons to the Taskbar

Windows 7 provides the ability to permanently "pin," or attach, frequently used program icons to the taskbar next to the Start button. Once there, the icons are always visible (unless you hide the taskbar), and the related program can be started by a single click. By default Windows 7 has three icons pinned to the taskbar: Internet Explorer, Windows Explorer, and Media Player. You can pin additional icons, you can remove those that are currently pinned, and you can rearrange the current icons.

PIN AN ICON TO THE TASKBAR

After you have used Windows 7 for a while, you may find that you use a program more often than others and would like to have it more immediately available. This is what pinning to the taskbar is for. You can do that by either:

Locating the program icon in Windows Explorer, any part of the Start menu, or on the desktop; right-clicking it; and clicking **Pin To Taskbar**.

–Or–

Figure 2-10: A taskbar can be moved to any of the four sides of the screen.

QUICKSTEPS

CHANGING TASKBAR PROPERTIES

A number of taskbar features can be changed through the Taskbar And Start Menu Properties dialog box (see Figure 2-11).

OPEN TASKBAR PROPERTIES

Right-click an open area of the taskbar, and click **Properties**. The Taskbar And Start Menu Properties dialog box appears with the Taskbar tab selected. (Click **Apply** to test a change without closing the dialog box.)

UNLOCK THE TASKBAR

By default, the taskbar is locked. To move or resize the taskbar, it must be unlocked.

> Click **Lock The Taskbar** to remove the check mark and unlock the taskbar.

HIDE THE TASKBAR

Hiding the taskbar means that it is not displayed unless you move the mouse to the edge of the screen containing the taskbar. By default, it is displayed.

> Click **Auto-Hide The Taskbar** to select the check box and hide the taskbar.

USE SMALL ICONS

If you want to conserve desktop space and you have good eyesight, you can make the icons smaller, the size they were in previous versions of Windows.

> Click **Use Small Icons** to add a check mark and make the icons smaller.

Continued . . .

Figure 2-11: You will use the taskbar often, so it should look and behave the way you want.

Start the program in any of the ways described in Chapter 1. When it has started, right-click its icon on the taskbar, and click **Pin This Program To Taskbar**.

You can pin a file or folder to the Windows Explorer icon on the taskbar by opening Windows Explorer, navigating to the file or folder, and dragging it to the Windows Explorer icon on the taskbar. Access the pinned file or folder by right-clicking the Windows Explorer icon and clicking the file or folder.

CHANGING TASKBAR PROPERTIES
(Continued)

CUSTOMIZE TASKBAR BUTTONS

There are three choices for customizing taskbar buttons:

- Always combine similar items and hide the labels, such as program names (this is the default).

- Combine similar items when the taskbar is full, but display the labels.

- Never combine similar items under any circumstances, but display the labels.

Combining similar items, for example, puts all Microsoft Word documents in one icon or all Internet pages in one icon so that they take up less room on the taskbar. By default, similar items are combined.

> Click the **Taskbar Buttons** down arrow, and make your choice.

USE AERO PEEK

Aero Peek allows you to see the desktop and what is under the open windows on the screen when you move the mouse to the Show Desktop button on the far right of the taskbar. This is turned on by default.

> Click **Use Aero Peek** to remove the check mark and this capability.

CLOSE TASKBAR PROPERTIES

After you've made any of these changes to the taskbar, click **OK** to enable them and close the Taskbar And Start Menu Properties dialog box.

REMOVE AN ICON PINNED TO THE TASKBAR

To remove a program icon pinned to the taskbar:

> Right-click the icon and click **Unpin This Program From Taskbar**.

REARRANGE ICONS PINNED TO THE TASKBAR

The icons that are pinned to the taskbar can be moved around and placed in any order.

> Drag icons pinned to the taskbar to where you want them.

If you have a program pinned to the taskbar, which is preferable if there is room, you don't also need it on your desktop.

Change How Windows 7 Operates

How Windows 7 operates is probably more important to you than how it looks. For that reason, Windows 7 has a number of facilities that allow you to customize its operation.

Set and Use the Date and Time

The time and date in the lower-right corner of the screen may seem simple enough, but significant capability lies behind these simple numbers.

1. Move the mouse until your cursor is on the time or date in the notification area. The current day and date will appear.

QUICKSTEPS

CHANGING THE NOTIFICATION AREA

The notification area on the right of the taskbar can also be changed through the Taskbar And Start Menu Properties dialog box (see the "Changing Taskbar Properties" QuickSteps for instructions on displaying the dialog box). The notification area, which can get crowded at times, contains program icons put there by Windows and other programs. You can control which icons are displayed along with their notifications, which icons are hidden but their notifications displayed, or which icons are not there at all. To change the notification area:

Click **Customize** under Notification Area. The Notification Area Icons window will appear, as shown in Figure 2-12.

CUSTOMIZE NOTIFICATION ICONS

To customize the behavior of icons in the notification area:

Click the drop-down list opposite the icon you want to change, and select the behavior you want.

DISPLAY SYSTEM ICONS

Up to five system icons—Action Center, Network, Volume, Power (on mobile computers), and Clock—are shown in the notification area by default. You can turn them off if you wish.

1. Click **Turn System Icons On Or Off**.

2. Click the drop-down list opposite an icon name, and click **Off** to not display it.

Continued . . .

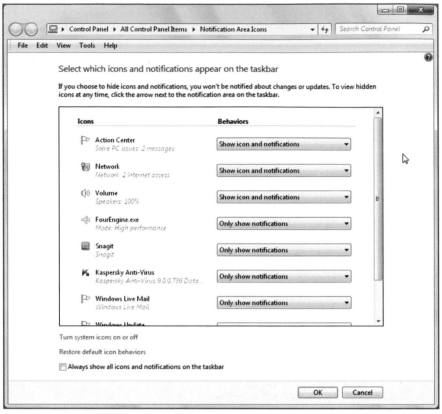

Figure 2-12: Turn off the notification area icons that are not useful to you.

2. Click the time. The full calendar and clock appear.

CHANGING THE NOTIFICATION AREA *(Continued)*

3. When you have made the changes you want, click **OK**.

CLOSE TASKBAR PROPERTIES

After you've made any of these changes to the notification area, click **OK** to enable them and close the Notification Area Icons window. Click **OK** again to close the Taskbar And Start Menu Properties dialog box.

NOTE

The blue and yellow shield on the Change Date And Time button tells you that the function being selected requires administrator permission. You must be an administrator or have a password for one.

3. Click **Change Date And Time Settings**. The Date And Time dialog box will appear, as shown in Figure 2-13.

Figure 2-13: Setting the date and time is normally automated using an Internet time server.

4. With the Date And Time tab selected, click **Change Date And Time**. The Date And Time Settings dialog box appears.

5. Use the arrows on the calendar to change the month. Or, click the month to display the year, use the arrows to change the year, click the month, and then click a day.

6. Double-click an element of time (hour, minute, second, AM/PM), and use the spinner to change the selected time element. Click **OK** to close the Date And Time Settings dialog box.

7. Click **Change Time Zone**, click the **Time Zone** down arrow, and click your time zone.

8. Click **Automatically Adjust Clock For Daylight Saving Time** if it isn't already selected and you want Windows 7 to do that. Click **OK** to close the Time Zone Settings dialog box.

9. Click the **Additional Clocks** tab to add one or two clocks with different time zones. Click **Show This Clock**, open the drop-down list box, and click a time zone. Enter a display name, and repeat for a second additional clock, if desired. (The additional times will appear when you point to the time in the notification area.) Click **OK** when done.

10. Click the **Internet Time** tab and see how your computer's time is currently being synchronized. If you want to change that, click **Change Settings**.

11. Click **Synchronize With An Internet Time Server** if it isn't already selected, open the drop-down list, click a time server, and click **Update Now**. Once turned on, Windows will check the time every seven days. Click **OK** to close the Internet Time Settings dialog box.

12. Click **OK** to close the Date And Time dialog box.

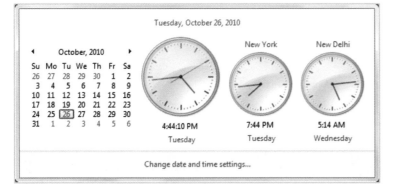

Change Ease-of-Access Settings

Ease-of-access settings (also called Accessibility Options) provide alternatives to the normal way the mouse and keyboard are used, as well as some settings that make the screen more readable and sounds more understandable, all of which are meant to make the computer easier to use with various physical limitations.

1. Right-click a blank area of the screen, click **Personalize**, and click **Ease Of Access Center** in the lower-left area. The Ease Of Access Center window will open, as shown in Figure 2-14.

   –Or–

   Press and hold the **Windows Flag** key while pressing **U**.

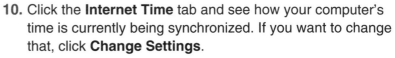

TIP

You can also turn on the most common ease-of-access options from the Windows 7 logon screen by clicking the **Ease Of Access** icon in the lower-left corner of the screen.

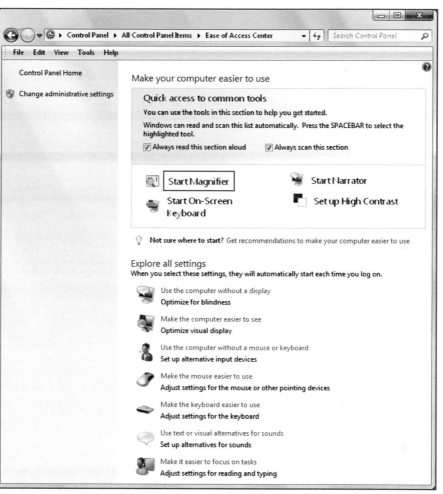

Figure 2-14: Ease-of-access settings let you work with Windows 7 and your programs in ways that facilitate use with various physical limitations.

2. Select the options you want to use in the common tools area at the top (see Table 2-1 for a description). You can also turn the options on or off using the keyboard shortcuts shown.

OPTION	DESCRIPTION	KEYBOARD SHORTCUT
Magnifier	Enlarges a part of the screen around the mouse.	
On Screen Keyboard	Displays an image of a keyboard on the screen that you can click to select the appropriate keys.	
Narrator	Reads aloud selected text on the screen.	
High Contrast	Uses high-contrast colors and special fonts to make the screen easy to use.	Press together left **SHIFT**, left **ALT**, and **PRINT SCREEN**.

Table 2-1: Ease-of-Access Common Tools

NOTE

By default, and if you have speakers and a sound card, Windows 7 will scan and read aloud the four options in the Quick Access section.

3. Click any of the blue text links in the lower part of the window to review, and possibly change, the ease-of-access settings that apply to various areas of the computer. Within links there are a number of assistive tools, shown in Table 2-2, that can be turned on, either in these links or with the keyboard shortcuts shown.

4. When you have set up the accessibility options you want, click **Close**.

OPTION	DESCRIPTION	KEYBOARD SHORTCUT
Mouse Keys	Uses the numeric keypad to move the mouse around the screen.	Press together left **SHIFT**, left **ALT**, and **NUM LOCK**.
Sticky Keys	Simulates pressing a pair of keys, such as CTRL+A, by pressing one key at a time. The keys SHIFT, CTRL, and ALT "stick" down until a second key is pressed. This is interpreted as two keys pressed together.	Press either **SHIFT** key five times in succession.
Filter Keys	Enables you to press a key twice in rapid succession and have it interpreted as a single keystroke; also slows down the rate at which the key is repeated if it is held down.	Hold down the right **SHIFT** key for eight seconds.
Toggle Keys	Hear a tone when CAPS LOCK, NUM LOCK, or SCROLL LOCK is turned on.	Hold down the **NUM LOCK** key for five seconds.

Table 2-2: Additional Ease-of-Access Tools

UICKSTEPS

Customize the Mouse

The mouse lets you interact with the screen and point at, select, and drag objects. You also can start and stop programs and close Windows using the mouse. While you can use Windows without a mouse, it is more difficult, making it important that the mouse operates in the most comfortable way possible. Change the way the mouse works through the Control Panel Mouse component.

1. Click **Start** and click **Control Panel**.
2. In Category view, click **Hardware And Sound**, and under Devices And Printers, click **Mouse**.

   –Or–

   In Large or Small Icons view, click **Mouse**.

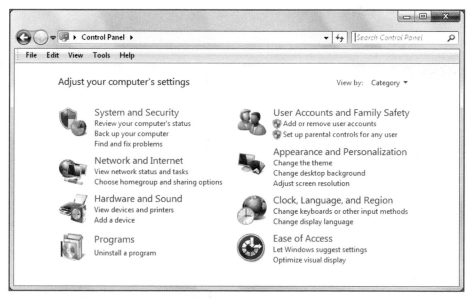

Figure 2-15: Category view provides a hierarchy of windows that leads you to the settings you want to change.

QUICKSTEPS

USING THE CONTROL PANEL (Continued)

OPEN A CONTROL PANEL CATEGORY

Category view groups components into categories that must be opened to see the individual components, although some subcategories are listed.

Click a category to open a window for it, where you can select either a task you want to do or open a Control Panel component represented by an icon.

OPEN A CONTROL PANEL COMPONENT

When Category view's secondary windows are opened in the previous step, the icons for individual Control Panel component icons are displayed. In either Large or Small Icons view, these component icons are directly displayed. To open a component:

Click the component's icon.

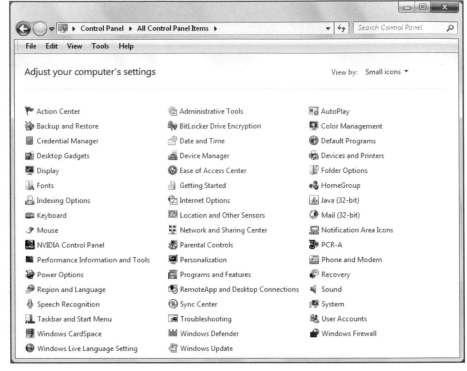

Figure 2-16: The Control Panel's Small Icons view shows all of the components in the Control Panel.

NOTE

Many Control Panel components are also available from other locations. For example, the Date And Time component opens the same dialog box that appears when you click the time/date in the taskbar and click **Change Date And Time Settings**.

Either way, the Mouse Properties dialog box will appear, as you can see in Figure 2-17.

3. If you want to use the mouse with your left hand, click **Switch Primary And Secondary Buttons**.

4. Double-click the folder in the middle-right area of the Buttons tab. If the folder opens, your double-click speed is okay. If not, drag the **Speed** slider until the folder opens when you double-click it.

5. Select the options you want to use on the **Buttons**, **Pointer Options**, **Wheel**, and **Hardware** tabs.

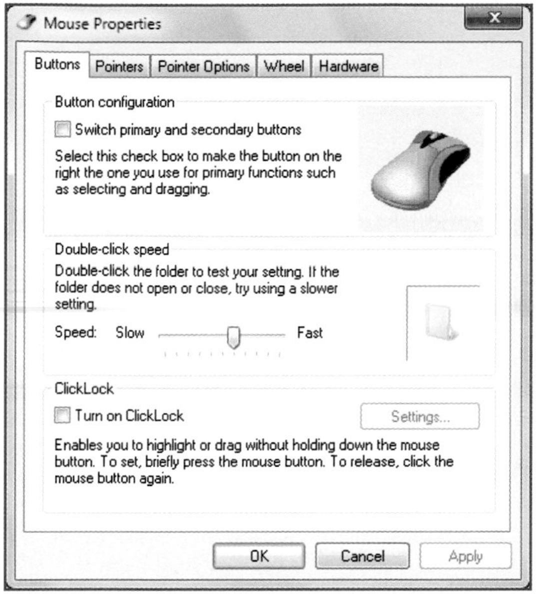

Figure 2-17: *The mouse is the primary way you operate in Windows 7.*

NOTE

If you have purchased a mouse separately from your computer and have installed its software, your tabs may be different and its features may not be as described here.

6. Click the **Pointers** tab. If you want to change the way the pointer looks, select a different scheme (see "Use a Different Mouse Pointer," earlier in the chapter).

7. When you have set up the mouse the way you want, click **OK**.

Customize the Keyboard

Windows requires a keyboard for manual communications (speech recognition can replace the keyboard in many instances). You can change the length of the delay before a key that is held down is repeated and the rate at which the key is repeated.

1. Click **Start** and click **Control Panel**.

2. In Category view, click **Large** or **Small Icons** view, and then click **Keyboard**. The Keyboard Properties dialog box appears.

3. Click in the text box in the middle of the dialog box, and press a character key to see how long you wait before the key is repeated and how fast the repeated character appears.

4. Drag the **Repeat Delay** slider in the direction desired, and then test the repetition again.

5. Drag the **Repeat Rate** slider in the direction desired, and then test the repetition again.

6. Drag the **Cursor Blink Rate** slider in the direction desired, and observe the blink rate.

7. When you have set up the keyboard the way you want, click **OK**.

Change Sounds

Windows 7 uses sounds to alert and entertain you. Through Control Panel's Sound component, you can select the sound scheme you want (see Figure 2-18).

1. Click **Start** and click **Control Panel**.

2. In Category view, click **Hardware And Sound**, and then click **Sound**.

   –Or–

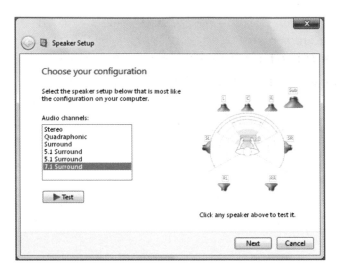

Figure 2-18: Windows 7 can handle up to a seven-speaker surround sound.

In Large or Small Icons view, click **Sound**.

In either case, the Sound dialog box appears.

3. Click **Speakers**, click **Configure** in the lower-left corner, select your configuration in the Audio Channels list, and click **Test** to test your setup. When you are ready, click **Next**.

4. If you have speakers in the configuration you choose that aren't actually present, click them, and click **Next**. Click the speakers that are full-range speakers, and click **Next**. When you are done, click **Finish**.

5. Double-click **Speakers**, click the **Levels** tab, and drag the sliders in the direction desired to set the volume. Click **OK** to close the Speakers Properties dialog box.

6. Click the **Sounds** tab, and select a different sound scheme to change it, if desired (see "Select the Sounds Windows 7 Plays" earlier in the chapter).

7. When you have set up the sounds the way you want, click **OK**.

Change Regional Settings

Windows 7 lets you determine how numbers, dates, currency, and time are displayed and used, as well as the languages that will be used. Choosing a primary language and locale sets all the other settings. You can customize these options through the Regional And Language Options component in the Control Panel.

1. Click **Start** and click **Control Panel**.

2. In Category view, click **Clock, Language, And Region**, and then click **Region And Language**.

   –Or–

   In Large or Small Icons view, click **Region And Language**.

   In either case, the Region And Language dialog box will appear, as you can see in Figure 2-19.

CAUTION

Changing the format used for dates and times might affect other Windows programs, such as Excel.

![Region and Language dialog box. Tabs: Formats, Location, Keyboards and Languages, Administrative. Format: English (United States). Date and time formats — Short date: M/d/yyyy; Long date: dddd, MMMM dd, yyyy; Short time: h:mm tt; Long time: h:mm:ss tt; First day of week: Sunday. What does the notation mean? Examples — Short date: 10/26/2010; Long date: Tuesday, October 26, 2010; Short time: 6:10 PM; Long time: 6:10:52 PM. Additional settings... Go online to learn about changing languages and regional formats. OK, Cancel, Apply.]

Figure 2-19: **Regional and language options allow Windows 7 to operate almost anywhere in the world.**

3. In the Formats tab, click the **Format** drop-down list, and select the primary language and region in which the computer will be used. This changes the standards and formats that will be used by default.

4. Customize the date and time formats by clicking the down arrow associated with each setting and selecting the option that you want.

5. Click **Additional Settings** and then go to the individual tabs for numbers, currency, time, and date; and set how you want these items displayed. Click **OK** when you are done.

6. Review the **Location**, **Keyboards And Languages**, and **Administrative** tabs, and make any desired changes.

7. When you have set up the regional settings the way you want, click **OK**.

Manage Gadgets

The Gadgets feature displays a clock and other gadgets—initially on the right side of the screen, but they can be moved. To manage gadgets:

1. Click **Start** and click **Control Panel**.

2. In Category view, click **Appearance And Personalization**, and then click **Desktop Gadgets**.

   –Or–

   In Large or Small Icons view, click **Desktop Gadgets**.

   In either case, the Gadgets window will open.

3. Double-click the gadgets that you want displayed.

4. If you want to see more gadgets, click **Get More Gadgets Online**. Internet Explorer will open and display the gadgets that are available. Under the gadget that you want, click **Get Now**. On the Windows Live page that appears, review the gadget, and click the **Download** button. If prompted, read the Unverified Submission notice and click **Install** if you want to continue. Click **Save**, navigate to a folder in which you want the gadget stored, and click **Save** again. Either a dialog box will open or a message will appear at the bottom of Internet Explorer, both of which will offer to open the folder that contains the downloaded gadget. Click **Open Folder** and double-click the gadget. Click **Install**. The new gadget appears on your desktop.

5. When you are ready, click **Close** to close the Gadgets window. Gadgets for headlines, weather, and central processing unit (CPU) meter (which tells you the amount of your computer resources you are using) are shown here on a desktop.

NOTE

Some gadgets that are available online cost money, and you need to be aware of that when you select them.

Chapter 3

Working with Information

The information on your computer—documents, email, photographs, music, and programs—are stored in **files**. So that your files are organized and more easily found, they are kept in **folders**, and folders can be placed in other folders for further organization. For example, a folder labeled "Ancestry," which is contained in the My Documents folder, contains separate folders for my parents, "J B Matthews" and "R S Matthews." The "J B Matthews" folder contains folders for my father's parents, as well as folders of photos and articles, and files for notes and lineage. Such a set of files and folders is shown in the My Documents folder in Figure 3-1.

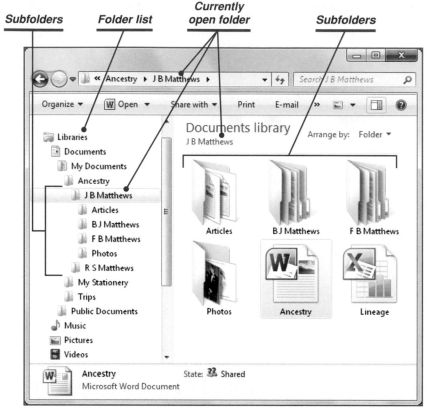

Subfolders   *Folder list*   *Currently open folder*   *Subfolders*

Figure 3-1: Windows stores files in folders, which can be within other folders.

> The term "objects" is used to refer to any mix of files, folders, and disk drives.

Work with Windows Explorer

The tool that Windows 7 provides to locate and work with files and folders is *Windows Explorer* (often called "Explorer," not to be confused with Internet Explorer discussed in Chapter 4). Windows Explorer has a number of components and features, most of which are shown in Figure 3-2 and described in Table 3-1. Much of this chapter is spent exploring these items and how they are used.

When you open Windows Explorer, you can choose what you want it to initially display from among the choices on the upper-right corner of the Start menu. These choices give you access to (from top to bottom):

- Your personal folder, which contains your documents, pictures, music, and games
- Your documents
- Your pictures
- Your music
- Your games
- The computer on which you are working

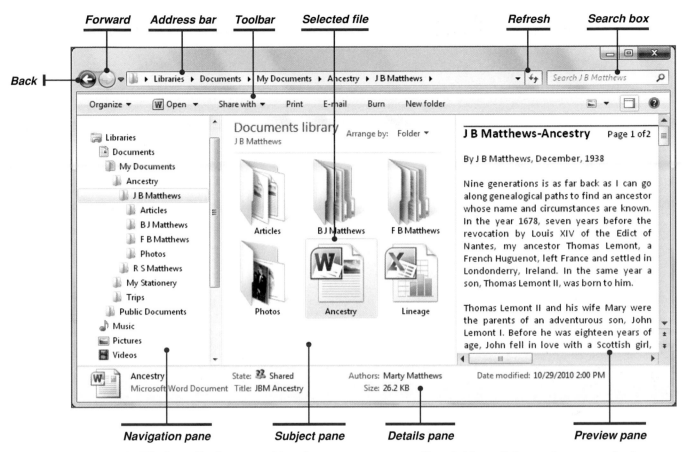

Forward   Address bar   Toolbar   Selected file   Refresh   Search box

Back

Navigation pane   Subject pane   Details pane   Preview pane

Figure 3-2: Windows Explorer provides the means to access files, folders, disks, and memory devices on your computer.

Start Windows Explorer

By default, Windows Explorer is pinned to the taskbar, and you can most easily start it by clicking this icon. For this example, though, start Windows Explorer using the Start menu.

1. Start your computer, if it's not running.

2. Click **Start**. The Start menu will open, and you'll see the Windows Explorer choices on the right of the menu.

AREA	FUNCTION
Back and Forward buttons	Displays an object previously shown.
Address bar	Displays the location of what is being shown in the subject pane.
Toolbar	Contains tools to work with objects in the subject pane.
Selected file	The object that is displayed in the preview pane and on which chosen operations, such as copy and delete, will be performed.
Refresh	Updates or refreshes the window specified in the address bar.
Search box	Allows you to search a folder or disk for specific text. Type the text you want to search for.
Preview pane	Displays the contents of the object selected in the subject pane.
Details pane	Provides information about the object selected in the subject pane.
Subject pane	Displays the objects stored at the address shown in the address bar.
Navigation pane	Facilitates moving around among the objects you have available.

Table 3-1: Windows Explorer Components

TIP

A good way to learn about the contents of your hard disk and how it is laid out is to simply explore it by clicking the many folders it contains. There are some folders, such as Windows and Programs that are not easily understood, but other folders, such as Users, have many files important to you, such as Contacts, Favorites, My Documents, and My Music. Knowing where these files are assists you in backing them up.

3. Click your personal folder (the one with your name on it). Explorer will open and display in the subject pane the files and folders that either come standard with Windows 7 or that have been placed there by you or somebody else, as shown in Figure 3-3. You can:

Click an object in the subject pane to *select* it and get information about it in the details pane, preview it in the preview pane (not shown in Figure 3-3 because an object is not yet selected), or use the toolbar tools with that object.

–Or–

Double-click an object in the subject pane to *open* it in Windows Explorer or its program, like Microsoft Word, so that you can see and work with its contents.

Change Windows Explorer

You can change how Windows Explorer looks and which features are available with the toolbar.

1. If Windows Explorer is not already open, click **Start** and click your personal folder.

2. Click **Pictures** in the navigation pane, and then double-click **Sample Pictures** in the subject pane. Windows 7's sample pictures should open, as you can see in Figure 3-4.

3. Click one of the pictures. The toolbar changes to something like what is shown in the illustration.

These toolbar options are specific to a picture. Selecting other types of files would have generated different options.

4. Click **Organize** to open the Organize menu. Here you can perform operations on the object you have selected using menu options such as Cut, Copy, Paste, Delete, and Rename, and perform folder-related operations with menu options such as Layout, Folder And Search Options, and Close.

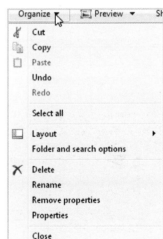

5. Click the **Change Your View** down arrow (not the button itself, which gives you another view of your folder—the down arrow is labeled "More Options") on the right of the toolbar. Drag the slider up and down to change first the size of the objects in your folder, and, as you continue downward, the arrangement of the objects.

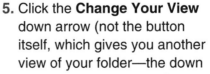

Figure 3-3: Windows 7 starts with a number of standard folders that are a part of your personal folder.

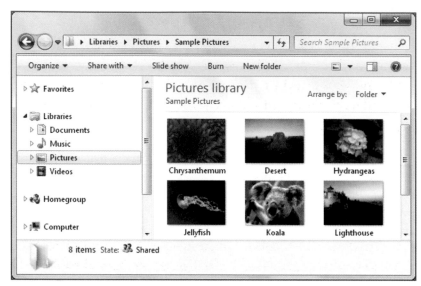

Figure 3-4: Windows Explorer's toolbar changes to provide commands for what is selected in the subject pane.

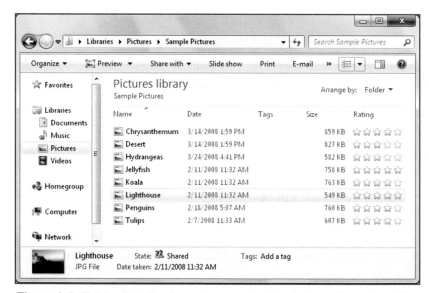

Figure 3-5: Folder Details view gives you further information about the objects in a folder.

6. Click the **Change Your Views** down arrow, and click **Details**, which is shown in Figure 3-5.

7. Click **Name** at the top of the left column in the subject pane. The contents of the subject pane will be sorted alphanumerically by name. Click **Name** again, and the contents will be sorted by name in the opposite direction.

8. Click one of the other column headings, and then click the same column heading again to see the contents sorted that way, first in one direction, and then in the other.

9. Click the Close button in the upper-right corner of the Explorer window to close it.

Locate and Use Files and Folders

The purpose of a file system, of course, is to locate and use the files and folders on your computer. Within your computer, there is a storage hierarchy that starts with storage devices, such as disk drives, which are divided into areas called folders, each of which may be divided again into subareas called subfolders. Each of these contains files, which can be documents, pictures, music, and other data. Figure 3-1 showed folders containing subfolders and eventually containing files with information in them. Figure 3-6 shows a computer containing disk drives, which in turn contain folders. Windows Explorer contains a number of tools for locating, opening, and using disk drives, folders, and files.

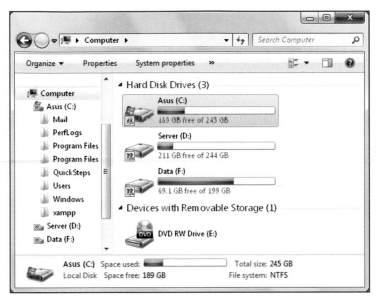

Figure 3-6: Your computer stores information in a hierarchy of disk drives and folders.

Recognize Storage Devices

Files and folders are stored on various physical storage devices, including disk drives, CD and DVD drives, memory cards and sticks, and Universal Serial Bus (USB) flash memory. You will have some, but not necessarily all, of the following:

- Primary floppy disk, labeled "A:"
- Primary hard disk, labeled "C:"
- CD or DVD drive, labeled "D:"
- Other storage devices, labeled "E:" and then "F:" and so on

Your primary floppy drive is always labeled "A:" (given that you still have one—most new computers don't). Your primary hard disk is always labeled "C:." Other drives have flexible labeling. Often, the CD or DVD drive will be drive "D:," but if you have a second hard disk drive, it may be labeled "D," as you can see in Figure 3-6.

Open Drives and Folders

When you open Windows Explorer and display the items in Computer, you see the disk drives and other storage devices on your computer, as well as several folders, including Program Files, Users, and Windows, as you saw in Figure 3-6. To work with these drives and folders, you must select them; to see and work with their contents, you must open them.

1. Click **Start** and click **Computer** to open Windows Explorer and display the local disk drives, similar to what was shown in Figure 3-6.

2. In the subject pane (right pane), click disk **(C:)**. Disk (C:) will be highlighted and its characteristics will be displayed in the details pane (bottom pane).

3. Double-click disk **(C:)** in either the navigation or subject pane. Disk (C:) will open and its folders will be displayed in the subject pane.

Figure 3-7: Double-clicking a drive or folder will open it in the subject pane.

4. Scroll down and double-click **Users** to open that folder and display your personal folder (the folder with your name on it) along with a Public folder.

5. Double-click your personal folder. The subject pane displays the files and folders in your folder. This will include Contacts, Desktop, My Documents, My Music, and others, as shown in Figure 3-7.

6. Keep double-clicking each folder to open it until you see the contents you are looking for.

Navigate Folders and Disks

Opening Windows Explorer and navigating through several folders—beginning with your hard disk—to find a file you want is fine. However, if you want to quickly go to another folder or file, you won't want to have to start with your hard disk every single time. The Windows 7 Explorer gives you three ways to do this: through the Libraries folder in the navigation pane, by using the folder tree in the navigation pane, or by using the address bar.

NAVIGATE USING LIBRARIES

The Windows 7 suggested way to navigate is through the Libraries folder, which contains links to the folders within your personal folder (called a "library" in this case, as shown next). By clicking a library in the navigation pane and then double-clicking folders within the subject pane, you can move around the folders and files within your personal folder. For example, given the folder structure shown Figure 3-1, here are the steps to open my J B Matthews folder.

1. Click **Start** and click **Documents**, which opens the Documents library within your personal Libraries folder.

TIP

It is easy to get confused with the various folders in the navigation pane. Both Favorites and Libraries are folders with *shortcuts*, or links to folders and files on your computer. The shortcuts in Libraries are links to the actual folders in the C:/Users/*Personal Folder*/My Documents, as you see in the section "Navigate Using Folders."

2. In the navigation pane, click the right-pointing triangle or arrow opposite the Documents library to open it (if the arrows are not visible, move your pointer into the navigation pane).

3. Still in the navigation page, click the right-pointing arrow opposite My Documents to open it.

4. If you had such a set of folders, you would repeat step 3 to open the Ancestry folder, and then click the **J B Matthews** folder to open it in the subject pane.

NAVIGATE USING FOLDERS

The portion of the navigation pane starting with Computer is a folder tree that contains all the disk drives, folders, and files on your computer in a tree, or hierarchical, structure. To open the same folder structure shown in Figure 3-1 through Computer:

1. Click **Start** and click **Computer**, which opens Computer. If you don't see the (C:) drive in the navigation pane, click the right-pointing arrow opposite Computer to open it there.

2. In the navigation pane, click the right-pointing arrow opposite (C:) disk drive to open it.

3. Still in the navigation pane, click the right-pointing arrow opposite Users to open it.

4. Repeat step 3 to open your personal folder and then the My Documents and Ancestry folders.

5. Click the **J B Matthews** folder to open it in the subject pane.

You can see that Libraries saves a couple of steps, but at the cost of possible confusion.

NAVIGATE USING THE ADDRESS BAR

Windows 7 gives you another way to quickly navigate through your drives and folders by clicking segments of a folder address in the address bar, as shown in the illustration.

If you click any segment of the address, you will open that level in the subject pane. If you click the arrow to the right of the segment, it displays a drop-down list of subfolders that you can jump to. By successively clicking segments and their subordinate folders, you can easily move throughout the storage space on your computer and beyond to any network you are connected to.

CREATE NEW FOLDERS

While you could store all your files within one of the ready-made folders in Windows 7—such as Documents, Music, or Pictures—you will probably want to make your files easier to find by creating several subfolders.

TIP

The small down arrow between the Forward button and the address bar displays a list of disks and folders that you recently displayed.

New folder

For example, to create the Ancestry folder discussed earlier:

1. Click **Start** and click **Documents**. Make sure nothing is selected.

2. Click **New Folder** on the toolbar. A new folder will appear in the Documents folder with its name highlighted.

3. Type the name of the folder, such as Ancestry, and press **ENTER**. Double-click your new folder to open it (you will see it's empty).

As an alternative to clicking New Folder on the toolbar, right-click the open area in the subject pane of Windows Explorer, click **New**, and click **Folder**. Type a name for the folder, and press ENTER.

Select Multiple Files and Folders

Often, you will want to do one or more operations—such as copy, move, or delete—on several files and/or folders at the same time. To select several files or folders from the subject pane of an Explorer window:

Move the mouse pointer to the upper-left area, just outside of the top and leftmost object. Then drag the mouse to the lower-right area, just outside of the bottom and rightmost object, adding shading across the objects, as shown in Figure 3-8.

–Or–

Click the first object, and press and hold **CTRL** while clicking the remaining objects, if the objects are noncontiguous (not adjacent to each other). If the objects are contiguous (next to each other), click the first object, press and hold **SHIFT**, and click the last object.

Use the Recycle Bin

If you do a normal delete operation in Explorer or the desktop, the deleted item or items will go into the Recycle Bin. Should you change your mind about the deletion, you can reclaim an item from the Recycle Bin, as explained in the "Renaming and Deleting Files and Folders" QuickSteps earlier in this chapter.

UICKSTEPS

RENAMING AND DELETING FILES AND FOLDERS

Sometimes, a file or folder needs to be renamed or deleted (whether it was created by you or by an application) because you may no longer need it for any number of reasons.

RENAME A FILE OR FOLDER

With the file or folder in view but not selected, to rename it:

In the subject pane, slowly click the name twice (don't double-click), type the new name, and press **ENTER**.

–Or–

In either the navigation or subject pane, right-click the name, click **Rename**, type the new name, and press **ENTER**.

DELETE A FILE OR FOLDER TO THE RECYCLE BIN

With the file or folder in view in either the navigation or subject pane, to delete it:

Click the icon for the file or folder to select it, press **DELETE**, and click **Yes** to confirm the deletion.

–Or–

Right-click the icon, click **Delete**, and click **Yes** to confirm the deletion.

Continued . . .

RENAMING AND DELETING FILES AND FOLDERS *(Continued)*

RECOVER A DELETED FILE OR FOLDER

To recover a file or folder that has been deleted:

Click the **Organize** menu, and click **Undo**. This only works if you perform the undo operation immediately after the deletion.

–Or–

Double-click the **Recycle Bin** on the desktop to display the Recycle Bin. Right-click the file or folder icon you want to undelete, and choose **Restore**.

Recycle Bin

PERMANENTLY DELETE A FILE OR FOLDER

If you're sure you want to permanently delete a file or folder:

Click the icon to select it, press and hold **SHIFT** while pressing **DELETE**, and click **Yes** to confirm the permanent deletion.

–Or–

Right-click the icon, press and hold **SHIFT** while clicking **Delete**, and click **Yes** to confirm the permanent deletion.

To select all objects in the subject pane, click **Organize** and click **Select All**; or click any object in the subject pane, and press **CTRL+A**.

Figure 3-8: Drag across multiple objects to select all of them.

The Recycle Bin is a special folder and it can contain both files and folders. You can open it and see its contents as you would any other folder by double-clicking its desktop icon or clicking it in the navigation pane (look under Favorites and Desktop). Figure 3-9 shows a Recycle Bin after deleting several files and folders. What makes the Recycle Bin special are the two special tasks in the toolbar:

- **Empty The Recycle Bin** permanently removes all of the contents of the Recycle Bin.

- **Restore All Items** returns all the contents to their original folders, in effect, "undeleting" all of the contents.

1 2 3 4 5 6 7 8 9 10

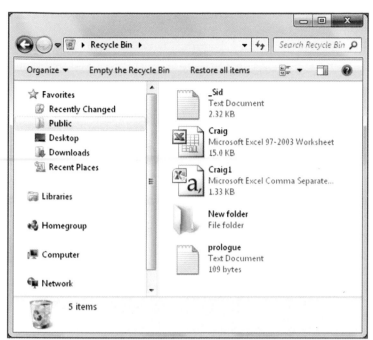

Figure 3-9: *The Recycle Bin holds deleted items so that you can recover them until you empty it.*

Obviously, there is a limit to how much the Recycle Bin can hold. You can limit the amount of space it takes so that it doesn't take over your hard disk. That and other settings are configured in the Recycle Bin's Properties dialog box.

1. Right-click the **Recycle Bin** on the desktop, and click **Properties**. The Recycle Bin Properties dialog box will appear, as you can see here.

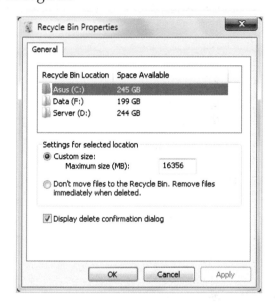

2. If you have multiple hard disks, select the drive you want to set. In any case, make sure **Custom Size** is selected, select the size, and type the number of megabytes you want to use ("16356" MB or megabytes is 16.356 gigabytes).

3. If you don't want to use the Recycle Bin, click **Don't Move Files To The Recycle Bin**. (This is strongly discouraged, however, since this means that files will be permanently deleted with no hope of recovery.)

4. If you don't need to see the deletion confirmation message, click that check box to deselect it. (Again this is discouraged, since it tells you what is happening to the files in case it is not what you want.)

5. When you are ready, click **OK** to close the dialog box.

TIP

Remember to empty your Recycle Bin. You'd be surprised how much stuff it will collect. Right-click the **Recycle Bin** on the desktop, and click **Empty Recycle Bin**.

Create Shortcuts

A shortcut is a link to a file or folder that allows you to quickly open the file or folder from places other than where it is stored. For example, you can start a program from the desktop even though the actual program file is stored in some other folder (a program shortcut is called a "link," as you can see in the illustrations here, but for our purposes it is the same as a shortcut). To create a shortcut:

1. In Windows Explorer, locate the program or other file or folder for which you want to create a shortcut.

2. If it is a program file (one that has the word "application" in the Type column), drag it to a different folder (as from a folder to the desktop).

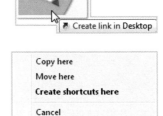

3. If it is any other file or folder, hold down the right mouse button while dragging the file or folder to a different folder, release the right mouse button, and then click **Create Shortcuts Here**.

–Or–

1. On the desktop or in the folder in Windows Explorer in which you want to create a shortcut, right-click a blank area, click **New**, and click **Shortcut**.

2. In the dialog box that appears, click **Browse**, and use the folder tree to locate and select the file or folder for which you want to make a shortcut.

3. Click **OK**, and click **Next**. Type a name for the shortcut, and click **Finish**.

UICKSTEPS

COPYING AND MOVING FILES AND FOLDERS

Copying and moving files and folders are similar actions, and can be done with the mouse alone, with the mouse and a menu, and with the keyboard.

COPY WITH THE MOUSE

To copy with the mouse, hold down **CTRL** while dragging any file or folder from one folder to another on the same disk drive, or drag a file or folder from one disk drive to another.

MOVE NONPROGRAM FILES ON THE SAME DISK WITH THE MOUSE

Move nonprogram files from one folder to another on the same disk with the mouse by dragging the file or folder.

MOVE NONPROGRAM FILES TO ANOTHER DISK WITH THE MOUSE

Move nonprogram files to another disk by holding down **SHIFT** while dragging them.

MOVE PROGRAM FILES WITH THE MOUSE

Move program files to another folder or disk by holding down **SHIFT** while dragging them.

COPY AND MOVE WITH THE MOUSE AND A MENU

To copy and move with a mouse and a menu, hold down the right mouse button while dragging the file or folder. When you release the right mouse button, a context menu opens and allows you to choose whether to copy, move, or create a shortcut (see "Create Shortcuts" in this chapter).

Copy here
Move here
Create shortcuts here

Cancel

Continued . . .

Search for Files and Folders

With large, and possibly several, hard disks, it is often difficult to find files and folders on a system. Windows Explorer's Search feature addresses that problem.

1. Click **Start** and notice the blinking cursor in the Search Programs And Files text box at the bottom of the menu.

2. Type all or part of the folder name, filename, or keyword or phrase in a file in the Search box. As you type, Windows 7 will start locating files and folders that match your criteria and display them in the top of the Start menu.

The search will be of all indexed files, the index for which is automatically built by Windows 7. After you have used the computer for a relatively short period, depending on the number of files you have, all nonprogram or not-system files will be indexed.

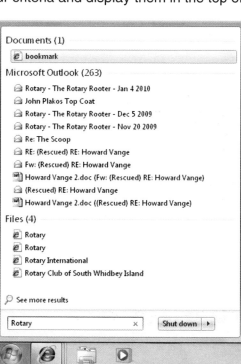

3. If you see the file or folder you are searching for, click it and it will be displayed in Windows Explorer (if a folder) or in the program that created it (if a file).

4. If you want to see more results, click **See More Results** at the bottom of the menu. Windows Explorer will open. Review the list in the subject pane; if you see the file or folder you want, click it to open it.

QUICKSTEPS

COPYING AND MOVING FILES AND FOLDERS *(Continued)*

COPY AND MOVE WITH THE KEYBOARD

Copying and moving with the keyboard is done with three sets of keys:

- **CTRL+C** ("Copy") copies the selected item to the Windows Clipboard.

- **CTRL+X** ("Cut") moves the selected item to the Windows Clipboard, deleting it from its original location.

- **CTRL+V** ("Paste") copies the current contents of the Windows Clipboard to the currently open folder. You can repeatedly paste the same Clipboard contents to any additional folders you want to copy to by opening them and pressing **CTRL+V** again.

To copy a file or folder from one folder to another using the keyboard:

1. In Windows Explorer, open the disk and folder containing the file or folder to be copied.

2. Select the file or folder, and press **CTRL+C** to copy the file or folder to the Clipboard.

3. Open the disk and folder that is to be the destination of the copied item.

4. Press **CTRL+V** to paste the file or folder into the destination folder.

5. If you still are not finding what you want, scroll the subject pane to the bottom and you'll see some additional options, as shown in Figure 3-10.

6. In the Search Again In options, you can choose one of three specific places to search, or click **Customize** to select one or more other places to search.

7. To filter the search results, click in the search text box in the upper-right corner of the Windows Explorer window. Two options will appear that let you filter the search results by the date it was modified and the size of the file.

8. To change search options, click **Organize** in the toolbar, and click **Folder And Search Options**. The Folder Options dialog box will appear. Click the **Search** tab. Make any change to the settings that you want, and click **OK**.

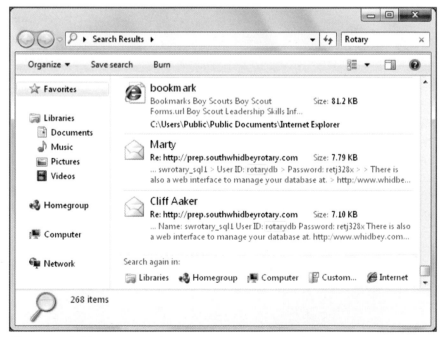

Figure 3-10: You may need to refine your search criteria to get only the files you are looking for.

TIP

You can also use the Cut and Copy commands in the object's context menu (by right-clicking the object) or Cut, Copy, and Paste from the Organize menu in Windows Explorer.

QUICK QUOTES

BOB FINDS SIMPLE IS EASIER

After being president of a succession of banks, I came into my retirement with little hands-on experience with computers, although I had overseen their introduction and use in our banks. Luckily, I had a number of friends and associates who helped me get set up and started using a personal computer. In this process, I picked up several pointers, primary among them, which I had known from other areas, was the K.I.S.S. principle of keeping it simple. I only have on my computers the programs I want to use frequently, and I have found that the simpler the set of folders I use, the easier it is to find what I need. It is easier to search through a number of files in a single folder than it is to search through a number of folders.

Bob O., 74, Washington

9. If you want to save the search, click **Save Search** on the toolbar, select the folder in which you want to store the file, type the filename, and click **Save**. If you don't select another folder, saved searches are available in the Searches folder by default. Saved searches also appear under Favorites in the navigation pane.

10. When you are done, close Windows Explorer.

Create Files

Files are usually created by applications or by copying existing files; however, Windows has an additional file-creation capability that creates an empty file for a particular application.

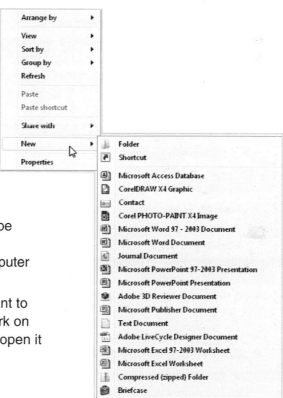

1. Click **Start**, click **Documents**, and open the folder in which you want to create the new file.

2. Right-click a blank area of the subject pane in Windows Explorer, and choose **New**. A menu of all the file types that can be created by the registered applications on your computer will appear.

3. Click the file type you want to create. If you want to work on the file, double-click it to open it in its application.

Continued . . .

Back Up Files and Folders

Backing up copies important files and folders on your disk and writes them on another device, such as a recordable CD or DVD, a USB flash drive, or to another hard disk. To start the backup process:

1. Click **Start** and click **Control Panel**. In Category view, click **System And Security**, and click **Backup And Restore**. If this is the first time you are doing a backup, you will have to set up Windows Backup.

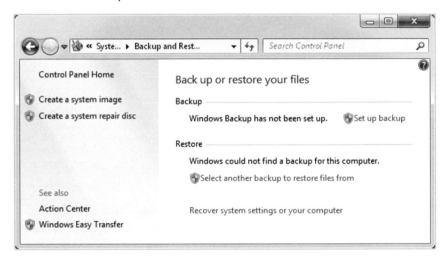

2. Click **Set Up Backup**. The Set Up Backup dialog box will appear, as shown in Figure 3-11.

3. Click a local backup destination drive or, if it is available on your computer, click **Save On A Network**.

4. If you chose to save on a network, click **Browse**, select a network drive and folder where you want the backup, click **OK**, and enter your network user name and password. Click **OK**. The network drive will appear on the list of destination drives. Click it.

5. Click **Next**. Accept the recommended **Let Windows Choose What To Backup** or click **Let Me Choose**, and then click **Next**.

UICKSTEPS

ZIPPING FILES AND FOLDERS

Windows 7 has a way to compress files and folders called "zipping." *Zipped* files are compatible with programs like WinZip and take up less room on a disk and are transmitted over the Internet faster.

CREATE A ZIPPED FOLDER

You can create a new zipped folder and drag files to it.

1. Click **Start** and click **Documents**.

2. Navigate to the folder that you want to contain the zipped folder.

3. Right-click in a blank area of the subject pane, click **New**, and click **Compressed (Zipped) Folder**. The zipped folder will appear.

New Compressed (zipped) Folder

4. Click the folder name, type a new name, and drag files and folders into it to compress them.

PACKAGE FILES OR FOLDERS TO A ZIPPED FOLDER

1. In Windows Explorer, select the files and/or folders you want zipped.

2. Right-click the selected objects, click **Send To**, and click **Compressed (Zipped) Folder**. A new zipped folder will appear containing the original files and/or folders, now compressed.

ZIPPING FILES AND FOLDERS
(Continued)

EXTRACT ZIPPED FILES AND FOLDERS

To unzip a file or folder, simply drag it out of the zipped folder, or you can extract all of a zipped folder's contents.

1. Right-click a zipped folder, and click **Extract All**. The Extract Compressed (Zipped) Folders dialog box will appear.

2. Enter or browse to the location where you want the extracted files and folders (or click **Make New Folder** if you want them in a new folder under the selected folder), and click **Extract**.

3. Close Windows Explorer when you are done.

TIP

When you zip a group of files, right-click the file whose name you want to give to the zip folder, and then click **Send To**. The file's name will automatically be given to the zip folder.

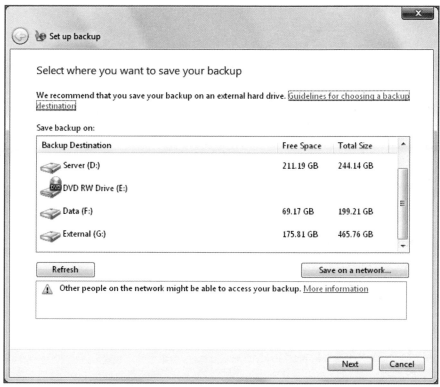

Figure 3-11: If possible, back up to an external drive.

6. If you chose the latter option, select the files and drives you want to back up, and click **Next**.

7. Review the Backup Summary that is presented. If it is not correct, click **Back** in the upper-left area, and return to the previous steps.

8. If the proposed schedule is not what you want, click **Change Schedule**. Select how often, what day, and what time you want to do the backup, and click **OK**.

NOTE

System and program files will not be backed up in an automatic scheduled backup.

9. Click **Save Settings And Run Backup**. Your next backup will be scheduled and the current backup will begin. You can stop the backup if you wish and change the settings in this window, which replaces the original Backup And Restore window.

10. When the backup is complete, you'll get a message that the backup has completed successfully. Click **Close**. The Backup And Restore window goes into its final form, shown in Figure 3-12. Click the **Close** button to close the Backup And Restore window.

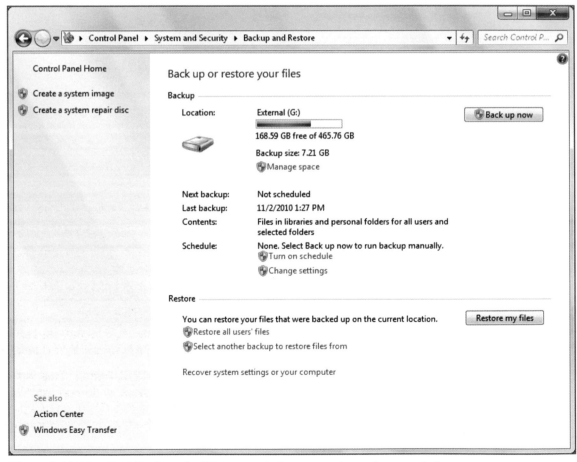

Figure 3-12: The final Backup And Restore window goes through several changes.

Write Files and Folders to a CD or DVD

Windows 7 allows you to copy ("burn" or record) files to a writable or rewritable CD or DVD. You must have a CD or DVD writing drive and blank media.

1. Place a blank recordable disc in the drive. You will be asked if you want to burn a CD or DVD using Windows Explorer or Windows Media Player, or possibly other programs on your computer.

2. Click **Burn Files To Disc**. Type a name for the disc. You will be shown two formatting options based on how you want to use the disc:

   • **Like A USB Flash Drive**, which is the default. This format, called *Live File System*, can only be read on a computer with Windows XP, Windows Server 2003 or 2008, Windows Vista, or Windows 7 operating systems. This option allows you to add one file or folder to the CD or DVD at a time, like you would with a hard disk or a USB flash drive. You can leave the disc in the drive and drag data to it whenever you want and delete previously added objects.

   • **With A CD/DVD Player**. This format, called Mastered, can be read by most computers, including older Windows and Apple computers and most stand-alone CD and DVD players. To use this format, you must gather all the files in one place and then burn them all at one time.

TIP

The Live File System that lets you use CD-R/DVD-R discs like CD-RW/DVD-RW is a super capability that you can use much like an additional hard disk.

MANAGING DISKS

Windows 7 provides three tools to help manage the files and folders stored on hard disks.

CLEAN UP A DISK

Disk Cleanup helps you get rid of old files on your hard disk. Windows looks through your hard disk for types of files that can be deleted and lists them, as shown in Figure 3-13. You can then select the types of files you want to delete.

1. Click **Start**, click **Computer**, right-click a disk drive you want to work on, and click **Properties**.

2. Click **Disk Cleanup**. Windows 7 will calculate how much space you could save.

3. Select the types of files to delete, and click **OK**. You are asked if you want to permanently delete these files. Click **Delete Files** to permanently delete them.

4. When you are ready, close the Properties dialog box.

CHECK FOR ERRORS

Error Checking tries to read and write on your disk, without losing information, to determine if bad areas exist. If it finds a bad area, that area is flagged so that the system will not use it. Error Checking automatically fixes file system errors and attempts recovery of bad sectors.

1. Click **Start**, click **Computer**, right-click a disk drive you want to work on, and click **Properties**.

Continued . . .

Use this format for music and video files that you want to play on automobile or stand-alone devices, such as MP3 and video players.

3. Click the option you want, and click **Next**. If you chose Like A USB Flash Drive, the disc will be formatted and, depending on the option you choose, a new AutoPlay dialog box may appear.

4. With the Live File System, in the AutoPlay dialog box, click **Open Folder To View Files**.

5. In either case, a Windows Explorer window will open with the subject pane message "Drag files to this folder to add them to the disc."

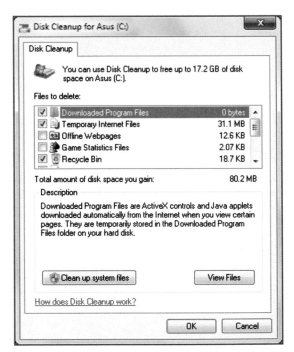

Figure 3-13: It is important to get rid of files and folders that you are no longer using.

MANAGING DISKS (Continued)

2. Click the **Tools** tab, and click **Check Now**. Select whether you want to automatically fix errors and/or attempt recovery of bad sectors, and click **Start**. You may be told you have to restart Windows to use Error Checking. If so, close any open applications, click **Schedule Disk Check** to do a disk check the next time you start your computer, and then restart your computer. Error Checking will automatically begin when Windows restarts.

You will be shown the status of the Error Checking operation and told of any problems that could not be fixed. When Error Checking is complete, your computer will finish restarting.

DEFRAGMENT A DISK

When files are stored on a hard disk, they are broken into pieces (or *fragments*) and individually written to the disk. As the disk fills, the fragments are spread over the disk as space allows. To read a file that has been fragmented requires extra disk activity and can slow down the performance of your computer. To fix this, Windows has a defragmentation process that rewrites the contents of a disk, placing all of the pieces of a file in one contiguous area.

1. Click **Start**, click **Computer**, right-click a disk drive you want to work on, and click **Properties**.

Continued . . .

6. Open another Windows Explorer window, locate the files and folders you want on the CD or DVD, and drag them to the CD/DVD drive subject pane.

● If you are using the Live File System format, as you drag the objects to the drive, they will be immediately written on the disc. When you have written all the files you want to the disc, right-click the drive and click **Close Session**. After the "Closing Session" message above the notification area disappears, you can remove the disc from the drive and insert it at a later time to resume adding or removing files and folders.

● If you are using the Mastered format, drag all the objects you want written on the disc to the drive. When all files and folders are in the drive's subject pane, click **Burn To Disc**. You are asked to confirm or change the title, select a recording speed, and click **Next**. When the burn is complete, the disc will be ejected and you can choose to burn the same files to another disc. In any case, click **Finish** when you are done. The temporary files will be erased, which might take a few minutes.

7. When you are done, click **Close** to close Windows Explorer.

QUICKSTEPS

MANAGING DISKS (Continued)

2. Click the **Tools** tab, and click **Defragment Now**. The Disk Defragmenter will open, as shown in Figure 3-14. You can choose to turn off the automatic defragmentation by deselecting the drives to be defragmented, or you can modify the schedule.

3. If you wish to go ahead manually, such as with an external drive not otherwise defragmented, shown in Figure 3-14, select the drive and click **Analyze Disk** to see if the disk needs defragmenting. If you wish to continue, click **Defragment Disk**. The process can take up to a couple of hours. Some fragments may remain, which is fine.

4. When you are ready, click **Close** to close the Disk Defragmenter window.

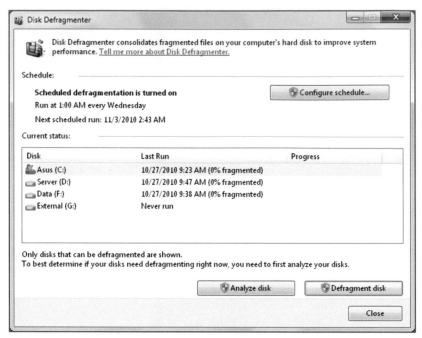

Figure 3-14: Defragmenting brings pieces of a file together into one contiguous area.

TIP

A very good way of backing up important information on your computer is to write the files to a CD and put the CD in your bank safety deposit box.

NOTE

By default, Windows 7 automatically defragments your drives on a periodic basis, so under most circumstances, you won't need to do it.

Chapter 4
Exploring the Internet

The Internet provides a major means for worldwide communication between both individuals and organizations, as well as a major means for locating and sharing information. For many, having access to the Internet is the primary reason for having a computer. To use the Internet, you must have a connection to it using one of the many means that are now available. You then can send and receive email; access the World Wide Web; watch movies; and participate in blogs, forums, and newsgroups, among many other things.

Connect to the Internet

You can connect to the Internet using a telephone line, a cable TV connection, a satellite link, or a land-based wireless link. Across these various types of connections there are a myriad of speeds, degrees of reliability, and costs. The most important factor is what is available to you at the location where you want to use it. In an urban area, you have a number of alternatives, from landline phone companies, cell phone companies, and cable TV companies, all with varying degrees of speed, reliability, and cost. As you move away from the urban area, your options will decrease the further away you are, until you have only a telephone dial-up connection and/or a satellite link available. With a telephone line, you can connect with a *dial-up* connection, a *DSL* (digital subscriber line) connection, or other high-speed connections of various types. DSL, cable, satellite, and some wireless connections are called *broadband* connections and offer higher speeds and are always on—you don't have to turn them on and off. You must have access to at least one of the forms of communication in order to connect to the Internet, and the Internet connection itself may need to be set up.

Research the types of connections available to you and their cost. Start by talking to your friends and neighbors, see what they use and how happy they are with their service. Then call your phone company and your cable TV company and ask them about their Internet offerings.

With most forms of Internet connections, you have a choice of speed and ancillary services, such as the number of free email accounts and possibly a personal website. Also, depending on the type of connection, you may need dedicated equipment, such as a modem, DSL router, or satellite-receiving equipment, which may or may not be included in the monthly cost. Also, make sure you know not only what your Internet service will initially cost, but what it will cost after the introductory period.

Set Up an Internet Connection

Broadband Internet services, including DSL, TV cable, satellite, and high-speed wireless, provide an Internet link with a device called a *router* that connects your computer to the service. Normally your

TIP

If you have to use a dial-up connection, which you should avoid if possible, contact your phone company and have them lead you through the process of getting set up and becoming familiar with its use. You may need to get a *modem*, a device to connect your computer to a phone line, or one may be built into your computer—your phone company will be able to tell.

NOTE

To connect to the Internet, you need to have an existing account with an ISP with a user name and password for your account. If you want to use Internet mail, you need to know your email address, the type of mail server, the names of the incoming and outgoing mail servers, and the name and password for the mail account. This information is provided by your ISP when you establish your account.

Internet service provider (ISP) will provide the router and physically install it. With a router in place, your computer is connected to a broadband service and you are connected to the Internet at all times. There may be nothing else you need to do to connect to a broadband service. The easiest way to check if you are connected to the Internet is to try it out by clicking the **Internet Explorer** icon normally pinned to the left of the taskbar.

If an Internet webpage is displayed, like the MSN page shown in Figure 4-1, then you are connected and you need do no more. If you did not connect to the Internet, then you need to run through the following steps:

1. Have you (or has someone else) contacted an ISP (such as your phone or cable company) and contracted to have Internet service connected to your computer? If so, go to the next question. If not, you need to locate an ISP and contract for the service. To find a good ISP, in addition to asking friends and neighbors who are using the Internet, ask the store where you bought your computer.

2. If you know that you have contracted for an Internet service, then is your computer connected to it? Can you physically see the connection? If you can answer "yes" to both those questions, go to the next question. If not, contact your ISP and ask them about connecting your computer. They will either send someone out to do it or they will lead you through the steps to do it yourself.

3. If you have a service and your computer is connected to it and you still cannot connect to the Internet, then you probably need to change some settings on your computer. Contact your ISP and have them lead you through the changes you need to make. This is their job. They need to make sure your connection is working properly.

Figure 4-1 shows Internet Explorer (IE) 9, which is just becoming available as this book is written. Originally Windows 7 came with IE 8, but in early 2011 Windows 7 started including IE 9. If you have an earlier version of Windows 7 with IE 8, you can download IE 9 from Microsoft.com, which I recommend you do. It is both cleaner and faster, and leaves more room to display a webpage. This book assumes you are using IE 8 or 9.

Figure 4-1: The easiest way to see if you have an Internet connection is to try to connect to the Internet.

Use the World Wide Web

The *World Wide Web* (or just the *Web*) is the sum of all the websites in the world—examples of which are CNN, Google, and MSN (which was shown in Figure 4-1). The World Wide Web is what you can access with a *web browser,* such as Internet Explorer, which comes with Windows 7.

Browse the Internet

Browse the Internet (also called "surf" the Internet) refers to using a browser, like Internet Explorer, to go from one website to another to see the sites' contents. You can browse to a site by directly entering a site address, by navigating to a site from another site, or by using the browser controls. First, of course, you have to start the browser.

START A BROWSER

To start your default browser (assumed to be Internet Explorer), click the **Internet Explorer** icon on the left of the taskbar.

ENTER A SITE DIRECTLY

To go directly to a site:

1. Start your browser and click the existing address, or URL (uniform resource locator), in the address bar to select it.

2. Type the address of the site you want to open, as shown next, and either click **Go To** (the right-pointing arrow) next to the address bar or press **ENTER**.

USE SITE NAVIGATION

Site navigation is using a combination of links and menus on a webpage to locate and open another webpage, either in the same site or in another site:

- **Links** are words, phrases, sentences, or graphics that always have an open hand displayed when the mouse pointer is moved over them and, when clicked, take you to another location. They are often underlined—if not initially, then when you move the mouse pointer to them.

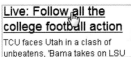

- **Menus** contain one or a few words in a horizontal list, vertical list, or both that always have an open hand displayed when the mouse pointer is moved over them and, when clicked, take you to another location.

Back · Address bar · Compatibility view · Stop

Forward · Pages recently entered · Refresh

USE BROWSER NAVIGATION

Browser navigation is using the controls within your browser to go to another location. Internet Explorer has two controls not discussed elsewhere that are used for navigation:

- **Back** and **Forward** buttons take you to the next or previous page in the stack of pages you have viewed most recently. Moving your mouse over these buttons will display a tooltip showing you the name of the page the button will take you to.

- **Pages recently entered** button displays a drop-down list of webpages that you have recently entered into the address bar, as well as a list of sites you recently visited (in IE 9).

Search the Internet

You can search the Internet in two ways: by using the search capability built into Internet Explorer and by using a search facility built into a website.

SEARCH FROM INTERNET EXPLORER

To use Internet Explorer's search box:

1. Click the **Internet Explorer** icon on the taskbar to open it.

2. In IE 8, click in the Search box on the right of the address bar, or in IE 9, click in the address bar. In either case, begin typing what you want to search for. (The first time you search in IE 9, click **Turn On Search Suggestions**.) Click one of the suggestions below the

Search box, and click **Search** (the magnifying glass in IE 8) on the right end of the Search box, or click **Go To** (IE 9), or press **ENTER**. By default, the Bing search site will open with the results of the search, as you can see in Figure 4-2.

3. Click the link of your choice to go to that site.

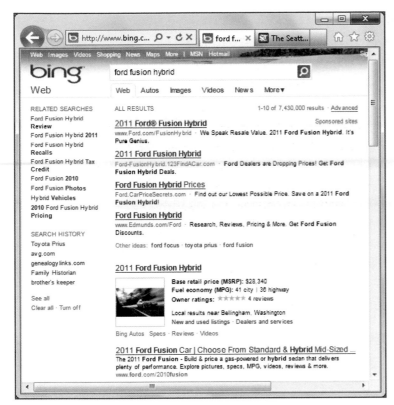

Figure 4-2: *The results of a search using Internet Explorer's Search box.*

SEARCH FROM AN INTERNET SITE

There are many independent Internet search sites. The most popular is Google.

1. In Internet Explorer, click the current address in the address bar, type google.com, and either click **Go To** (the blue arrow) or press **ENTER**.

2. In the text box, type what you want to search for. As you type, Google will display some guesses based upon what you have typed, with the resulting websites for those guesses shown in a full webpage, as illustrated in Figure 4-3.

3. Click the link of your choice to go to that site.

Figure 4-3: *The results of a search using Google.*

Save a Favorite Site

Sometimes you visit a site that you would like to return to quickly or often. Internet Explorer has a memory bank called Favorites to which you can save sites for easy retrieval.

ADD A FAVORITE SITE

To add a site to Favorites:

1. In Internet Explorer, open the webpage you want to add to your Favorites list, and make sure its correct address (URL) is in the address bar.
2. In IE 8, click **Favorites** in or above the tab row. In IE 9, click the **Favorites** icon on the right of the tab row.
3. In either case, click **Add To Favorites**. The Add A Favorite dialog box appears. Adjust the name as needed in the text box (you may want to type a name you will readily associate with that site), and click **Add**.

OPEN A FAVORITE SITE

To open a favorite site you have saved:

In Internet Explorer 8, click **Favorites** above the tab row. In IE 9, click the **Favorites** icon on the right of the tab row. In either case, click the site you want to open.

Use Tabs

Internet Explorer 8 and 9 allow you to have several webpages open at one time and easily switch between them by clicking the tab associated with the page. The tabs reside on the *tab row,* immediately above the displayed webpage, which also has the address bar in IE 9, as shown in Figure 4-4. Originally, only one page was open at a time in versions of Internet

Close Tab   New Tab

Figure 4-4: Tabs allow you to quickly switch among several websites.

QUICKSTEPS

CHANGING YOUR HOME PAGE

When you first start Internet Explorer, a webpage is automatically displayed. This page is called your *home page*. When you go to other webpages, you can return to this page by clicking the **Home** icon on the tab row. When IE starts, you can have it open several pages in addition to the home page, with the additional pages displayed as tabs (see "Use Tabs" in this chapter), which will also be opened when you click the Home Page icon. To change your home page and the other pages initially opened:

1. In Internet Explorer, directly enter or browse to the site you want as your home page. If you want additional pages, open them in separate tabs.

2. In IE 9 right-click the **Home Page** icon, and click **Command Bar**. In either IE 8 or in the IE 9 Command bar, click the **Home Page** down arrow, and click **Add Or Change Home Page**. The Add Or Change Home Page dialog box will appear.

Continued . . .

Explorer before IE 7. If you opened a second page, it replaced the first page. IE 7 and on, however, give you the ability to open multiple pages as separate tabs that you can switch among by clicking their tabs.

OPEN PAGES IN A NEW TAB

To open a page in a new tab instead of opening the page in an existing tab:

1. Open Internet Explorer, with at least one webpage displayed.

2. Click **New Tab** on the right end of the tab row, or press **CTRL+T**, and open another webpage in any of the ways described earlier in this chapter.

   –Or–

   Hold down **CTRL** while clicking a link in an open page. (If you just click the link, you'll open a page in the same tab.) Then click the new tab to open the page.

3. Repeat any of the alternatives in step 2 as needed to open additional pages.

SWITCH AMONG TABS

To switch among open tabs:

Click the tab of the page you want to open.

–Or–

Press **CTRL+TAB** to switch to the next tab to the right, or press **CTRL+ SHIFT+TAB** to switch to the next tab to the left.

–Or–

Press **CTRL+***n*, where *n* is a number from 1 to 8 to switch to one of the first eight tabs numbered from the left in the order they were opened.

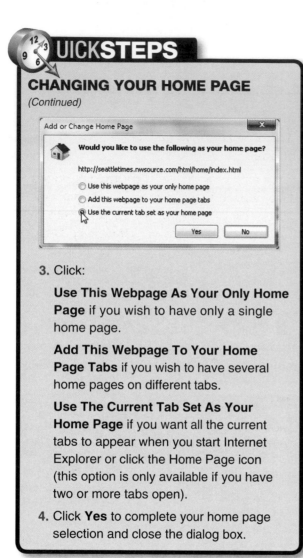

CHANGING YOUR HOME PAGE
(Continued)

3. Click:

Use This Webpage As Your Only Home Page if you wish to have only a single home page.

Add This Webpage To Your Home Page Tabs if you wish to have several home pages on different tabs.

Use The Current Tab Set As Your Home Page if you want all the current tabs to appear when you start Internet Explorer or click the Home Page icon (this option is only available if you have two or more tabs open).

4. Click **Yes** to complete your home page selection and close the dialog box.

(You need to use a number key on the top of the main keyboard, *not* on the numeric keypad on the right). You can also press **CTRL+9** to switch to the last tab that was opened, shown on the right of the tab row.

CLOSE TABS

To close one or more tabs:

Right-click the tab for the page you want to close, and click **Close Tab** on the context menu; or click **Close Other Tabs** to close all of the pages except the one you clicked.

–Or–

Press **CTRL+W** to close the current page.

–Or–

Click the tab of the page you want to close, and click the **X** on the right of the tab.

Access Web History

Internet Explorer keeps a history of the websites you visit, and you can use that history to return to a site. You can set the length of time to keep sites in that history, and you can clear your history.

USE WEB HISTORY

To use the Web History feature:

1. Click Favorites or its icon, and click the History tab or press **CTRL+H** to open the History pane.

2. Click the down arrow on the History tab bar to select how you want the history sorted. Depending on what you select, you will be able to further specify the type of history you want to view. For example, if you click View By Date, you can then click the day, website, and webpage you want to open, as shown in Figure 4-5.

Figure 4-5: The Web History feature allows you to find a site that you visited in the recent past.

TIP

To view and use Internet Explorer's menus, press just the **ALT** key.

QUICKSTEPS

ORGANIZING FAVORITE SITES

After a while, you will probably find that you have a number of favorite sites and it is becoming hard to find the one you want. Internet Explorer provides two places to store your favorite sites: a Favorites list, which is presented to you in the form of a menu you can open, and a Favorites bar, which can be displayed at all times. There are several ways to organize your favorite sites.

REARRANGE THE FAVORITES LIST

The items on your Favorites list are displayed in the order you added them, unless you drag them to a new location.

In Internet Explorer, click **Favorites** or the icon, locate the site you want to reposition, and drag it to the location in the list where you want it.

CREATE NEW FOLDERS

Internet Explorer (both 8 and 9) comes with several default folders added by Microsoft or by the computer's manufacturer. You can also add your own folders within the Favorites list.

1. In Internet Explorer, click **Favorites** or the icon, click the **Add To Favorites** down arrow, and click **Organize Favorites** to open the Organize Favorites dialog box, shown in Figure 4-6.

Continued . . .

DELETE AND SET HISTORY

You can set the length of time to keep your Internet history, and you can clear this history.

1. In Internet Explorer, click **Tools** or its icon at the right end of the tab row, and click **Internet Options**.

2. In the General tab, under Browsing History, click **Delete** to open the Delete Browsing History dialog box. If needed, select the check box opposite History to delete it. Select any other check box to delete that information, although you should keep the Preserve Favorites Website Data check box selected to *keep* that information (it is a confusing dialog box). Click **Delete**.

3. Click **OK** again to close the Internet Options dialog box.

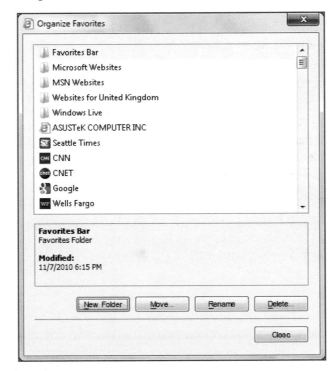

Figure 4-6: As with files, organizing your favorite websites helps you easily find what you want.

ORGANIZING FAVORITE SITES

(Continued)

2. Click **New Folder**, type the name for the folder, and press **ENTER**.

3. Drag the desired site links to the new folder, drag the folder to where you want it on the list, and then click **Close**.

PUT FAVORITES IN FOLDERS

You can put a site in either your own folders (see "Create New Folders") or the default ones when you initially add it to your Favorites list.

1. Open the webpage you want in your Favorites list, and make sure its correct address or URL is in the address bar.

2. Click **Favorites** or the icon, click **Add To Favorites**, adjust the name as needed in the text box, click the **Create In** down arrow, select the folder to use, and click **Add**.

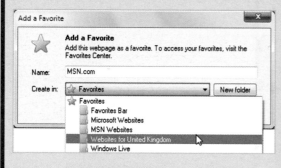

ADD A SITE TO THE FAVORITES BAR

In IE 8, by default, a Favorites bar is displayed on the same row with and to the right of the Favorites menu. In IE 9, you can turn on the

Continued . . .

Copy Internet Information

You may occasionally find something on the Internet that you want to copy—a picture, some text, or a webpage.

COPY A PICTURE FROM THE INTERNET

To copy a picture from a webpage to a folder on your hard disk:

1. Open Internet Explorer and locate the webpage containing the picture you want.

2. Right-click the picture and click **Save Picture As**. Locate the folder in which you want to save the picture, enter the filename you want to use, and file type, if it is something other than the default .jpg, and click **Save**.

> Open link
> Open link in new tab
> Open link in new window
> Save target as...
> Print target
>
> Show picture
> Save picture as...
> E-mail picture...
> Print picture...

3. Close Internet Explorer if you are done.

COPY TEXT FROM THE INTERNET TO WORD OR EMAIL

To copy text from a webpage to a Microsoft Word document or email message:

1. Open Internet Explorer and locate the webpage containing the text you want.

2. Drag across to highlight the text, right-click the selection, and click **Copy**.

3. Open a Microsoft Word document or an email message in which you want to paste the text. Right-click where you want the text, and click **Paste**.

4. Save the Word document and close Internet Explorer, Microsoft Word, or your email program if you are done with them.

COPY A WEBPAGE FROM THE INTERNET

To make a copy of a webpage and store it on your hard disk:

1. Open Internet Explorer and locate the webpage you want to copy.

QUICKSTEPS

ORGANIZING FAVORITE SITES

(Continued)

Favorites bar by right-clicking any of the three icons (Home, Favorites, and Tools) on the right of the tab row and clicking **Favorites Bar**. By default, the Favorites bar has two sites on it, but you can add others.

Open the site you want to add to the Favorites bar. In either IE 8 or IE9, if the Favorites bar is open, click the **Add To Favorites Bar** button on the left of the Favorites bar.

–Or–

In either IE 8 or 9, click **Favorites**, click the **Add To Favorites** down arrow, and click **Add To Favorites Bar**.

DELETE A FAVORITE SITE

You can delete a favorite site from either the Favorites list or the Favorites bar by right-clicking it and then clicking **Delete**.

CAUTION

Material you copy from the Internet is normally protected by copyright; therefore, what you can do with it is limited. Basically, you can store it on your hard disk and refer to it. You cannot put it on your own website, sell it, copy it for distribution, or use it for a commercial purpose without the permission of the owner.

2. In IE 8, click **Page** on the tab row, and click **Save As**. In IE 9, click the **Tools** icon, click **File**, and click **Save As**.

3. In the Save Webpage dialog box, select the folder in which to save the page, enter the filename you want to use, and click **Save**.

4. Close Internet Explorer if you are done.

Play Internet Audio and Video Files

You can play audio and video files on the Internet with Internet Explorer directly from a link on a webpage. Many webpages have links to audio and video files, such as the one shown in Figure 4-7. To play these files, simply click the links. If you have several audio players installed (for example, Windows Media Player and Real Player),

Figure 4-7: Play an audio or video file on a webpage by clicking the link.

you will be asked which one you want to use. Make that choice, and the player will open to play the requested piece.

Chapter 10 discusses working with audio and video files in depth, including how to play these files in several ways.

Use the Internet

The Internet is a major way in which you can connect with the world that provides information, shopping, contact with government agencies, getting directions and maps, and planning and purchasing travel, to name only a fraction of what you can do. In later chapters of this book we'll look at using the Internet for email, social networking, digital photography, music and video, personal finance, and genealogy. For the rest of this chapter we'll look at using the Internet in a number of other, possibly more general, ways.

Get Information

The start of many things you do on the Internet is through a search. As you have seen earlier in this chapter, searching the Internet is easy through either the Internet Explorer's Search box, which by default is the Microsoft Bing search engine, or a search website like Google .com. While there are a number of other search sites, for example, Ask.com, I've found that Google and Bing are as good as any and handle all that I want to do.

You can search for almost anything and in most cases find it. Sometimes you need to be more diligent than other times, but often you can find what you are looking for. Several examples of searches follow.

SEARCH FOR HISTORICAL FIGURES

In the last several years there have been movies and television programs on England's King Henry VIII and Queen Elizabeth I, his daughter. In these, two historical figures named Mary come up: Mary Tudor and Mary Queen of Scots. Let's say you are curious and want to know more about these two people and how they are related.

1. In Internet Explorer's address bar highlight the current contents and type <u>google.com</u>.

2. In Google's text box, type <u>Mary Tudor and Mary Queen of Scots</u> and press **ENTER**. The Google page similar to that shown in Figure 4-8 will open.

3. Review the first several entries, and click the first one you want to see. A page similar to the one shown in Figure 4-9 will open.

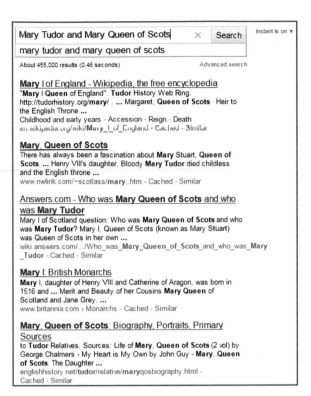

Figure 4-8: A search can be a question, a statement, a word, or a phrase. Often a question can be truncated, as it is here, where "who were" has been left off.

NOTE

Searches on the Internet are seldom the same, as it is a dynamic and changing environment. New pages, re-ordered pages, and obsolete pages are constantly changing and creating new results for searches.

Figure 4-9: Sometimes a search can quickly lead you to the answer you want.

4. If the results of the first entry do not satisfy your curiosity, click **Previous** in Internet Explorer's address bar to return to the list of search results and click another entry.

SEARCH FOR RECIPES

The Internet is a tremendous resource for recipes. All you have to do is search. Here is an example with white bean soup.

1. In the Internet Explorer Search box (in IE 8) or in the address bar (in IE 9) type white bean soup. By default the Bing search engine is used and as you are typing, search suggestions will appear below the Search box.

Figure 4-10: If you like to cook, the Internet is a great resource for you.

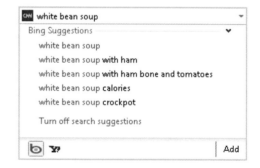

2. If you want one of the suggestions, click it. Otherwise press **ENTER**. A list of sites with a recipe for this dish appears, similar to what you see in Figure 4-10.

Be sure and look beyond the first page of search results. Often you'll find some great resources off the first page.

Get the News

With the Internet's almost immediate communication, it is a great vehicle for getting news of all types, including local and national newspapers, general and specialized magazines, and newsletters of all types. Several examples follow.

READ ONLINE NEWSPAPERS

Most newspapers have been online for some time. Generally, you can go right to their site by putting their name directly into the address bar followed by ".com" without searching for them. For example, the following URLs all work:

- ajc.com (*Atlanta Journal Constitution*)
- bostonherald.com
- chicagotribune.com
- denverpost.com
- kcstar.com (*Kansas City Star*)
- latimes.com (*Los Angeles Times*)
- miamiherald.com
- times.com (*New York Times*)
- philly.com (*Philadelphia Inquirer*)
- seattletimes.com
- wsj.com (*Wall Street Journal*)
- washingtonpost.com

READ ONLINE MAGAZINES

Many magazines that once had paper editions are now only online, while others are now charging for their online editions. For example *Consumer Reports* (consumerreports.org, .com also works) and *Cook's Illustrated* (cooksillustrated.com), which give you their home page for free, ask you to pay when you want to see the detail, as you can see in Figure 4-11. For the most part, you can directly use the magazine title with ".com" in Internet Explorer's address bar.

READ NEWSLETTERS

There are a great many newsletters on the Internet. Practically every organization that has an Internet presence has a newsletter, either as

Figure 4-11: While the majority of Internet news and information content is free, an increasing number of sites are beginning to charge for it.

a part of their site or one that is emailed to you. If you belong to or are otherwise a part of an organization, inquire about looking at their newsletter online or receiving it by email.

Contact Government Agencies

Most government agencies from the local to the federal level have an online presence that can be very useful in finding out about government programs, learning about public officials, and getting the results of elections. Three examples are the Social Security Administration, researching the position of a congressperson, and looking at the results of a statewide election.

SOCIAL SECURITY ADMINISTRATION

Probably the fastest way of locating a website is to search the name of the entity; similarly, the fastest way to find what you want in a site is to do an intrasite search. Let's say you want to find the current eligibility requirements for Social Security.

1. In the Internet Explorer Search box (in IE 8) or in the address bar (IE 9), type <u>social security</u> and press **ENTER**. One of the entries that appears is titled "Social Security Online - The Official Website…"

2. In the search box under "Search within www.ssa.gov", type <u>eligibility requirements</u> and click **Search**.

3. Review the search results and click the entry that is most likely to give you the information you need.

4. Follow any additional links that you need to get your information.

KEN FINDS NEW WAYS TO PURSUE HOBBIES

I am a retired civil/structural engineer and as such, I have had a rather lengthy exposure to computers of all sizes. I have now been using personal computers for over ten years and would find it very hard, if not impossible, to be without them. I use them for email, banking, paying bills, and monitoring credit cards, as well as researching medical questions, things we are thinking of buying, and low-cost travel. Probably most important to me is the support that a personal computer provides in the photography and video areas. I have had a long-time hobby of taking pictures and making movies, and what I can now do with my computer in that area constantly amazes me. I do video editing; photograph touch-ups, organization, and storage and burning both photographs and videos to CDs and DVDs. I even have a device that transfers film negatives and photographic slides to my computer so I can edit and store them. The personal computer has given me many tools in this area that I never dreamed about before they appeared.

Ken H., 70, Derbyshire, UK

RESEARCH A CONGRESSPERSON

If you would like to determine the views of your congressperson and you don't remember his or her name or the district number he or she represents, you can find all that online.

1. In the Internet Explorer address bar, type google.com.

2. In the Google search box, type your state name and congressional districts, and press **ENTER**. Your results should be similar to the illustration.

> **washington state congressional districts**   ✕   Search
>
> About 9,010,000 results (0.23 seconds)   Advanced search
>
> ▸ Statewide Map of Washington Legislative Districts
> History of the **State** Legislature ... You may use the information below to find your legislative district and **congressional district**. ...
> apps.leg.**wa**.gov/**District**Finder/ - Cached
>
> Washington's Representatives - **Congressional District Maps (WA ...**
> The two senators from **Washington** are Sen. Cantwell, Maria [D-**WA**] and Sen. ... The map to the right shows the **congressional districts** in this **state**. ...
> www.govtrack.us › Congress › Members of Congress - Cached - Similar
>
> Washington State Legislature
> Congress - the Other **Washington** ... Legislator Information, Find Your **District**, Bill Search ... (List of legislators, their committees, **districts**, ...
> Bill Information - Find Your Legislator - RCW
> www.leg.**wa**.gov/ - Cached - Similar

3. Click the entry with "Congressional District Maps" in its title with the URL govtrack.us. The result should look similar to Figure 4-12, except for your state.

4. Note your district, scroll down to locate your congressperson, and click his or her name. A page about your congressperson should open. From here, you can see a brief or official biography, track his or her voting record, find out who donated to his or her campaign, and the bills that he or she alone sponsored.

5. Follow any of the links that interest you.

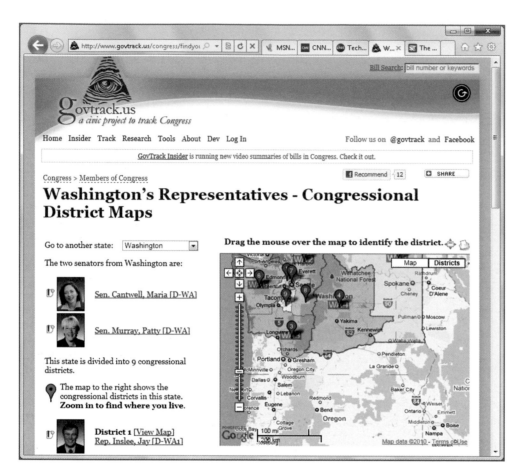

Figure 4-12: The Internet has a number of resources to help you understand and work with local, state, and federal governments.

STATEWIDE ELECTION

Most governmental jurisdictions (cities, counties, and states) maintain a page with the most recent election results. To find the results for a statewide race:

1. In Internet Explorer's Search box (IE 8) or address bar (IE 9), type the name of your state and the words "state election results," and press **ENTER**. A list of related topics should appear.

> **Washington Elections** Information
> Ballot, voter registration, current initiative, and general information for **elections** as reported through the **Washington** Secretary of **State's** office.
> www.secstate.wa.gov/elections · Cached page

2. Click the entry that looks most promising to you. A related detail page will open. Review that page and determine if you need to go further or if the information you want is available there.

Get Maps and Directions

Google and Microsoft, as well as other sites, have excellent and very detailed maps and driving directions. Here's how each works.

USE MICROSOFT MAPS

1. In Internet Explorer's Search box (IE 8) or address bar (IE 9), type an address or location you want to see on a map, and press **ENTER**. Among the search results is a small map.

2. Click **View Large Map** to see a full-sized map of the location or address you entered, as shown in Figure 4-13.

3. On this map you can:

- Zoom in for more detail or zoom out for area references by clicking or dragging in the scale on the upper left of the map.

- Drag the map around to see areas not currently in view by moving the mouse onto the map and dragging it in the direction you want it moved.

- View the map as a road map or as an aerial photograph in either straight down Aerial view or the slightly angled Bird's Eye view using the option on the top-right corner.

- Get driving directions from another location by clicking the auto icon on the bottom left of the page.

- Locate restaurants, businesses, malls, and hotels by clicking the options on the left side of the page.

Figure 4-13: Excellent maps are available online with many features not available any other way.

USE GOOGLE DIRECTIONS

Both Google and Microsoft provide very detailed driving directions between two or more locations.

1. In the Internet Explorer address box, type google.com to open the Google search site. At the top of the page you should see a row of options, either immediately or after a few seconds.

2. Click **Maps**. In the page that opens, note that you can put in an address or a location just as you did with Bing. Here, though, we'll get driving directions.

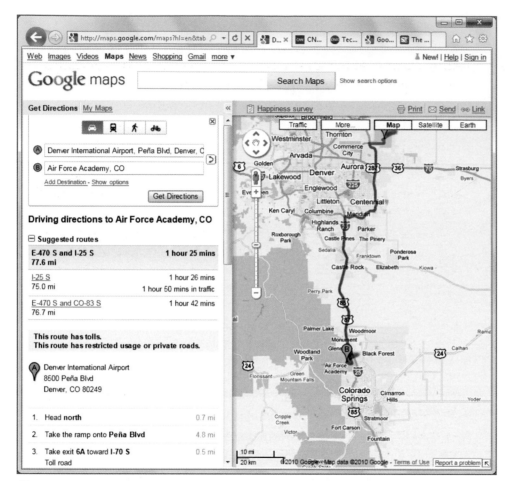

Figure 4-14: *With the advent of online maps and directions, you can more easily find your way.*

3. Click **Get Directions**. In the first text box, labeled "A," type the starting location. This can be a street address, a city or airport, or some other location identifier.

4. Press **TAB** and type the ending location or the location's first intermediate point. If you want to enter more locations, click **Add Destination**, and type that location.

5. Click **Get Directions**. A map will appear along with a detailed set of directions, as you can see in Figure 4-14. Click **Print** above the map to print the directions. If you want the map printed, click **Include Large Map**, and then click **Print** again.

6. Close the Print window. Back on the map, if you want to change your route, simply drag the blue line that represents it. You'll see the line move and the directions change accordingly.

7. As with the Bing map, you zoom by simply double-clicking the map, drag the map to show other areas, and look at it either as road map or as a satellite photograph.

Shop on the Internet

Shopping is one of the great benefits of having access to the Internet. You don't have to leave your home, you have access to far more outlets than are available in most places, prices are generally modest, and you have the ability to do comparison shopping to find the best products at the best prices. Look at three examples of online shopping for a digital camera, narrow shoes, and airline tickets.

Figure 4-15: For electronics, there is a wealth of information that allows you to find what you want, compare alternatives, and shop for the best price and terms.

TIP

When comparison shopping, make sure that you compare the price with shipping and tax, because, as you will see, not all stores are the same.

DIGITAL CAMERA

You may be aware that digital cameras are improving quickly and getting cheaper at the same time. If you are interested in getting a new one, you may be in a quandary as to which one to buy. Start by searching for camera reviews and then do some comparison shopping before finally buying a camera (you can't do this with all products, but electronics in particular can be handled in this way).

1. In either the Google or Internet Explorer Bing search box, type digital camera reviews and press **ENTER**. A page of sites that review digital cameras will appear.

2. Open several of the sites and look at what they offer. Some may be more comparison shopping than reviews of cameras. One site that I have found to be good is CNET Reviews. Click that link to open it.

> Digital cameras: compare **digital camera reviews** - CNET **Reviews**
> **Digital camera reviews** and ratings, video **reviews**, user opinions, most popular **digital cameras**, **camera** buying guides, prices, and comparisons.
> reviews.cnet.com/digital-cameras · Cached page

3. On the CNET site, in the middle of the page, click **Digital Camera Product Finder** to pick the camera that is right for you. Click the size you want and click **Next**, click the level of sophistication desired and click **Next**, click the features you want and click **See Results**. A page of possibilities is displayed, an example of which you can see in Figure 4-15.

4. Pick the camera you want to investigate further, and click the title of the camera to open a page devoted to it. Read the review and other information on the page.

5. Click **Compare Prices** in the Price Range section. Here you see a list of several stores with their customer rating, price, and whether the camera is in stock and has free shipping (enter your ZIP code to determine this).

6. If you are ready to go ahead, click **Shop Now** and follow the instructions to purchase the camera.

AIRLINE TICKETS

Airlines now prefer and reward buying tickets online. You often save money, sometimes a lot, may also be entitled to fast electronic check-in at the airport, and sometimes get bonus miles. There are many sources of airline tickets on the Internet, including the airlines themselves and numerous travel sites. Sometimes the sites can save you money, but often the cheapest fares are from the airlines, and some airlines, such as Southwest, do not allow sales through the travel sites, so you need to look at both the airlines and the travel sites. Also, some travel sites, such as Fly.com, will compare the fares on several other travel sites. What I recommend is that you start by comparing travel sites with Fly.com, then go to the site that looks best, and finally go to the airline that looks best. Also, if you are going along a Southwest route, you want to check them (Southwest does not charge for up to two pieces of checked luggage, which on other airlines can be $25 to $35 a bag).

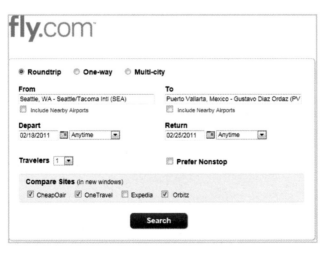

1. In Internet Explorer's address bar, type fly.com and press **ENTER**. Type the from and to cities, select the departure and return dates and times and the number of travelers, and click the travel sites you want to compare, as shown in the illustration.

2. Click **Search**. Your screen becomes very busy, and you may see a message that a pop-up window has been blocked. Click to allow the pop-up. You see a Fly.com summary, shown next, and then a narrow window for each of the travel sites you selected, as you can see in Figure 4-16.

Priceline.com has a Name Your Own Price program that allows you enter from and to locations and the dates you want to fly, and then enter the round-trip fare before taxes and fees that you want to pay. (You can also do this for hotels and rental cars.) Priceline says you can save up to 40 percent on flights. The catch is that you have to pay for the tickets ahead of time, you can't specify the airline or the time of day you will fly, the ticket must be roundtrip and for economy class only. If your price is accepted, your money is nonrefundable and nontransferable, the ticket cannot be changed, and you don't get mileage credits. Priceline does promise that domestic flights will leave only between 6 A.M. and 10 P.M. unless the city pairs require off-peak travel and that there will be no more than one connection each way. If you have some flexibility, it can save you some money.

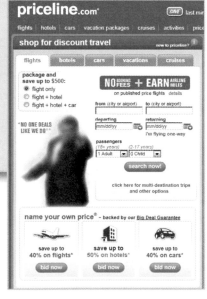

3. Expand (click **Maximize** on the right of the title bar) and review each of the travel sites (be sure to get the total price with both taxes and fees included, not just the advertised price.

4. Pick an airline and enter their name in the Internet Explorer address bar (don't click their name in Fly.com or another travel site because you want the best fare the airline itself will offer). Re-enter the from and to cities and dates and times. Click **Search** or the equivalent button (Alaska Airlines uses "Shop"). The results for that airline will be displayed. It may surprise you.

5. If Southwest flies the route you want to fly (type southwest.com in the address bar and enter your from and to cities), check their fares. Initially the fares are displayed one-way without fees and taxes, so you need to select a departing and a returning flight. Click **Continue** to go to the Price page and see the total cost.

It may take some work and perseverance to find the lowest fare.

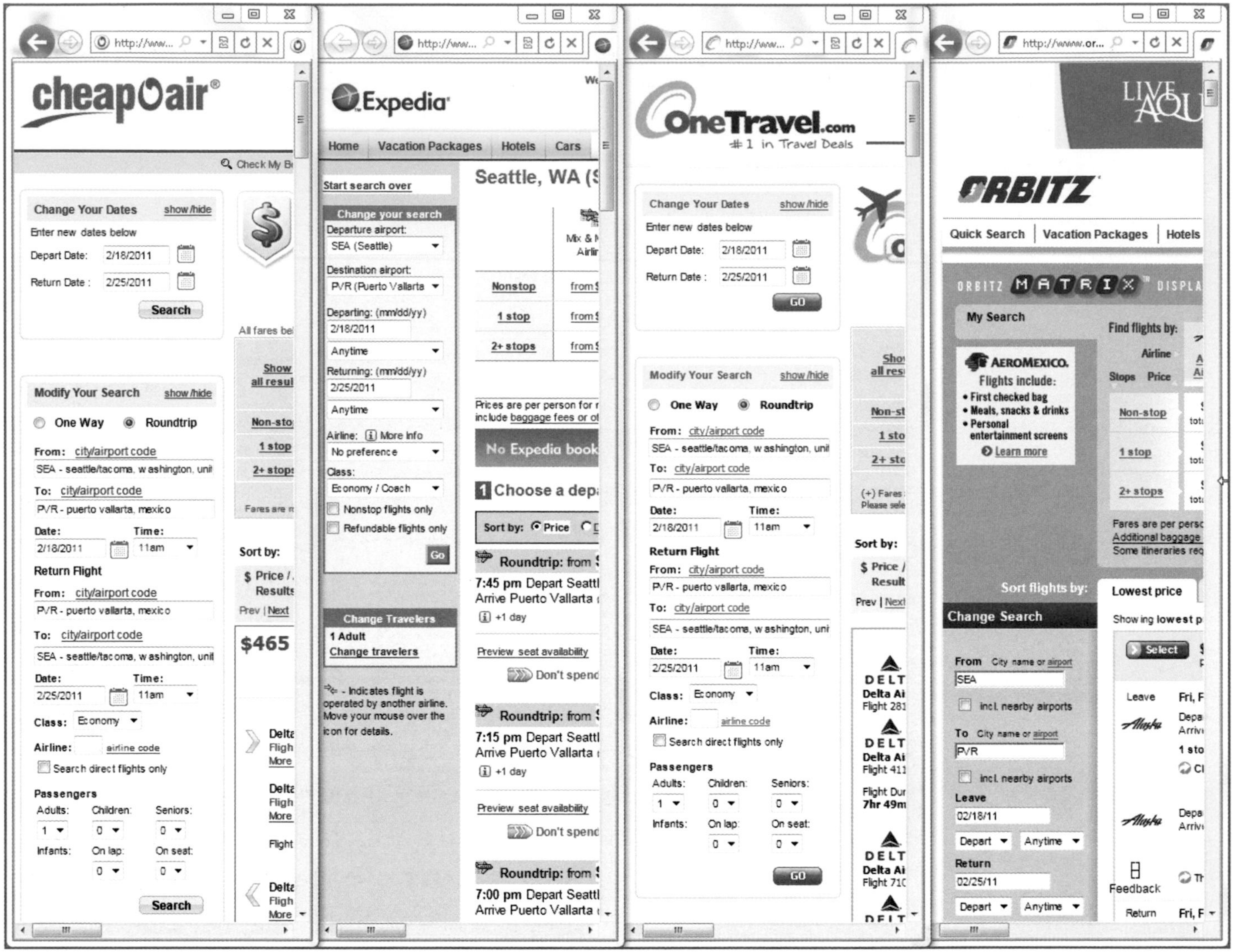

Figure 4-16: Fly.com provides a comparison of the fares on several travel sites.

Chapter 5

Sending and Receiving Email

For many seniors, having access to the Internet and email are the primary reasons for having a computer. The Internet provides a major means for worldwide communication between both individuals and organizations, allowing you to send and receive email, as well as communicate using blogs, forums, and newsgroups. In this chapter we'll talk about how to get, set up, and use Windows Live Mail, including creating, sending, and receiving messages; handling spam; adding attachments and signatures; and applying formatting. We'll also briefly look at two web-based alternatives for email, as well as how to use the Calendar, participate in newsgroups, and use Windows Live Messenger.

Use Internet Email

Windows 7 does not include a mail program, but you can download Windows Live Mail from Microsoft for free as part of Windows Live Essentials. Windows Live Mail allows you to send and receive email and to participate in newsgroups. You can also send and receive email through a Web mail account using Internet Explorer or another browser. This section will primarily describe using Windows Live Mail. See the "Using Web Mail" QuickSteps for a discussion of that subject.

Figure 5-1: *By downloading Windows Live Essentials, Microsoft assures that you have the very latest software and allows other manufacturers the opportunity to have you use their software.*

Get Windows Live Mail

For email with Windows 7, this book describes the use of Windows Live Mail because it works well, is freely available from Microsoft, and is designed for Windows 7. There are a number of other alternatives that you can buy or get for free, including Outlook from Microsoft, Eudora, Mozilla Thunderbird, and Opera. Conduct an Internet search on "Windows Mail Clients."

To get Windows Live Mail, you must download Windows Live Essentials from Microsoft. To do that:

1. If you have a new computer or new installation of Windows 7, click **Start**, click **Getting Started**, and click **Go Online To Get Windows Live Essentials**.
   If you are using Windows 7 (assumed in this book) and don't see the Getting Started menu, click **Start**, click **All Programs**, click **Accessories**, click **Getting Started**, and double-click **Go Online To Get Windows Live Essentials**, as shown in Figure 5-1.

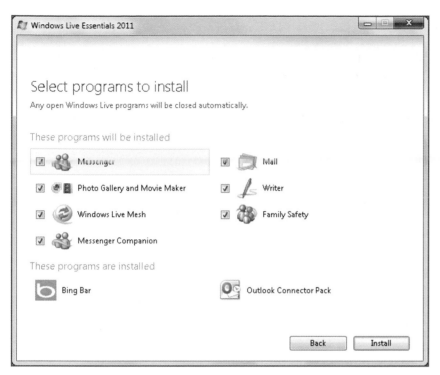

*Figure 5-2: **Windows Live Essentials includes email, instant messaging, blogging, movie making, and more.***

2. Click **Download Now** and in the File Download - Security Warning box, click **Run**. If a User Account Control dialog box opens, click **Yes** to allow the installation. The Windows Live site will open.

3. Click **Choose The Programs You Want To Install**, choose what you would like (I recommend all, but think it is a good idea to look at what you are installing; see Figure 5-2), and click **Install**. If you are asked to close Internet Explorer and possibly other programs, click **Continue**, and the programs will be closed for you.

4. The downloading and installation of Windows Live Essentials will begin and take from one to ten minutes with a broadband Internet connection. When this is completed, you may be asked to restart your computer. If so, make sure all other programs are closed and click **Restart Now**.

5. When your computer restarts, you are asked to select various settings that, if selected, tend to lock you into Microsoft's Bing search engine and Microsoft's MSN website. This may be subtle, like telling you that several add-ons are ready to use. Click **Enable** if you want the add-ons or click **Don't Enable** otherwise (my recommendation).

6. If you do not have a Windows Live, Hotmail, Messenger, or Xbox Live account, you will need to create one. Click **Sign Up** and follow the instructions on the screen to establish an account. If you already have one of those accounts, sign in as indicated.

7. If a Windows Live Messenger window has opened, click **Close**. It will be opened and discussed at the end of this chapter.

Establish an Email Account

To send and receive email with Windows Live Mail, you must have an Internet connection, an email account established with an Internet service provider (ISP), and that account must be set up in Windows Live Mail.

For an email account, you need:

- Your email address, for example: mike@anisp.com
- The type of mail server the ISP uses (POP3, IMAP, or HTTP—POP3 is the most common)
- The names of the incoming and outgoing mail servers, for example: mail.anisp.com
- The name and password for your mail account

With this information, you can set up an account in Windows Live Mail.

1. Click **Start**, click **All Programs**, and click **Windows Live Mail** if you see it on the Start menu; if not, click the **Windows Live** folder, and then click **Windows Live Mail**.

2. If Windows Live Mail has not been previously set up, the Add Your Email Accounts dialog box will appear; if it doesn't, click the **Accounts** tab, and click **Email** on the left to open it.

3. Enter your email address, press **TAB**, enter your email password, press **TAB**, enter the name you want people to see when they get your email, select the **Manually Configure Server Settings** check box, and click **Next**.

4. Select the type of mail server your ISP uses (commonly POP 3), enter the name of your ISP's incoming mail server (such as mail.anisp.com), and whether this server requires a secure connection (most don't, but your ISP will tell you if it does and how to handle it). Unless your ISP tells you otherwise, leave the default port number and logon authentication.

TIP

You need to get your email address and password from your ISP before you set up an email account.

5. Enter your logon ID or user name, the name of your ISP's outgoing server (often the same as the incoming server), leave the default port number, and select the check box if your ISP tells you the server requires a secure connection or authentication.

6. When you have completed these steps, click **Next** (if you have other email accounts you want to add, click **Add Another Email Account** and repeat the necessary steps), and then click **Finish**. (Before Windows Live Mail can read messages from certain accounts, it might need to download the existing folders in those accounts. Click **Download** to do that. Windows Live Mail will open. Figure 5-3 shows it after receiving several email messages.

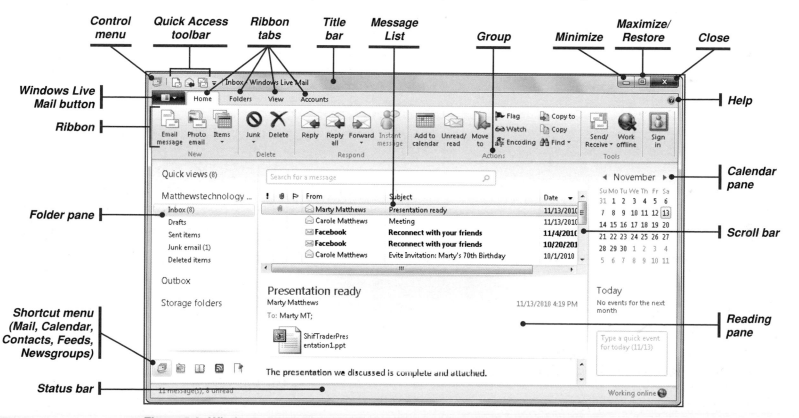

Figure 5-3: Windows Live Mail provides access to email, a calendar, contacts, feeds, and newsgroups.

To quickly start Windows Live Mail with a single click, if it isn't already running, start it as described in "Establish an Email Account," right-click the **Windows Live Mail** icon on the taskbar, and click **Pin This Program To Taskbar**. The icon now will always be available on the taskbar to open the program.

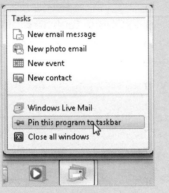

Use the next two sections, "Create and Send Email" and "Receive Email," to test your setup.

Create and Send Email

To create and send an email message:

1. Open Windows Live Mail, as described in the previous section, and in the Home tab, click **Email Message** in the New group. The New Message window will open, similar to the one in Figure 5-4.

2. Start to enter a name in the To text box. If the name is in your Contacts list (see the "Using the Contacts List" QuickSteps in this chapter), it will be automatically completed and you can press **ENTER** to accept that name. If the name is not automatically completed, finish typing a full email address (such as billg@microsoft.com).

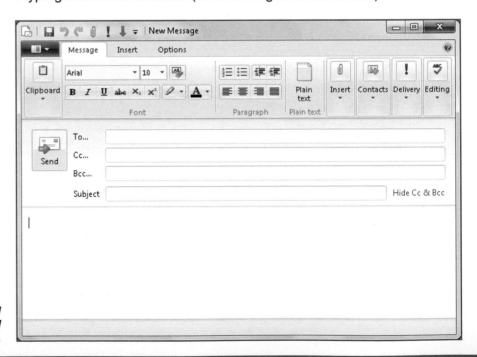

*Figure 5-4: **Sending email messages is an easy and fast way to communicate.***

UNDERSTANDING THE RIBBON

The *ribbon* is the container at the top of both the Windows Live Mail and New Message windows for the tools and features you are most likely to use to accomplish the task at hand (see Figure 5-3). The ribbon collects tools in *groups;* for example, the New group provides the tools to start an email message or add a new event to the calendar. Groups are organized into tabs, which bring together the tools to work on broader tasks. For example, the Folders tab contains groups that allow you to add and work with folders.

The ribbon provides space so each of the tools (or commands) in the groups has a labeled button you can click. Depending on the tool, you are then presented with additional options in the form of a list of commands, a dialog box or task pane, or galleries of visibly accurate choices that reflect what you'll see in your work.

Other features that are colocated with the ribbon include the Windows Live Mail button on the left of the tab row and the Quick Access toolbar on the left of the title bar. The Windows Live Mail button lets you work *with* your mail, as opposed to the ribbon, which centers on working *in* your mail. The Quick Access toolbar provides an always available location for your favorite tools. It starts out with a default set of tools, but you can add to it.

3. If you want more than one addressee, type a semicolon (;) and a space after the first address, and then type a second one as in step 2.

4. If you want to differentiate the addressees to whom the message is principally being sent from those for whom it is just information, click **Show Cc & Bcc**, if they are not already displayed, press **TAB**, and put the second or subsequent addressees in the Cc text box as you did in the To text box.

5. If you want to send the message to a recipient and not have other recipients see to whom it is sent, click **Show Cc & Bcc**, if they are not already displayed, click in the **Bcc** text box, and type the address to be hidden. (Bcc stands for "blind carbon copy.")

6. Press **TAB**, type a subject for the message, press **TAB** again, and type your message.

7. When you have completed your message, click **Send** opposite the addresses. For a brief moment, you may see a message in your outbox and then, if you open the Sent Items folder, you will see the message in its folder. If you are done, close Windows Live Mail.

Receive Email

Depending on how Windows Live Mail is set up, it may automatically receive any email you have when you are connected to your ISP, or you may have to direct it to download your mail. To open and read your mail:

1. Open **Windows Live Mail**, and click **Inbox** in the Folders list on the left to open your inbox, which contains all of the messages you have received and haven't deleted or organized in folders.

2. If new messages weren't automatically received, in the Home tab click the top of the **Send/Receive** area in the Tools group. You should see messages being downloaded.

3. Click a message in the inbox Message List to read it in the reading pane on the bottom or right of the window, as shown in Figure 5-3

5

TIP

Have a friend send you an email message so you know whether you are receiving messages. Then send the friend a message back and ask them to let you know when they get it so you know you are sending messages.

TIP

Normally, the contents of your Message List are sorted by the date and time in the Date column, with the most recent message at the top. You can sort on any of the elements in the message by clicking in the column heading for that element. Click in the column heading a second time to sort in the opposite direction. You can also click **Sort By** in the View tab Arrangement group and click the element you want to sort on.

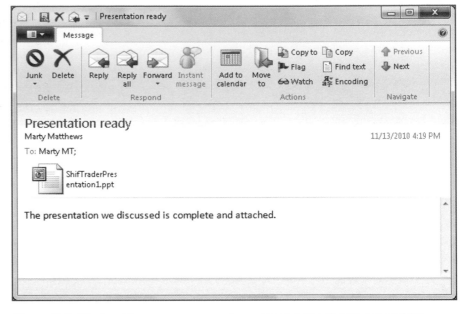

Figure 5-5: *Work with a message you have received in the Message List (see Figure 5-3) or in its own window (shown here).*

(which shows the message on the bottom), or double-click a message to open the message in its own window, as shown in Figure 5-5.

4. Delete a message in either the inbox or its own window by clicking the relevant button on the toolbar. Close Windows Live Mail if you are finished with it.

Respond to Email

You can respond to messages you receive in three ways. First, click the message in your Message List or open the message in its own window, and then in the Home tab of the inbox or the Message tab of the message, click:

- **Reply** to return a message to just the person who sent the original message.

   –Or–

TIP

If the sender of an email is not in your Contacts list, you can easily add her or him by clicking **Add Contact** next to the From email address.

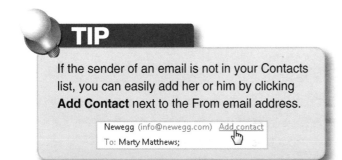

TIP

If you see an email address in an email message that you want to add to your Contacts list, right-click the email address, and click **Add To Contacts**. This opens the Add A Contact window so that you can enter the necessary information.

Randall Le
arke; Tina

Add to contacts
Send email
Add to safe senders list
Add to blocked senders list

QUICKSTEPS

USING THE CONTACTS LIST

The Contacts list, shown in Figure 5-6, allows you to collect email addresses and other information about the people with whom you correspond or otherwise interact.

OPEN THE CONTACTS LIST

To open the Contacts list:

Click **Contacts** 📖 in the lower-left area of Windows Live Mail.

ADD A NEW CONTACT

To add a new contact to the Contacts list:

1. With Contacts Windows Live Mail open, click **Contact** in the Home tab New group. The Add A Contact dialog box opens.

2. Enter as much of the information as you have or want. For email, you need a name and an email address, as shown in the Quick Add category. If you have additional information, such as a nickname, several email addresses, several phone numbers, or a home address for the contact, click the other categories on the left and fill in the desired information.

Continued . . .

- **Reply All** to return a message to all the people who were addressees (both To and Cc) in the original message.

–Or–

- **Forward** (upper half) to relay a message to people not shown as addressees on the original message.

In all three cases, a window similar to the New Message window opens and allows you to add or change addressees and the subject, and add a new message.

Figure 5-6: The Contacts list provides a place to store information about the people with whom you correspond.

USING THE CONTACTS LIST

(Continued)

3. When you are done, click **Add Contact** to close the Add A Contact dialog box.

ADD CONTACT CATEGORIES

You can group contacts by category and then send messages to everyone in the category. To categorize a group of contacts:

1. In the Contacts Windows Live Mail window, click **Category** in the Home tab New group. The Create A New Category dialog box appears.

2. Enter the category name, and click the names in your Contacts list that you want in the category. When you have selected all the names, click **Save**.

3. When you are done, click the **Mail** icon in the lower left to close the Contacts list and reopen Windows Live Mail.

When you want to address a message to a category of people, start typing the category, and its name will be displayed. Click the category name to send the message to everyone in the category. Click the plus sign on the left of the category to expand it and list the contacts that are included in it.

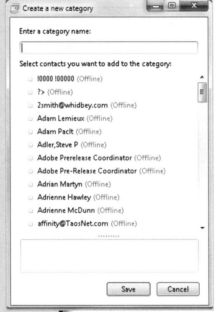

When you have several email addresses in a single contact's record, they are all displayed when you go to enter the contact in an email message so you can select the address you want.

Deal with Spam

Spam, or unsolicited email, often trying to sell something, from Viagra to designer watches, can be harmful as well as irritating. Spam can contain viruses or malware buried inside a harmless-looking link or sales offer. If you do not handle spam, it can overwhelm your inbox. There are essentially three ways to deal with it:

- **Your ISP often can filter email for their clients if the clients choose**. If you are suffering from too much spam, your first attack is to ask your ISP to increase the filtering level for your account. They capture email that is suspicious and present it to you in a list for you to check. If you see valid email, you can rescue it. If your ISP cannot do this, or doesn't guide you through finding a way to do it, you might look for a different ISP. This can be a serious problem.

- **Your email program, such as Windows Live Mail, will usually have a filtering mechanism available**. You may have several options.

ANNE FINDS EMAIL A MIXED BLESSING

Email allows me to stay current on what's going on in others' lives. I see it as a surface connection, and often follow up by interacting on the telephone. I can't imagine not having email, although I find it a mixed blessing.

I try to save email communication for family, friends, and professional peers, but I confess I haven't managed to keep the intruders out. Email address information has become a standard question on most applications now, be it for employment or opening a bank account. Who knows who has access to my address from there, so it seems virtually impossible to keep it all private. At one time I considered changing my email address, but I believe that would only be a short-term diversion.

I have been encouraged to find an antispam product, and perhaps that is my way out of my dilemma. I know that there must be something out there that will solve this problem—there are too many people out there who have had to march down this same road. Somewhere there is an answer . . .

Anne T, 61, New Mexico

Windows Live Mail, for example, can set a level for email protection, filter for phishing attacks (phishing is described in the following section), block specific senders, allow specific senders, restrict international email, use digital IDs, or block images in email and put the offending messages in a Junk email folder (see Figure 5-7). To access these features in Windows Live Mail, see "Set Safety Options in Windows Live Mail."

• **You can find third-party software that specializes in filtering email and providing a way for you to safely sift through your email without a lot of hassle**. I have used MailWasher for this with good results (see mailwasher.net for a free download). You can get a list of products that are rated from cnet.com. Type http://cnet.com into your browser address text box, type anti spam software into the search text box, and click **Search** (the magnifying glass). You'll find a list of reviewed antispam software (look at the date and make sure it is a current review).

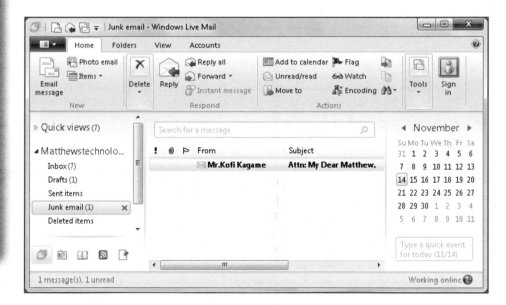

*Figure 5-7: **To keep from being inundated with spam, it is important to use all the filtering mechanisms at your disposal.***

NOTE

Many malware protection packages labeled "Internet Security" include antispam capability. Examples of two highly rated programs include Norton Internet Security 2011 and Kaspersky Internet Security 2011.

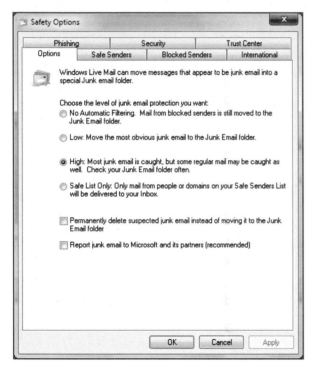

Figure 5-8: You can set safety options for dealing with spam and other threats to your email in Windows Live Mail.

SET SAFETY OPTIONS IN WINDOWS LIVE MAIL

To set the options for handling spam and other email threats in Windows Live Mail:

1. Click the **Windows Live Mail** tab on the left of the tab bar (left of the Home tab), click **Options**, and then click **Safety Options**. You'll see a dialog box, shown in Figure 5-8, with several approaches to safely dealing with email.

   - **Options**, the default tab, allows you to set a level of protection you want. High, the default, is a good choice, although you may prefer Low if you already have a good ISP or third-party spam handler. If you don't want to deal with suspected spam at all, you might click **Permanently Delete Suspected Junk Email Instead Of Moving It To The Junk Email Folder**. Although this can be a viable solution, I don't recommend it, as there are occasional valid emails that get trapped this way—you'll lose the ability to rescue them.

   - **Safe Senders**, allows you to enter specific email addresses or domain names that you trust. Click **Add** and enter the email address/ domain name. Click **Also Trust Email From My Contacts** to allow people from your Contact list to be automatic trusted senders.

   - **Blocked Senders** blocks specific email addresses or domain names. If you have a specific offender, you can simply block them. Click **Add** and enter the address/domain name. You can also choose to send an offending email to the sender or unsubscribe to the mailing list. I don't recommend either of these in order to retain your privacy.

   - **International** allows you to block email from specific countries or languages. Click **Blocked Top-Level Domain List**, and click the check box to block messages from countries on the list based on their top-level domain, such as BE for Belgium or RU for Russia. Click **Blocked Encoding List**, and click the check box to block the selected languages based on the way they are encoded.

   - **Phishing** is when an email message pretends to be from a reputable organization and tries to get you to give them sensitive information like a credit card number or your password. This tab allows you to remove suspicious emails that potentially contain invalid links to the source of the message (it says it is from one source, but is really from another). Select both check boxes to protect against phishing and to place the email in your Junk email folder. You'll want to check your Junk folder occasionally and delete the contents after you verify that no valid email was selected.

- **Security** gives you several opportunities for protection. You can select a "security zone" to use. I recommend the Internet Zone; otherwise, it is too restrictive. I also select the **Warn Me When Other Applications Try To Send Mail As Me**. I do not recommend blocking the downloading of images. Again, this is too restrictive. It is better to just open images from trusted sources. Do not open forwarded images without knowing who it is from and trusting that they are discriminating. Finally, you can purchase a digital ID and use it to send and receive email that contains a digital signature. You can encrypt the contents and attachments for all your email or digitally sign your outgoing email. These are fairly strict security measures that I do not use. However, if you have a special need for them, they are available.

2. Click **OK** to save your changes and close the dialog box.

Apply Formatting

The simplest messages are sent in plain text without any formatting. These messages take the least bandwidth and are the easiest to receive. If you wish, you can send messages with formatting using Hypertext Markup Language (HTML), the language with which many websites are created. You can do this for an individual message and for all messages.

APPLY FORMATTING TO ALL MESSAGES

To turn HTML formatting on or off:

1. Click the **Windows Live Mail** tab on the left of the tab bar (left of the Home tab), click **Options**, and then click **Mail**.

2. Click the **Send** tab. Under Mail Sending Format, click **HTML** if you want it and it is not selected, or click **Plain Text** if that is what you want (see Figure 5-9).

3. Click **OK**, and, if desired, close Windows Live Mail.

CAUTION

Not all email programs can properly receive HTML messages, which results in messages that are not very readable. However, most programs released in the last ten years can handle HTML.

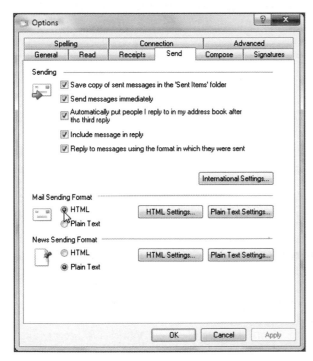

Figure 5-9: *If you send your mail using HTML instead of plain text, you can apply fonts and color and do many other things not available with plain text.*

SELECT A FONT AND A COLOR FOR ALL MESSAGES

To use a particular font and font color on all of your email messages (you must send your mail using HTML in place of plain text—see "Apply Formatting to All Messages"):

1. Click the **Windows Live Mail** tab, click **Options**, and then click **Mail**.

2. Click the **Compose** tab. Under Compose Font, click **Font Settings** opposite Mail.

3. Select the font, style, size, effects, and color that you want to use with all your email; click **OK** twice; and then, if desired, close Windows Live Mail.

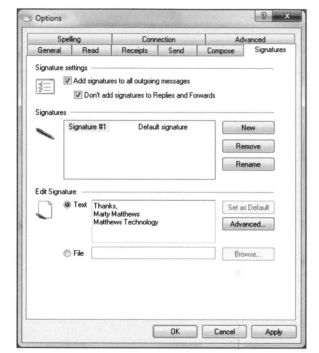

Figure 5-10: *A "signature" in Windows Live Mail is really a closing.*

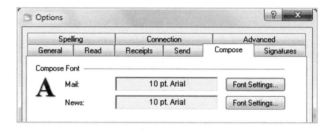

ATTACH A SIGNATURE

To attach a signature (a closing) on all of your email messages:

1. Click the **Windows Live Mail** tab, click **Options**, and then click **Mail**.

2. Click the **Signatures** tab, and click **New**. Under Edit Signature, enter the closing text you want to use, or click **File** and enter or browse to the path and filename you want for the closing. The file could be a graphic image, such as a scan of your written signature, if you wished.

3. Click **Add Signatures To All Outgoing Messages**, as shown in Figure 5-10, and click **OK**. Then, if desired, close Windows Live Mail.

NOTE

If you have several email accounts, you can click **Advanced** in the Signatures tab of the Options dialog box and select the account(s) with which to use a selected signature.

UICKSTEPS

USING WEB MAIL

Web mail is the sending and receiving of email over the Internet using a browser, such as Internet Explorer, instead of an email program, such as Windows Live Mail. There are a number of web mail programs, such as Windows Live Hotmail (hotmail.com), Yahoo! Mail (mail.yahoo.com), and Google's Gmail (gmail.com). So long as you have access to the Internet, you can sign up for one or more of these services. The basic features (simple sending and receiving of email) are often free. For example, to sign up for Windows Live Hotmail:

1. Open Internet Explorer. In the address bar, type hotmail.com, and press **ENTER**.

2. If you already have a Windows Live account, enter your ID and password, and click **Sign In**. Otherwise, under Windows Live Hotmail, click **Sign Up**, fill in the requested information, and click **I Accept**.

3. When you are done, the Windows Live Hotmail page will open and display your mail, as shown in Figure 5-11.

4. Click the envelope icon to open and read a message.

5. Click **New** on the toolbar to write an email message. Enter the address, a subject, and the message. When you are done, click **Send**.

6. When you are finished with Hotmail, close Internet Explorer.

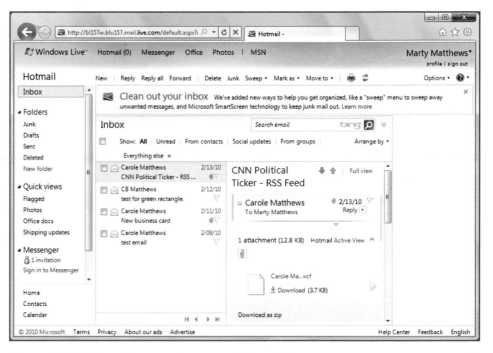

Figure 5-11: *Web mail accounts are a quick and free way to get one or more email accounts.*

A way to quickly open Windows Live Hotmail is to add it to your Favorites list or Favorites bar. With Hotmail open in Internet Explorer, click the **Favorites** icon ☆ in the upper-right corner of the Internet Explorer window, click **Add To Favorites**, change the name, and then click **Add**; or click the **Add To Favorites** down arrow, and click the **Add To Favorites Bar**. Windows Live Hotmail will appear either in the Favorites list or on the Favorites bar. In either place, click it once to open Windows Live Hotmail.

Attach Files to Email

You can attach and send files, such as documents or images, with email messages.

1. Open Windows Live Mail, and click **Email Message** in the Home tab New group.

2. Click **Attach File** in the Message tab Insert group. Select the folder and file you want to send, and click **Open**. The attachment will be shown below the subject.

3. Address, enter, and send the message as you normally would, and then close Windows Live Mail.

Subject: Gettysburg Address

📎 📄 The Gettysburg Address formatted.docx

Use Calendar

The Windows Live Mail Calendar, which you can use to keep track of scheduled events, is open by default in the right pane, as you have seen in several figures in this chapter, beginning with Figure 5-3.

To close the Calendar or open it if it is closed:

Click the **View** tab, and click **Calendar Pane** in the Layout group. The calendar pane will close, or open if it was closed.

You can also expand the Calendar to fill the Windows Live Mail window.

Click the **Calendar** icon in the lower-left corner of the Windows Live Mail window. The Calendar opens, as you can see in Figure 5-12.

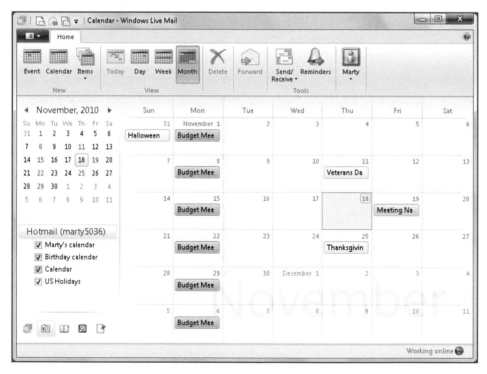

Figure 5-12: The Calendar provides a handy way to keep track of scheduled events, especially those scheduled through email.

To return from the Calendar to Windows Live Mail:

Click the **Mail** icon in the lower-left corner of the Windows Live Mail window.

DIRECTLY ADD EVENTS TO A CALENDAR

To add an event to a calendar date:

1. With the calendar pane open, right-click a date on the Calendar, and click **Create New Event**. The New Event window will open.

2. Enter the subject, location, dates and times, and a message, as shown in Figure 5-13.

3. If you have multiple calendars, click the **Calendar** down arrow, and select the calendar you want to use. Also, select how you want the calendar to reflect your time during the event.

4. If the event will happen on a repeated basis, click the **Recurrence** down arrow, and click the period for this event.

5. When you have completed the event, click either **Save & Close** to store the event on your Calendar or **Forward** to send this to others for their schedules.

6. If you selected Forward, an email message will open. Address it, make any desired changes to the message, and click **Send**.

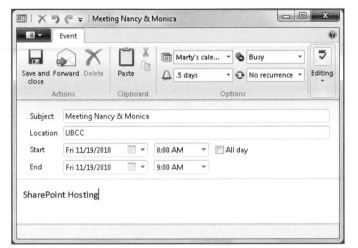

Figure 5-13: *The Windows Live Mail Calendar allows you to send scheduled events to others to put on their calendars.*

ADD AN EMAIL MESSAGE TO A CALENDAR

When you receive an email message with scheduling ramifications, you can directly add its information to your Calendar.

1. In Windows Live Mail, click the message that has calendar information, and click **Add To Calendar** in the Home tab Actions group.

   –Or–

   Right-click the message and click **Add To Calendar**.

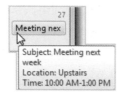

In both cases, an event window will open. Unfortunately, the subject and the body are the only fields that are filled in for you from the e-mail (the current date is in the Start and End date, but you probably need to change that). You must fill in the location, dates and times, and whether it is recurring.

2. After filling in the pertinent information, click **Save & Close**. The event will appear on your Calendar.

Participate in Newsgroups

Newsgroups are organized chains of messages on a particular subject. Newsgroups allow people to enter new messages and respond to previous ones. To participate in one or more newsgroups, you need to set up a newsgroup account, then locate and open a particular newsgroup, and finally send and receive messages within the newsgroup.

SET UP A NEWSGROUP ACCOUNT

Setting up a new account for a newsgroup is similar to setting up the account for your email. To set up a newsgroup account, you need the name of the news server and, possibly, an account name and password.

1. Open Windows Live Mail, and click the **Newsgroups** icon in the lower-left corner of the window. During your initial use of the Newsgroups window you will be asked if you want Windows Live Mail to be your default news client. If you don't have another newsgroup reader, click **Yes**.

2. To participate in newsgroups, click the **Accounts** tab, and click **Newsgroup**. Enter the name you want displayed showing from whom your messages are being sent, and click **Next**. Enter your email address if not already displayed, and click **Next**.

3. Enter the name of your news server. Your ISP or sponsoring organization will give you this. One you can try is news.microsoft.com. If you do not need to enter an account name and password, your ISP or sponsoring organization also will tell you this, and you can skip to step 6.

4. To enter an account name and password, click **My News Server Requires Me To Log On**, and click **Next**. Enter your account name and password, and click **Remember Password** (if desired).

5. Click **Next**, click **Finish**, and click **OK** to show available newsgroups. You will get a message that you are not subscribed to any newsgroups and asking if you would like to see a list of newsgroups. If so, click **View Newsgroups**.

6. A list of newsgroups will appear. If you wish to just view a newsgroup, select that newsgroup and click **Go To**. If you wish to view a newsgroup over a given period, click **Subscribe**. Newsgroups will be downloaded from your news server. This could take several minutes. A new account will appear in the Newsgroup Subscriptions window and a list of newsgroups will be displayed.

SUBSCRIBE TO A NEWSGROUP

Most general-purpose news servers, such as those maintained by ISPs, have a great many newsgroups, probably only some of which might interest you. To subscribe to a newsgroup (meaning to read and reply to messages they contain on a recurring basis):

1. If you have just come from setting up a newsgroup account, skip to step 2. Otherwise, open Windows Live Mail and click the **Newsgroups** icon.

2. Click the news server you want to use in the left column, and click **View Newsgroups**.

3. To search for a particular newsgroup, type a keyword (such as Computers) in the Display Newsgroups That Contain text box, and press **ENTER** (if newsgroups start popping up as you type your search keywords, you may not need to press **ENTER**).

4. Double-click the newsgroups to which you want to subscribe. An icon appears to the left of each newsgroup you double-click. After you have selected the newsgroups, click **OK**. You are returned to the Windows Live Mail Newsgroups window.

NOTE

To unsubscribe to a newsgroup, right-click the newsgroup name in the list of groups on the left of the newsgroup window, and click **Unsubscribe**. Click **OK** to confirm.

READ AND POST MESSAGES IN A NEWSGROUP

You can read and send messages like email messages for newsgroups to which you have subscribed, but with two differences. You can choose to reply to the newsgroup or to the individual, and a new message is called a write message. If someone replies to this message, it is added to the end of the original message, thereby creating a chain, or *thread*, of messages on a given subject.

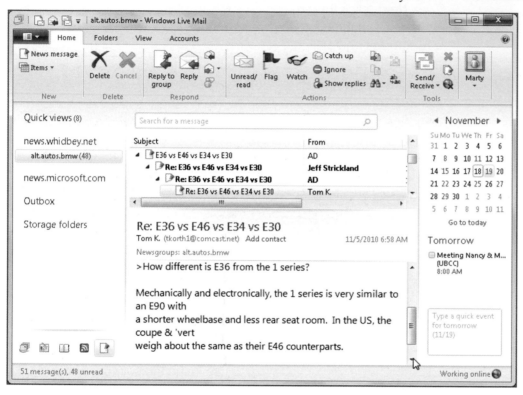

Figure 5-14: **A newsgroup provides a thread on a given topic to which you can add your comments.**

1. Open Windows Live Mail, open your news server, and click a newsgroup you want to open. A list of messages will be displayed.

2. Click the triangular icon on the left of a message (this identifies that there are replies) to open the related messages.

3. Click a message to display it in the bottom pane, as shown in Figure 5-14 (you may need to click **Click Here** or press **SPACEBAR** to open the message). Or, double-click the message to have it displayed in its own window.

4. To initiate a newsgroup thread or respond to a newsgroup thread:

- Click **News Message** in the Home tab New group to create a public message that will begin a new thread.

- Click **Reply To Group** in the Home tab Respond group to create a public message in the thread you have selected.

- Click **Reply** in the Home tab Respond group to create a private message to the person who wrote the message you have selected.

- Click **Reply All** in the Home tab Respond group to create individual messages to all who have contributed to the message you have selected.

- Click **Forward** in the Home tab Respond group to send a copy of the message you have selected to one or more individuals.

5. Create and send the message as you would any email message. When you are done, click **Mail** to return to Windows Live Mail.

Use Windows Live Messenger

Windows Live Messenger allows you to instantly send and receive instant messages (or *chat*) with others who are online at the same time as you. This is frequently called "instant messaging" or IM. Windows Live Messenger provides a quick way to chat, share photos, and exchange files with family, friends, and associates online.

Set Up Windows Live Messenger

When you downloaded and installed Windows Live Essentials to get Windows Live Mail, you probably also installed Windows Live Messenger; it is selected by default. If so, its icon may be on your taskbar, or at least it is in the Start menu. If you didn't install it and want to now, return to the "Get Windows Live Mail" section and follow the instructions there.

The use of Windows Live Messenger requires that you first have a Microsoft Live account or an MSN or Hotmail account, which you may have done earlier in this chapter in the "Using Web Mail" QuickSteps. Once you have an account, you are able to set up your contacts and personalize Messenger to your tastes.

ESTABLISH A WINDOWS LIVE ACCOUNT

With Windows Live Messenger installed, open it and establish a Windows Live account.

1. Click **Start**, click **All Programs**, and click **Windows Live Messenger**; or click the **Windows Live** folder, and click **Windows Live Messenger**. The Windows Live Messenger window will open, as you can see here.

2. If you already have a Windows Live account, enter your email address and password, and click **Sign In**. Go to the next section, "Add Contacts to Messenger."

3. If you don't have a Windows Live account, click **Sign Up**. Internet Explorer will open and the Windows Live registration will appear. Enter the information requested, click **I Accept**, and when you are told you have successfully registered your email address, close your browser. You will be returned to Windows Live Messenger.

4. Enter your email address and your password, and then click **Sign In**.

ADD CONTACTS TO MESSENGER

To use Windows Live Messenger, you must enter contacts for people you want to "talk" to.

1. If Windows Live Messenger is not already open, click its icon in the taskbar. If the icon isn't there, click **Start**, click **All Programs**, and click **Windows Live Messenger**.

2. The first time you start Windows Live Messenger you will see some introductory screens asking if you want to connect with Facebook and other social media sites. Following that you are asked if you would like either Social Highlights or MSN news in a side panel of Messenger. Click your choice. If you choose Social Networks, you are given a choice of Facebook, MySpace, or LinkedIn. Again, click your choice.

3. Click **Add** in the upper-right corner of the Windows Live Messenger window to open a context menu of choices for IM contacts. Click:

- **Add A Favorite**   This opens your list of contacts so you can select one or more that you want to contact with IM. Click in the **Search Contacts** text box, and type the person's name as best you can. People who fit what you have typed will appear (you can see if that person is online). Double-click the name you want.

- **Create A Group**   Click **OK** to start a group so you can have group conversations. Type a name for the group, and click **Next**. Click **Select From Your Contact List**, click the contacts you want, and click **OK**. Click **Next**, and then click **Done**. After the contacts accept your invitation, they will become members of the group.

- **Create A Category**   Click **OK** to create a new category, such as "church" or "club," within which you can organize your contacts. Type a name for the category, click to select the contacts you want in the category, and click **Save**.

- **Add A Friend**   Type your friend's email address; optionally, if you want to send text messages, select a country and type the friend's cell phone number, and click **Next**. If you want to make the person a favorite, click that option and click **Next**. An invitation will be sent to the friend. Depending on the person's status—whether they are online and whether they accept your invitation—you will get a response accordingly. Click **Add More Friends**, if desired, or click **Close**.

- **Search For Someone**   In the Windows Live search page, type the name you want to search for. As you type the name, a drop-down list appears with options to search your contacts, your documents, or the Web; or you can select a few choices. Click your choice. Depending on your choice, a Bing search window will open and display a list matching your search or list of people in your contacts or documents will be displayed. Click the one you want to find.

- **Add People From Other Services**   Type a name or email address, and click **Next** to add people in that way; or click one of the services and follow the instructions to connect that service with Windows Live. If you see a box labeled "Set Up Your Privacy Settings," choose among **Public**, **Limited**, or **Private** settings, and click **Save**.

4. When you are done adding contacts, close Internet Explorer. Back in Windows Live Messenger, you should now have a list of contacts. If you want to exit Windows Live Messenger, click **Close**.

CUSTOMIZE MESSENGER

There are several ways to customize Windows Live Messenger.

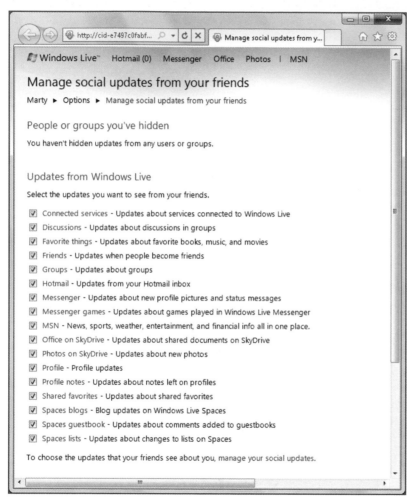

Figure 5-15: *Setting Windows Live Messenger options allows you to customize how your services work with mail.*

1. Open **Windows Live Messenger**. Change from full view, shown in Figure 5-11, to compact view, shown on the left, by clicking the **Switch To Compact View** icon in the upper-right corner of the window.

2. Assuming you have connected with social networking sites, click the **Edit Messenger Social Settings** icon . You are presented with a number of options for working with the various services you have selected, as shown in Figure 5-15.

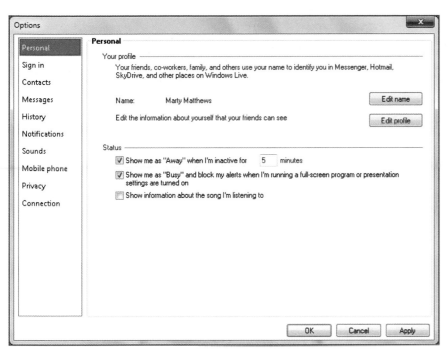

Figure 5-16: **You can customize Windows Live Messenger in a number of areas using the Options dialog box.**

3. When you have chosen the options you want, click **Save** and close Internet Explorer.

4. In Windows Live Messenger, click the down arrow to the right of your name. Here you can choose how you appear to IM users and a number of other options.

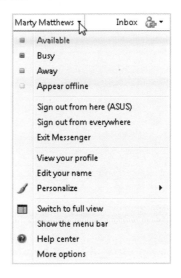

5. Click **More Options** to open the Options dialog box. Here you have a number of options you can use to customize Messenger, as you can see in Figure 5-16.

6. Click each of the areas on the left, and review the options and selections on the right. Make the changes that are correct for you, and then click **OK**.

Use Windows Live Messenger

Using Windows Live Messenger is simple: double-click a contact. If they are online, the Conversation window will open, as shown in Figure 5-17. If they are not online, you will be told the contact will be given the message the next time they are online.

NOTE

Windows Live Messenger does not normally create a permanent record of your conversation unless you specifically choose to do that. To do this, click the down arrow opposite your name, click **More Options**, click **History**, click **Automatically Save My Conversation History**, and click **OK**.

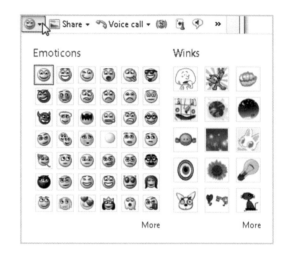

Figure 5-17: *When a conversation is in process, you can see who said what in the Conversation window.*

SEND A MESSAGE

With the Conversation window open (done by double-clicking a contact), send a message by typing it in the bottom pane and pressing **ENTER**. You can add emoticons (smiley faces), change the font, and/or change the message background with the icons below the text box.

RECEIVE A MESSAGE

With a conversation in process, a received message appears in the Conversation window, as you can see in Figure 5-17. If someone sends you an instant message without a Conversation window open, you will get a little pop-up message from your notification area. Double-click this message to open a Conversation window with the sender.

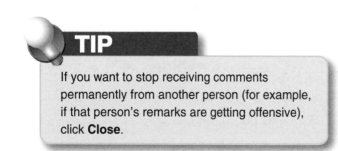

TIP

If you want to stop receiving comments permanently from another person (for example, if that person's remarks are getting offensive), click **Close**.

Chapter 6
Controlling Security

Computing, like most things in life, requires prudent caution. You should not let yourself be petrified by it; on the other hand, you want to do what's needed to protect yourself, your information, and your computer. There have been a number of articles in *AARP The Magazine* and elsewhere about the perceived vulnerability of seniors to computer scams and fraud, implying that seniors are not as able to take care of themselves on a computer as the younger generation. I think that is misguided. Most of us got to where we are today because we successfully learned how to protect ourselves from many different threats. The computer is no different. You simply need to learn how to protect yourself in that environment. It is well worth the effort to get the many benefits that using a computer provides.

Protecting yourself on a computer is a multifaceted subject because of the different aspects of computing that need protection. In this chapter you'll see how to control who uses your computer, control what other users do, protect data stored in the computer, and review the security you need with the Internet.

Control Who Is a User

Controlling who uses a computer means identifying the users to the computer, giving them a secure way of signing on to the computer, and preventing everyone else from using it. This is achieved through the process of adding and managing users and passwords.

With Windows 7, like previous versions of Windows, the first user of a computer is, by default, an administrator; however, the Windows 7 administrator operates like a standard user until there is a need to be an administrator. Then a Windows 7 feature called *User Account Control* (UAC) pops up and asks if the administrator started the process. If so, click **Continue** to proceed. A person who is not an administrator in the same circumstance would have to enter an administrator's password to continue.

Even though you may initially be an administrator, *it is strongly recommended that your normal everyday account be as a standard user.* The reason for this is that if you are signed on as an administrator and a hacker or malevolent software (called "malware") enters your system at the same time, the hacker or software might gain administrator privileges through you. The best solution is to use a separate administrator account with a strong password just for installing software, working with users, and performing other tasks that require extensive administrator work.

NOTE

This book talks about setting up *local* user accounts, which are those that are set up on and use a local computer, as well as smaller or workgroup local area networks (LANs). If your computer is part of a domain (generally found in larger organizations), it is important to use domain user accounts that are set up on a domain controller rather than local user accounts.

Set Up Users

If you have several people using your computer, each person should be set up as a separate user. To add users to your computer, or even to change your user characteristics (as well as to perform most other tasks in this chapter), you must be logged on as an administrator, so you first need to accomplish that. Then you may want to change the characteristics of your account and add a Standard User account for yourself. Finally, if you have multiple people using your computer, you may want to set up separate user accounts and have each user sign in to his or her account.

LOG ON AS AN ADMINISTRATOR

The procedure for logging on as an administrator depends on what was done when Windows 7 was installed on your computer:

- If you installed Windows 7 on your computer, or if you bought a computer with it already installed and did nothing special to the default installation regarding administrator privileges, you should be the administrator and know the administrator's password (if you established one).

- If you did not do the installation or you got the computer with Windows 7 already installed and you are unsure about your administrator status or password, the instructions here will help you log on as an administrator. The first step is to determine the administrator status on your computer.

Click **Start** and in the Start menu click **Control Panel**. In Category view, click **User Accounts And Family Safety**, and then in any view click **User Accounts**. The User Accounts window opens, as shown in Figure 6-1.

Figure 6-1: **Setting up users provides a way of protecting each user from the others and the computer from unauthorized use.**

TIP

If your personal account on your computer is currently set up as an Administrator account, it is strongly recommended that you create a new Standard User account and use that for your everyday computer use. Only use the Administrator account for installing software, changing and adding user information, and performing other tasks requiring an administrator.

QUICKFACTS

UNDERSTANDING USER ACCOUNT CONTROL

Windows 7 has a feature called User Account Control, or UAC. UAC monitors what is happening on the computer, and if it sees something that could cause a problem, like installing a program, adding a new user, or changing a password, it interrupts that process and asks for physical user verification. When it does this, it also freezes all activity on the computer so that nothing can happen until verification is provided—either using the mouse or the keyboard. If the user has administrator privileges, this person is asked if he or she wants to allow changes to be made and, if so, to click Yes. If the user doesn't have administrator privileges, he or she is asked for the administrator's password. By requiring a physical action, UAC ensures that an actual

Continued . . .

If the window shows you are an administrator, you can skip these steps. To make changes to an account, see "Change Your Account" later in this chapter.

–Or–

If you are not an administrator, someone else on your computer must be. Ask that administrator to change your account type or facilitate your signing on as an administrator. Once that is done, skip to "Change Your Account" later in the chapter.

CHANGE YOUR ACCOUNT

You can change an account name, the display picture, add or change a password, and possibly change the account type.

1. Click **Start** and click **Control Panel**. In Category view, click **User Accounts And Family Safety**, and then in any view click **User Accounts**.
2. Click **Change Your Account Name**. If you are not already logged on as an administrator, the User Account Control dialog box will appear and ask you to type an administrator's password.
3. Type a new name, and click **Change Name**.

In a similar manner, you can change your display picture. If you are the only administrator, you will not be allowed to change your account type or delete your account. Changing and setting passwords are discussed in the "Setting Passwords" QuickSteps in this chapter.

SET UP ANOTHER USER

To set up another user account, possibly a Standard User account for your use:

1. Click **Start** and click **Control Panel**. In Category view, click **User Accounts And Family Safety**, and then in any view click **User Accounts**. The User Accounts window opens.
2. Click **Manage Another Account**, and, if needed, type a password and click **Yes** to open the Manage Accounts window, as shown in Figure 6-2.

UNDERSTANDING USER ACCOUNT CONTROL *(Continued)*

person is sitting at the computer and that malware is not attempting to modify it.

All operations that require administrative privileges have a little shield icon beside them, as you can see in Figure 6-1.

For a while, especially if you are installing several programs, the UAC dialog boxes can be irritating. You can turn it off in the User Accounts Control Panel, but this is strongly discouraged. If you do turn it off while you are installing several programs, it is strongly recommended that you turn it back on when you are finished.

○ Standard user
    Standard account users can use most software and change system settings that do not affect other users or the security of the computer.

○ Administrator
    Administrators have complete access to the computer and can make any desired changes. Based on notification settings, administrators may be asked to provide their password or confirmation before making changes that affect other users.

Figure 6-2: **The Manage Accounts window allows you to create and manage user accounts.**

3. Click **Create A New Account**. Type a name of up to 20 characters. Note that it cannot contain just periods, spaces, or the @ symbol; it cannot contain " / \ [ ] : ; | = ,+ * ? < >; and leading spaces or periods are dropped.

4. Accept the default account type, **Standard User**, or click **Administrator** as the account type. You can see a summary of the privileges available to each user type.

5. Click **Create Account**. You are returned to the Manage Accounts window. Changing other aspects of the account is described in later sections of this chapter.

Reset a Password

Windows 7 allows you to reset a password you have forgotten if you have previously created a password reset disk, which can be a USB flash drive, CD, or floppy disk.

With a password reset disk, anyone can reset a password. Therefore, it is important to store the reset disk in a safe place.

CREATE A RESET DISK

1. Insert a USB flash drive in its socket, or insert a writable CD or a formatted and unused floppy disk into its respective drive. Close the AutoPlay window if it opens.

2. Click **Start** and click **Control Panel**. In Category view, click **User Accounts And Family Safety**, and then in any view click **User Accounts**. The User Accounts window opens.

3. Click **Create A Password Reset Disk** in the list of tasks on the left. If needed, type a password and click **Yes**.

4. The Forgotten Password Wizard starts. Click **Next**. Click the drive down arrow, and select the drive on which you want to create the password key. Click **Next**.

5. Type the current user account password, and again click **Next**. The disk will be created. When this process is done, click **Next**. Then click **Finish**. Remove and label the disk, and store it in a safe place.

6. Close the User Accounts window.

USE A RESET DISK

If you have forgotten your password and there isn't another person with administrator permissions on your computer who can reset it, you can use a reset disk you have previously created.

1. Start your computer. When you see the Welcome screen, click your user name. If you have forgotten your password, click the right arrow. You will be told that the user name or password is incorrect.

2. Click **OK** to return to the password entry, and look at your hint.

SETTING PASSWORDS

Passwords are the primary keys used to allow some people to use a computer and to keep others away. While there are recent alternatives to passwords (see "Replace Passwords" in this chapter), most computer protection depends on them.

CREATE A PASSWORD

After setting up a new user account, you can add a password to it that will then be required to use that account.

1. Click **Start** and click **Control Panel**. In Category view, click **User Accounts And Family Safety**, and then in any view click **User Accounts**. The User Accounts window opens.

2. If it is not your account that you want to add a password to, click **Manage Another Account**. If needed, type a password, click **Yes**, and click the account you want. In your account or in the other account that opens (this cannot be the Guest account because that cannot have a password), click **Create A Password**.

   The Create Password window will open, as shown in Figure 6-3. Note the warning message. This is true only if the user already has a password that has been used to encrypt files, create certificates, and access websites and network resources. If you create a new password for this person, it will replace the old one,

Continued . . .

3. If the hint isn't of any help, click **Reset Password**. The Password Reset Wizard starts.

4. Click **Next**. Insert your reset disk in its socket or drive. Click the drive down arrow, select the drive the reset disk is in, and again click **Next**. Type a new password, confirm it, type a password hint, click **Next**, and click **Finish**. (You do not have to create a new reset disk with your new password; Windows updates the reset disk for you.) Remove the reset disk.

5. Enter your new password, and press **ENTER**.

Figure 6-3: *Creating, changing, or deleting a password will lose all items that are based on passwords, such as encrypted files, certificates, and other passwords.*

SETTING PASSWORDS *(Continued)*

and all the places where the old one has been used will no longer be available even with the new password. This is the case every time you create, change, or delete a password.

3. Type the new password, click in the second text box, type the new password again to confirm it, click in the third text box, type a nonobvious hint to help you remember the password, and click **Create Password**.

4. Close the Change An Account window.

CHANGE A PASSWORD

It is a good idea to change your password periodically in case it has been compromised.

1. Click **Start** and click **Control Panel**. In Category view, click **User Accounts And Family Safety**, and then in any view click **User Accounts**. The User Accounts window opens.

2. If it is not your account that you want to change, click **Manage Another Account**. If needed, type a password, click **Yes**, and click the account you want to change. In your account or in the other account that opens, click **Change The Password**.

3. In your account, type the current password, and click in the second text box. In either your or another's account, type a new password, click in the next text box, and

Continued . . .

For a password to be *strong*, it must be eight or more characters long; use both upper- and lowercase letters; and use a mixture of letters, numbers, and symbols, which include ! # $ % ^ & * and spaces. It also should *not* be a recognizable word, name, or date. Instead of a password such as "mymoney," consider using something like this: "my$Money23."

Switch Between Users

When you have multiple users on a computer, one user can obviously log off and another log on; however, with the Welcome screen, you can use Fast User Switching (which is not available in the Starter Edition of Windows 7). This allows you to keep programs running and files open when you temporarily switch to another user. To use Fast User Switching:

1. Click **Start**, click the **Shut Down** right arrow, and click **Switch User**. The Welcome screen will appear and let the other person click his or her account and log on.

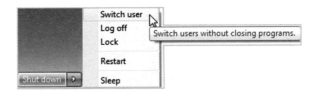

2. When the other person has finished using the computer and has logged off (by clicking **Start**, clicking the **Shut Down** right arrow, and clicking **Log Off**), you can log on normally. When you do, you will see all your programs exactly as you left them.

SETTING PASSWORDS *(Continued)*

type the new password again to confirm it. Click in the final text box, type a nonobvious hint to help you remember the password, and click **Change Password**.

4. Close the Change An Account window.

REMOVE A PASSWORD

If you move a computer to a location that doesn't need a password—for example, if it is not accessible to anyone else, or if you want to remove a password for some other reason—you can do so.

1. Click **Start** and click **Control Panel**. In Category view, click **User Accounts And Family Safety**, and then in any view click **User Accounts**. The User Accounts window opens.

2. If it is not your account in which you want to remove the password, click **Manage Another Account**. If needed, type a password, click **Yes**, and click the account you want. In your account or in the other account that opens, click **Remove The Password**.

3. If it is your account, type the current password, and, in any case, click **Remove Password**.

4. Close the Change An Account window.

Control What a User Does

User accounts identify people and allow them to log on to your computer. What they can do after that depends on the permissions they have. Windows 7 has two features that help you control what other users do on your computer: Parental Controls and the ability to turn Windows features on and off for a given user. In addition, Windows 7's New Technology File System (NTFS) allows the sharing of folders and drives as well as the assignment of permissions to use a file, a folder, a disk, a printer, and other devices. The permissions are given to individuals and to groups to which individuals can belong. So far, you've seen two groups: Administrators and Standard Users (also called just "Users"), but there are others, and you can create more.

You can limit the sharing of files and folders to the *Public folder* within the Users folder on your computer. To do so, you must create or move the files and folders you want to share into the Public folder. The other option is to share directly the other folders on your computer. This is made easier by the *inheritance* attribute, where subfolders automatically inherit (take on) the permissions of their parent folder. Every object in Windows 7 NTFS, however, has its own set of *security descriptors* that are attached to it when it is created; with the proper permission, these security descriptors can be individually changed. When permissions are appropriately set, other users on your computer can access and optionally change your files and folders.

Set Parental Controls

If you have a child or grandchild as one of the users on your computer and you are an administrator with a password, you can control what your child can do on your computer, including hours of usage, programs he or she can run, and access to the Internet. When your child encounters a blocked program, game, or website, a notice is displayed, including a link the child can click to request access. You, as an administrator, can allow one-time access by entering your user ID and password.

1. Click **Start** and click **Control Panel**. In Category view, click **User Accounts And Family Safety**, and then in any view click **Parental Controls**. If needed, type an administrator password and click **Yes**. You may be asked if you want to sign up for online Family Safety through Windows Live. If you want, enter your Windows Live user name and password, and click **Sign In** to see how it works. Otherwise, click **Cancel**.

2. When you are back in Windows and the Parental Controls window has opened, click the user for whom you want to set Parental Controls to open the individual User Controls window.

3. Click **On** under Parental Controls, as shown in Figure 6-4.

4. Click **Time Limits**, drag the hours to block or allow (you only need to select one or the other, and you can drag across multiple hours and days), and then click **OK**.

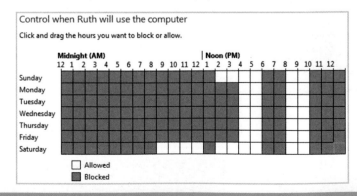

Figure 6-4: *Parental Controls allows you to determine what a child can do and see on your computer.*

5. Click **Games** and choose if any games can be played. Click **Set Game Ratings**, choose if games with no rating can be played, click a rating level, choose the type of content you want blocked, and click **OK**. Click **Block Or Allow Specific Games**, click whether to block or allow specific games installed on the computer, and click **OK**. Click **OK** again to leave Game Controls.

6. Click **Allow And Block Specific Programs**, and choose whether to allow the use of all programs or only the ones you choose. If you choose to pick specific programs to allow, a list of all the programs on the computer is presented. Click those for which you want to allow access, and click **OK**.

7. Click **OK** to close the User Controls window.

Control What Parts of Windows Can Be Used

As an administrator, you can control what parts of Windows 7 each user can access.

1. Log on as the user for whom you want to set Windows feature usage.

2. Click **Start** and click **Control Panel**. In Category view, click **Programs** and then in any view click **Programs And Features**.

3. Click **Turn Windows Features On Or Off** in the left column. If needed, type a password and click **Yes**. The Windows Features dialog box appears.

4. Click an unselected check box to turn a feature on, or click a selected check box to turn a feature off. Click the plus sign (+) where applicable to open the subfeatures and turn them on or off.

5. When you have selected the features the user will be allowed to use, click **OK**.

6. Close the Programs And Features window.

JEREMY IS COMFORTABLE WITH HIS SECURITY PRECAUTIONS

I am a small book publisher working out of my home. I depend very heavily on my computer and do a large part of my business over the Internet, frequently using PayPal for handling payments and keeping all my records on my computer. You would think in that situation I would be very concerned about computer security. I'm actually not. I do all the prudent things like using the latest software, doing all the recommended updates, running the latest antivirus software—again with the latest updates—doing recurring backups of my files, and maintaining the recommended security settings. None of these steps, though, is extreme, and none take much effort to implement and maintain. I believe that I have moderate-to-low exposure to security risks by working out of my home, where only my wife has access to my computer, and by following the basic security steps just mentioned. I believe that it is easy to get overly concerned about computer security, but if you look at what is the real risk if someone got control of your computer, generally, if you have taken the basic precautions, the answer is not much.

Jeremy B., 61, Michigan

Set File and Folder Sharing

Files are shared by being in a shared folder or drive. Folders and drives are shared by their creator or owner or by an administrator. To share folders and drives, as well as printers and other devices, both locally and over a network, you must address three components of Windows 7 that allow you to control access to your computer and its components (see Figure 6-5):

- **The Windows Firewall**, which protects your computer and its contents from network access
- **The Network And Sharing Center**, which is the primary means of controlling sharing in Windows 7
- **Sharing individual drives and folders**, which lets you determine if a drive, folder, or other device is shared; who has permission to access it; and what they can do with the contents

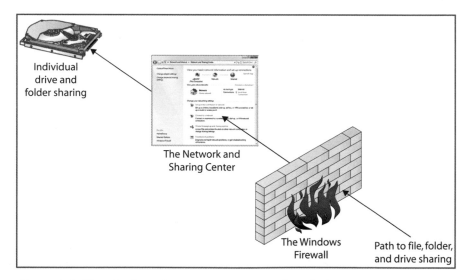

*Figure 6-5: **The sharing of your computer requires that you set up your firewall, the Network And Sharing Center, and the individual drives and folders to accomplish that.***

SET UP THE WINDOWS FIREWALL

Windows 7 includes the Windows Firewall, whose objective is to slow down and hopefully prevent anybody from accessing your computer without your permission, while at the same time allowing those who you want to use your computer to do so. The Windows Firewall is turned on by default. Check to see if it is; if it isn't, turn it on.

1. Click **Start** and click **Control Panel**. In Category view, click **System And Security**, and then in any view click **Windows Firewall**. The Windows Firewall window opens and shows your firewall status.

2. If your firewall is not turned on, or if you want to turn it off, click **Turn Windows Firewall On Or Off** in the pane on the left. If needed, type a password and click **Yes**. The Windows Firewall Customize Settings window opens. Click the respective option button to turn on your firewall (highly recommended) or to turn it off (not recommended). You can do this for both your local network and for a public network to which you may be connected. Click **OK**.

3. To change the settings for what the firewall will and won't let through, click **Allow A Program Or Feature Through Windows Firewall** at the top of the left column. The Allowed Programs window opens, as shown in Figure 6-6.

4. In the Programs And Features list, select the services running on your computer that you want to allow people from the Internet to use. To share information across a LAN, click the following items:

   - Core Networking
   - File And Printer Sharing

TIP

In the Windows Firewall Allowed Programs window, you can determine what each option does by highlighting it and clicking **Details** at the bottom of the dialog box.

NOTE

You will probably have other programs selected, such as Internet Explorer and Windows Live Messenger, that can be used on the Internet.

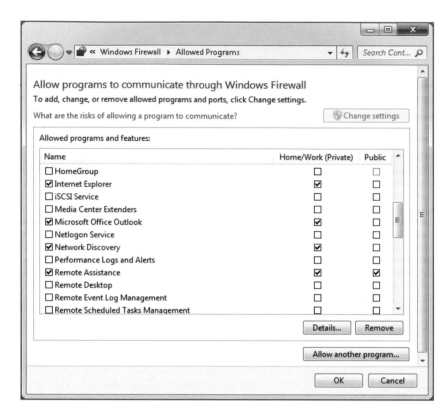

Figure 6-6: *The Windows 7 Firewall can be configured to allow certain programs and features to come through.*

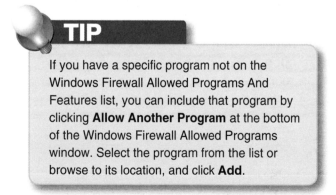

TIP

If you have a specific program not on the Windows Firewall Allowed Programs And Features list, you can include that program by clicking **Allow Another Program** at the bottom of the Windows Firewall Allowed Programs window. Select the program from the list or browse to its location, and click **Add**.

- HomeGroup
- Network Discovery
- Windows Collaboration Computer Name Registration Service (optional)
- Windows Peer To Peer Collaboration Foundation (optional)

5. Click to select each program or feature you want to allow through the firewall. Click **OK** to close the Windows Firewall Allowed Programs window, and then click **Close** to close the Windows Firewall Control Panel.

USE THE NETWORK AND SHARING CENTER

The second layer of file-sharing protection in Windows 7 is controlled with the Network And Sharing Center, shown in Figure 6-7, which allows you to turn on or off the primary components of sharing information among users on a computer and across a network.

The first time Windows 7 was run, a choice was made between a public and private network. The Network And Sharing Center allows you to change that. If you are primarily sharing your computer with other computers within an organization or a residence, you should select either **Home Network** or **Work Network**, where network sharing is relatively simple. If you are primarily using public wireless or cable Internet connections and very little sharing of your computer, select **Public**, which makes it more difficult for someone to get into your computer.

1. Click **Start** and click **Control Panel**. In Category view, click **Network And Internet**, and then in any view click **Network And Sharing Center**. The Network And Sharing Center window opens, as shown in Figure 6-7.

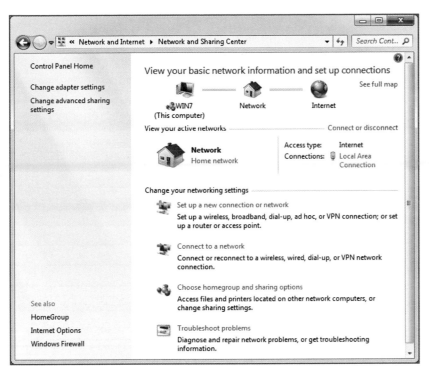

Figure 6-7: *The Network And Sharing Center is the primary means of sharing your computer.*

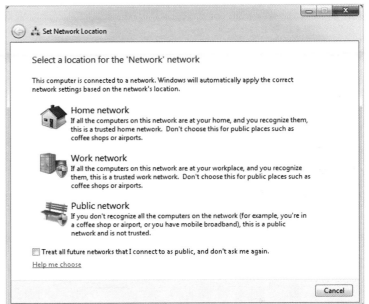

2. If you want to change the type of network (home, work, or public) you are connected to, click the current type of network to the right of the icon (in Figure 6-7, it is Home Network). The Set Network Location dialog box will appear.

3. Read the conditions that are expected in each network type, and then click the type that is correct for you. If needed, type a password and click **Yes**. Your choice will be confirmed. Click **Close**.

4. Each type of network has sharing settings that are automatically set. Home Network is the most open, with just about everything shared; Public Network is the other extreme.

5. When you have finished with the Network And Sharing Center, click **Close**.

USE HOMEGROUP FOLDER SHARING

The final layer of sharing settings is the determination of the disks and folders you want to share. Windows 7's HomeGroup makes sharing files and folders within the homegroup much easier. When Windows 7 is first installed or started, you are asked if you want a home, work, or public network. If you choose Home, which may also be a good idea for small businesses, a homegroup is either set up or joined, depending on whether a homegroup already exists. You are then shown a list of your libraries and asked if you want to share them. By default, your pictures, music, printers, and videos are shared for anyone to read, view, or use but not to change. Documents are not shared, but you can change this at the time of installation or at a later time. You can make these changes at the library level or at the disk and folder level. To do this at the library level:

1. Click **Start** and click **Control Panel**. In Category view, click **Network And Internet**, and then in any view click **HomeGroup**. The HomeGroup window opens.

   If this is the first time you are looking into HomeGroup, you'll be asked if you want to share any libraries. Click **Choose What You Want To Share**. The HomeGroup wizard will appear and walk you through the selection of what to share within the network and to create a password to join other Windows 7 computers to the HomeGroup. When you are done, and if you have previously reviewed the HomeGroup, the Control Panel HomeGroup window will open, as shown in Figure 6-8.

2. Make any changes that you feel you need, and then, if you made changes, click **Save Changes**. If needed, enter the password and click **Yes**. Otherwise, click **Cancel**.

To go beyond the sharing of libraries within the homegroup, and even then only for someone to read, view, or use your libraries, you need to go to the individual drives and folders. You can change

*Figure 6-8: **The HomeGroup default is to share three of your libraries plus your printer within your homegroup.***

the sharing of libraries so that other users can change contents in addition to reading or viewing them. To do that:

1. Click **Start** and click **Computer**. In the folders (left) pane, click **Libraries** so the detail libraries (documents, music, pictures, or videos) are shown in the right pane.

2. Right-click the library whose sharing you want to change, and click **Share With**. The context menu and file-sharing submenu will appear.

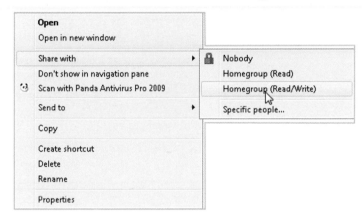

3. By default, the libraries are shared among the homegroup to be read-only. You can allow homegroup members both read and write access to your libraries, or you can select specific people and give them specific permissions. Click the option you want, and, when you are finished, close the Windows Explorer window.

Back Up Your Information

Computers are a great asset, but like any machine, they are prone to failures of many kinds. Once you have started using your computer regularly, it becomes important to make a copy of your information and store it in another location should your hard drive fail or something else happen to your computer.

NOTE

Windows 7 Starter and Home Basic editions can only join a homegroup and can't establish one or change the sharing of one.

TIP

It usually takes losing important information three times before people get religious about backing up their data. Don't wait that long. You don't need to back up everything—just the most important things that would really cause you a problem if you lost them. Figure out the simplest way for you to back up your most important items like your financial records, your contact lists, your writing, and possibly your genealogy information, and do it often.

There are several solutions to copying and saving your information. The term normally used for this is *backup* (or to back up—the verb form). This means storing a copy of your information in a location other than on your computer. You can back up both on your computer and on the Internet.

BACK UP ON YOUR COMPUTER

Within your computer, you can back up your information to a CD or DVD, to another drive that is connected to your computer (including an external hard drive and a USB flash or thumb drive), or to a hard drive on another computer. You may want to perform backups to a couple of these items on a periodic basic, and a couple of times a year back up your data to a CD and put it in your bank safety deposit box.

Windows 7 has a backup program, but without a lot of setup, it backs up things you don't really care about, like your programs you already have on CDs or DVDs. A simpler way to do a backup is to simply copy your files from the hard disk in your computer to an external device, like a CD, DVD, USB flash drive, or external hard drive. Here's how to copy some files to a writable (or "burnable") CD.

1. Click **Start**, click **Computer**, and open (click the triangle on the left) the drive and folders in the left column needed to display the files you want to back up in the right column, as you see in Figure 6-9.

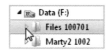

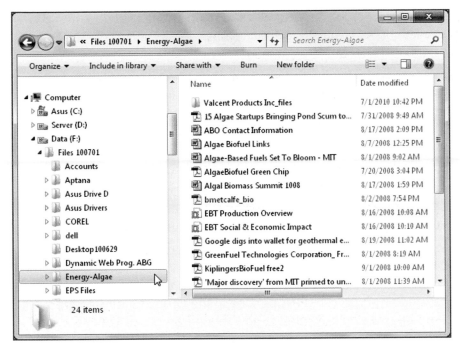

Figure 6-9: *You must first locate the files on your computer that you want to back up.*

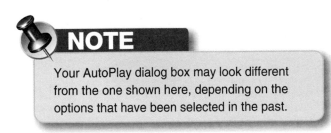

NOTE

Your AutoPlay dialog box may look different from the one shown here, depending on the options that have been selected in the past.

2. Open your CD/DVD drive, insert a blank writable disc, and close the drive. An AutoPlay dialog box will open offering you several options.

3. Click **Burn Files To Disc** to open the Burn A Disc dialog box. Type a title, click **Like A USB Flash Drive**, and click **Next**. You will see a message that the disc is being formatted and then another AutoPlay dialog box will appear.

4. Click **Open Folder To View Files** to open another window with a blank right pane with the message "Drag Files To This Folder To Add Them To The Disc."

5. In your original folder, similar to the one shown in Figure 6-9, select the files you want to back up by clicking the first file, pressing and holding **SHIFT** while clicking the last file if the files are contiguous, or pressing and holding **CTRL** while individually clicking the other files if they are not contiguous.

6. When all the necessary files in a folder are selected, drag them (point at the selected files, press and hold the left mouse button, and move the mouse) to the right pane of the new folder for the CD or DVD, as you can see in Figure 6-10, and release the mouse button.

7. You can open other folders and drives and drag other files to the CD/DVD folder. Periodically look at how much space on the CD/DVD has been used by right-clicking the drive in the left pane of its window and clicking **Properties** in the context menu. In the Properties dialog box, look at how much free space you have left, and then click **OK**.

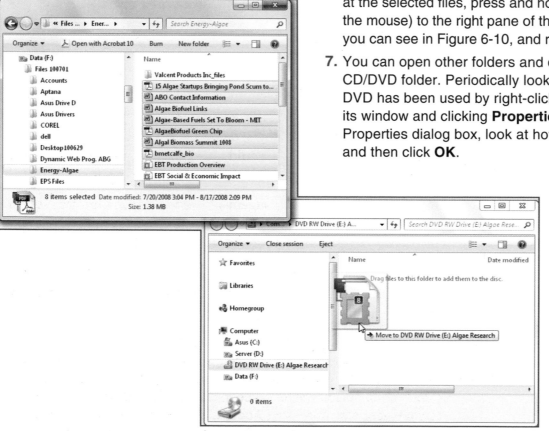

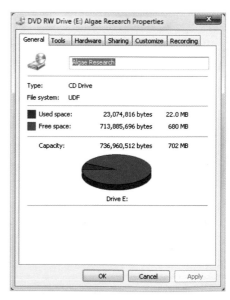

Figure 6-10: **An easy way to back up files is to drag them to an external disc or drive.**

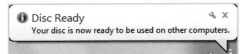

Disc Ready   ❌
Your disc is now ready to be used on other computers.

NOTE

A disc created with the Like A USB Flash Drive option can be put into the CD/DVD disc drive again and have files deleted and added to it, as well as edited and restored to the disc.

8. When you have all the files you want to back up in the CD/DVD, click **Close Session**. You'll see a message that the disc is being closed. When that is done, you'll see a message that the disc is ready. Click **Eject**, remove the disc, label it with a soft felt-tip pen, and store it with a paper or plastic sleeve in safe place, preferably away from your computer and in a fireproof container.

BACK UP OVER THE INTERNET

Recently, many people are choosing to save their information to the *cloud*, meaning that they back up the data on their computer to a location (a server) accessed through the Internet. This method makes it easy to access your data from any location, as well as your new computer, should your old computer fail. These services are reasonable in cost or even free and are easy to set up.

Some programs, once you have subscribed to them, install a small software program on your computer. These programs work behind the scenes, copying new photos, data files, deposits, or letters to a secure, encrypted location. Should your old computer break down, you can restore your files and data to your new computer.

Some personal financial management programs also offer this service for their data. For example, Quicken's Online Backup service charges a nominal fee per month to protect your financial information.

An example of a currently free cloud service is Microsoft's SkyDrive. Microsoft gives you 25GB of storage. You'll need to set up an account with a user ID and a password.

1. Click the **Internet Explorer** icon on the taskbar to open it. In the address bar, type skydrive.live.com and press **ENTER**. Windows Live will open, and if you are not already signed up as a Windows Live or Hotmail client, you will be asked to do that. Click **Sign Up**, fill out the form that opens, and click **I Accept**. Your SkyDrive page will open, where you can use existing folders or set up your own, as you can see in Figure 6-11.

*Figure 6-11: **Online, "cloud" Internet storage is a good and safe way to back up important files.***

2. Click a folder you want to use to open it, and then click **Add Files**; or click **New**, click **Folder**, enter a name for the folder, click **Create Folder**, and then click **Add Files**. In either case, a window will open inviting you to drop documents there or select documents from your computer.

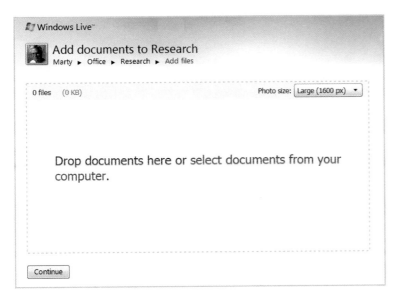

3. You can use steps 1, 5, and 6 under "Back Up on Your Computer" and drag the files to the window shown in the previous step; or you can click **Select Documents From Your Computer**, select the files as in step 5, and click **Open**.

4. You'll see the files being added. When the files have been added, you can remove individual files by clicking the X after the file size of each file. You can add files using either method in step 3.

5. When you have added all the files you want, click **Continue**. A list will appear of the files you have added. You can select a particular file and share, move, copy, rename, and delete it. If the file is for Microsoft Word, Excel, or PowerPoint, you can edit it directly in your browser (Internet Explorer) using the Microsoft Office Web Apps.

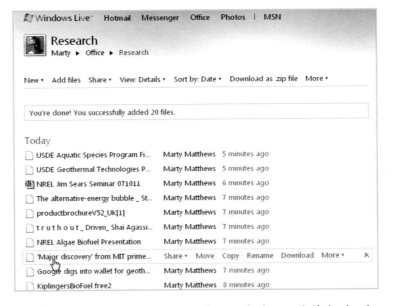

6. When you are done, close the skydrive.live website and, if desired, Internet Explorer.

Other cloud sites work similarly.

QUICKSTEPS

LOCKING A COMPUTER

By default, when your screen saver comes on and you return to use your system, you must go through the logon screen. If you have added a password to your account, you have to enter it to get back into the system, which is a means of preventing unauthorized access when you are away from your running computer. If you don't want to wait for your screen saver to come on, you can click **Start**, click the **Shut Down** right arrow, and click **Lock**; or you can press ⊞ (the Windows flag key) +**L** to immediately bring up the logon screen, from which your screen saver will open at the appropriate time.

Depending on your environment, having to go through the logon screen every time you come out of the screen saver may or may not be beneficial. To turn off or turn back on the screen saver protection:

1. Right-click the desktop and click **Personalize**. Click **Screen Saver**.

2. Select or deselect **On Resume, Display Logon Screen**, depending on whether you want to display the logon screen upon returning to your system (see Figure 6-12).

3. Click **OK** to close the Screen Saver Settings dialog box, and close the Personalization window.

Figure 6-12: *You can password-protect your system when you leave it unattended by having the logon screen appear when you return after using the screen saver.*

Protect Yourself on the Internet

Your connection through your computer to the Internet is your doorway to the cyberworld. It allows you to communicate with others through email and social networking; it allows you to shop for virtually anything without leaving your home; and it provides an enormous resource for gathering information and news. It also is a doorway that can let in things that can harm you, your computer, and your data. It is like the front door to your house—you need it to see and interact with other people, but it also has locks on it to keep out the people you don't want to let in. Similarly, there are a number of barriers you can place in the way of people who want to do damage via the Internet.

Understand Internet Threats

As the Internet has gained popularity, so have the threats it harbors. Viruses, worms, spyware, and adware have become part of our vocabulary. Look at each of these threats to understand what each can do and how to guard your computer and data, as described in Table 6-1.

Use an Antivirus or Security Program

To counter the various Internet threats, you need to install an antivirus or security program. A number of such programs are available, both free and at a cost. You can buy these in computer stores and on the Internet. There is a lot of variability in the pricing,

TIP

Malware is a catch-all term for viruses, worms, spyware, adware, and any other harmful Internet critter.

PROBLEM	DEFINITION	SOLUTION
Virus	A program that attaches itself to other files on your computer. There are many forms of viruses, each performing different, usually malevolent, functions on your computer.	Install an antivirus program with a subscription for automatic updates, and make sure it is continually running.
Worm	A type of virus that replicates itself repeatedly through a computer network or security breach in your computer. Because it keeps copying itself, a worm can fill up a hard drive and cause your network to malfunction.	
Trojan horse	A computer program that claims to do one thing, such as play a game, but has hidden parts that can erase files or even your entire hard drive.	
Adware	The banners and pop-up ads that come with programs you download from the Internet. Often, these programs are free, and to support them, the program owner sells space for ads to display on your computer every time you use the program.	Install an anti-adware program.
Spyware	A computer program that downloads with another program from the Internet. Spyware can monitor what you do, keep track of your keystrokes, discern credit card and other personally identifying numbers, and pass that information back to its author.	Install an antispyware program.

*Table 6-1: **Security Issues Associated with the Internet and How to Control Them***

NAME	WEBSITE	LIST PRICE (AS OF 3/2011)
AVG Antivirus Free Edition	free.avg.com	Free
AVG Internet Security	avg.com	$54.99 for one PC, one year
BitDefender Internet Security	bitdefender.com	$49.95 for three PCs, one year
Kaspersky Internet Security	Kaspersky.com	$79.95 for three PCs, one year
Microsoft Security Essentials	microsoft.com/security_essentials	Free
Norton Internet Security	Symantec.com	$69.99 for three PCs, one year

Table 6-2: *Antivirus and Security Programs*

and the opinion of which is the best also varies widely. Table 6-2 shows a few of these programs with which I have had direct experience. The best thing for you to do is go on the Internet and do a search of "antivirus program reviews." Look for the toptenreviews.com site—it gives you a quick comparison, but look at several sites and read the reviews, because there is considerable difference of opinion. When you have decided on the program you want, determine the version to get. Most companies have a basic antivirus program, an Internet security program, and an overall security program. My opinion is that the Internet security programs are a good middle ground. Finally, do some price hunting, making sure you are looking at the version you want. At the time this was written, Amazon.com, for example, was offering substantial discounts (as compared to purchasing on the company's website, shown in Table 6-2). There have been mail-in rebate deals that allow you to get the program for the price of shipping after the rebate.

Control Internet Security

Internet Explorer allows you to control three aspects of Internet security. You can categorize sites by the degree to which you trust them, determine how you want to handle cookies placed on your

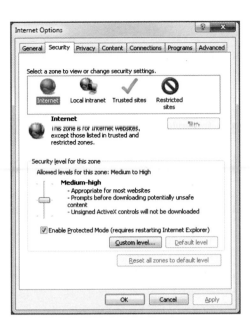

*Figure 6-13: **Internet Explorer allows you to categorize websites into zones and determine what can be done within those zones.***

NOTE

Protected Mode—which you can turn on or off for each zone at the bottom of the Security tab (the notice for which you'll see at the bottom of Internet Explorer)—is what produces the messages that tells you a program is trying to run in Internet Explorer or that software is trying to install itself on your computer. In most cases, you can click in a bar at the top of the Internet Explorer window if you want to run the program or install the software. You can also double-click the notice at the bottom of Internet Explorer to open the Security tab and turn off Protected Mode (clear the **Enable Protected Mode** check box).

computer by websites, and set and use ratings to control the content of websites that can be viewed. These controls are found in the Internet Options dialog box.

In Internet Explorer, click **Tools** on the tab row, and click **Internet Options**.

CATEGORIZE WEBSITES

Internet Explorer allows you to categorize websites into zones: Internet (sites that are not classified in one of the other ways), Local Intranet, Trusted Sites, and Restricted Sites (as shown in Figure 6-13).

From the Internet Options dialog box:

1. Click the **Security** tab. Click the **Internet** zone. Note its definition.
2. Click **Custom Level**. Select the elements in this zone that you want to disable, enable, or prompt you before using. Alternatively, select a level of security you want for this zone, and click **Reset**. Click **OK** when you are finished.
3. Click each of the other zones, where you can identify either groups or individual sites you want in that zone.

HANDLE COOKIES

Cookies are small pieces of data that websites store on your computer so that they can remind themselves of who you are. These can save you from having to constantly enter your name and ID. Cookies can also be dangerous, however, letting people into your computer where they can potentially do damage.

Internet Explorer lets you determine the types and sources of cookies you will allow and what those cookies can do on your computer (see Figure 6-14).

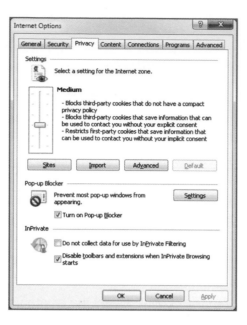

*Figure 6-14: **Determine how you will handle cookies that websites want to leave on your computer.***

From the Internet Options dialog box:

1. Click the **Privacy** tab. Select a privacy setting by dragging the slider up or down.
2. Click **Advanced** to open the Advanced Privacy Settings dialog box. If you wish, click **Override Automatic Cookie Handling**, and select the settings you want to use.
3. Click **OK** to return to the Internet Options dialog box.
4. In the middle of the Privacy tab, you can turn off the pop-up blocker, which is on by default (it is recommended that you leave it on). If you have a site that you frequently use that needs pop-ups, click **Settings**, enter the site address (URL), click **Add**, and click **Close**.
5. At the bottom of the Privacy tab, you can determine how to handle InPrivate Filtering and Browsing. See the Note on InPrivate later in this chapter.

CONTROL CONTENT

You can control the content that Internet Explorer displays.

From the Internet Options dialog box:

1. Click the **Content** tab. Click **Parental Controls**. If you are not an administrator, this will display the User Controls window similar to what you saw in Figure 6-4 when setting Parental Controls with Windows. To make changes in Parental Controls, you must make them as an administrator in Windows itself, not Internet Explorer.
2. Click **Enable** to open the Content Advisor dialog box. Individually select each of the categories, and drag the slider to the level you want to allow. Detailed descriptions of each area are shown in the lower half of the dialog box.
3. Click **OK** to close the Content Advisor dialog box.

When you are done, click **OK** to close the Internet Options dialog box. (Other parts of this dialog box are discussed elsewhere in this book.)

NOTE

Internet Explorer 8 and 9 have added a new way to browse and view sites, called *InPrivate*, that is opened by clicking **Safety** on the tab row of IE 8 or clicking **Tools** and then **Safety** in IE 9 and then in either case clicking **InPrivate Browsing**. This opens a separate browser window with this in the address bar: InPrivate about:InPrivate . While you are in this window, your browsing history, temporary Internet files, and cookies are not stored on your computer, preventing anyone looking at your computer from seeing where you have browsed. In addition, with InPrivate Filtering, also opened from Safety in the tab row, you can control how information about you is passed on to Internet content providers.

Chapter 7
Using and Maintaining Windows 7

Windows 7 facilitates whatever you want to do on your computer. It is the means by which you can run other programs, access the Internet, print documents and photos, capture digital pictures from your camera, send faxes, and connect to other computers. In this chapter we'll look at using and maintaining many of the facilities of Windows 7 not discussed elsewhere, including setting up the starting and stopping of programs in a number of different ways, as well as the maintenance and enhancement of Windows 7 and the setting up of Remote Assistance so that you can have someone help you without that person actually being in front of your computer.

NOTE

In many of the steps in this chapter, you will be interrupted and asked by User Account Control (UAC) if you want to allow system changes. So long as it is something you started and want to do, you should click **Yes** or enter a password. To simplify the instructions in this chapter, the UAC instructions have been left out. Chapter 6 discussed UAC in more detail.

NOTE

While there is a possibility that you will need one of the ancillary ways of starting a program shown in this chapter, the majority of the time you won't need to remember them; you only need the ways explained in earlier chapters, including using the Start menu, the desktop, and the taskbar.

Start and Stop Programs

Previous chapters discussed starting programs from the Start menu, through All Programs, through a shortcut on the desktop or taskbar, and by locating the program with Windows Explorer. All of these methods require a direct action by you. Windows also provides several ways to automatically start programs and to monitor and manage them while they are running.

Start Programs Automatically

Sometimes, you will want to start a program automatically and have it run in the background every time you start the computer. For example, you might automatically run an antivirus program or an Internet phone program (such as Skype, which your kids or grandkids may be pestering you to get so you can talk to them at a cheaper cost). To automatically start a program, open a folder, or open a file in a program:

1. Click **Start**, click **All Programs**, right-click **Startup**, and click **Open All Users**. The Startup folder will open.

2. Click **Start** and click **Computer** to open Windows Explorer. Position the Explorer window so that you can see both it and the Startup window on the desktop at the same time (right-click the taskbar and click **Show Windows Side By Side** to arrange both windows).

3. In Explorer, open the drive and folders needed to display the program file you want to automatically start, or the folder or disk drive you want to automatically open, or the file you want to automatically start in its program.

4. Hold the right mouse button while dragging (right-drag) the program file, the folder, or the file to the open Startup folder, as you can see in Figure 7-1. When you reach the Startup folder, click **Create Shortcuts Here**.

5. Close the Startup folder and Windows Explorer. The next time you start your computer, the action you want will take place.

Start Programs Minimized

Sometimes, when you start programs automatically, you want them to run in the background—in other words, minimized. To do that:

1. Click **Start**, click **All Programs**, right-click **Startup**, and click **Open All Users** to open the Startup folder.

2. Right-click the program you want minimized, and click **Properties**. Click the **Shortcut** tab.

*Figure 7-1: **Programs in the Startup folder are automatically started when you start Windows 7.***

Figure 7-2: *Minimizing a program, when it has automatically started, lets it run in the background.*

NOTE

Many programs, such as Backup and antivirus programs, use their own scheduler to run automatically on a scheduled basis.

3. Click the **Run** down arrow, and click **Minimized**, as shown in Figure 7-2.

4. Click **OK** to close the Properties dialog box, and then close the Startup folder.

Schedule Programs

You can schedule a program to run automatically, send an email, or display a reminder on your screen using Windows 7's Task Scheduler.

1. Click **Start**, click **All Programs**, click **Accessories**, click **System Tools**, and click **Task Scheduler**. The Task Scheduler window will open, as you can see in Figure 7-3.

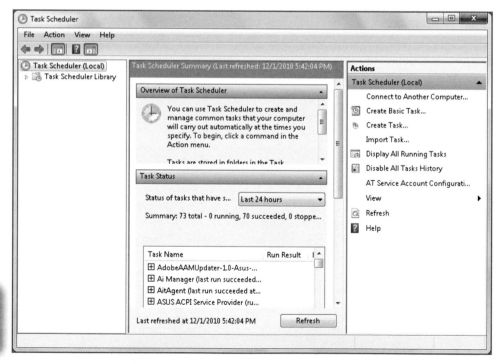

Figure 7-3: *The Task Scheduler is used by Windows 7 for many of its tasks, but you can also use it to repeatedly perform a task you want.*

2. Click **Create Basic Task** in the actions pane or in the Action menu. The Create A Basic Task Wizard opens. Type a name and description, and click **Next**. Select when you want the task to start, and again click **Next**.

3. Depending on when you want the task to start, you may have to select the start date and time and enter additional information, such as the day of the week for a weekly trigger. Click **Next**.

4. Choose whether you want to start a program, send an email, or display a message, and click **Next**.

5. If you want to start a program, select it either from the list of programs or by browsing to it, add any arguments that are to be passed to the program when it starts, and indicate if you would like the program to be looking at a particular folder when it starts (Start In).

–Or–

If you want to send an email, type the From and To email addresses, the subject, and text; browse to and select an attachment; and type your SMTP email server (this is your outgoing mail server that you entered when you set up Windows Mail—see Chapter 5).

–Or–

If you want to display a message, type a title and the message you want it to contain.

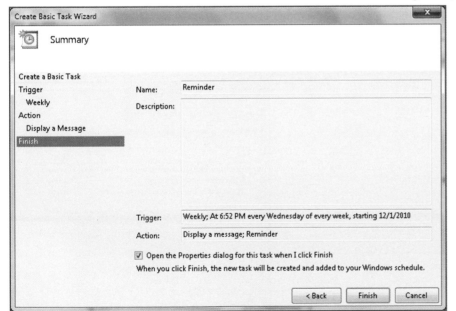

Figure 7-4: The Task Scheduler can be used to send email messages and display a message on your screen, as well as to start a program.

6. Click **Next**. The Summary dialog box will appear, as shown in Figure 7-4. Click **Open The Properties Dialog For This Task When I Click Finish**, and click **Finish**. The Task Properties dialog box will appear.

NOTE

The Create Task dialog box, basically identical to the Task Scheduler Properties dialog box, can be used to set up a scheduled task instead of using the Task Scheduler Wizard. Click **Create Task** instead of Create Basic Task.

TIP

In the left pane of the Task Scheduler, click **Task Scheduler (Local)**, in the center pane scroll down to display Active Tasks, and within that scroll down and double-click a Task Scheduler to work with it using the actions in the right pane.

QUICKSTEPS

SWITCHING PROGRAMS

You can switch programs that are running on the desktop, on the taskbar, and on the task list. You can also switch them using the Task Manager (see "Control Programs with the Task Manager" later in this chapter).

SWITCH PROGRAMS ON THE DESKTOP

If you have several programs running and arranged so that you can see all of them, switch from one to another by clicking the program you want to be active. However, if you have more than two or three programs running, it may be hard to see them on the desktop and, therefore, to select the one you want.

Continued . . .

7. Look at each of the tabs, review the information you have entered, and determine if you need to change anything.

8. When you are done reviewing the scheduled task, click **OK**. Click **Task Scheduler Library** in the left pane. You should see your scheduled task in the center pane. Close the Task Scheduler window.

Control Programs with the Task Manager

The Windows Task Manager, shown in Figure 7-5, performs a number of functions, but most importantly, it allows you to see what programs and processes (individual threads of a program) are running and to unequivocally stop both. A display of real-time graphs and tables also shows you what is happening at any second on your computer, as you can see in Figure 7-7. To work with the Task Manager:

1. Press **CTRL+ALT+DELETE** simultaneously and click **Start Task Manager**. Alternately, you can right-click a blank area of the taskbar, and click **Start Task Manager**.

*Figure 7-5: **The Task Manager shows you what programs are running and allows you to stop them.***

UICKSTEPS

SWITCHING PROGRAMS (Continued)

SWITCH PROGRAMS ON THE TASKBAR

If you have up to five or six programs running, you should be able to see their tasks on the taskbar. Clicking the task will switch to that program.

If you have multiple instances of a single program open, they will, by default, be grouped in a single icon. For example, in the following illustration, the taskbar icon indicates (note the right edge of the icon) that there are multiple instances open for both Internet Explorer and Windows Explorer.

To select a particular instance of a program when there are multiple instances running, mouse over the icon on the taskbar to open thumbnails of the several instances, then mouse over the one you want to see enlarged. Finally, when you are ready to fully open one particular instance, click the thumbnail for that instance, as you can see in Figure 7-6.

SWITCH PROGRAMS ON THE TASK LIST

The oldest method of switching programs, which predates Windows 95 and the taskbar, is using the task list.

1. Press **ALT+TAB** and hold down **ALT**. The task list will appear.

Continued . . .

2. Click the **Applications** tab. You'll see a list of the programs you are running, as shown in Figure 7-5.

3. Click a program in the list. Click **End Task** to stop the program, or click **Switch To** to activate that program.

4. Click **New Task** to enter a program you want to start.

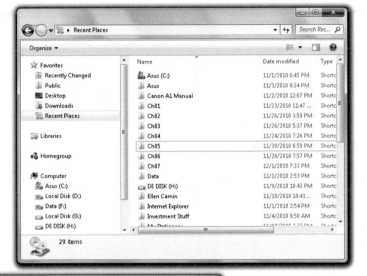

*Figure 7-6: **You can select one of several instances of a running program by mousing over the taskbar icon and the thumbnails, and then clicking the thumbnail you want.***

QUICKSTEPS

SWITCHING PROGRAMS *(Continued)*

2. While continuing to hold down **ALT**, press **TAB** repeatedly until the highlight moves to the program and instance you want or the desktop on the right. Then release **ALT** or click an icon to select the program you want.

C:\Users\Marty\Downloads

TIP

If you don't want tasks grouped on the taskbar, right-click an empty area of the taskbar, click **Properties**, click the **Taskbar Buttons** down arrow, and click **Never Combine**. Click **OK** to close the Properties dialog box. This not only doesn't combine, it also adds a title to each task or icon—taking up a lot of room. This method is not recommended.

Taskbar location on screen:	Bottom
Taskbar buttons:	Always combine, hide labels
	Always combine, hide labels
	Combine when taskbar is full
	Never combine
Notification area	
Customize which icons and notifications appear in the notification area.	Customize...

CAUTION

It is generally not a good idea to end a process. Instead, stop the program in the Applications tab that is generating the process.

5. Click the **Processes** tab. Here you see a list of all the processes that are currently running and their CPU (percentage) and memory (KB) usage. Most of these processes are components of Windows 7.

6. Click the **Services** tab. This is a list of the Windows 7 services that are active and their status. There is nothing that you can do here except observe it.

7. Click the **Performance** tab. This tab graphically shows the CPU and memory usage (see Figure 7-7), while the Networking tab shows the computer's use of the network. The Users tab shows the users that are logged on to the computer. You can disconnect them if they are coming in over the network or log them off if they are directly logged on.

8. When you are done, close the Windows Task Manager.

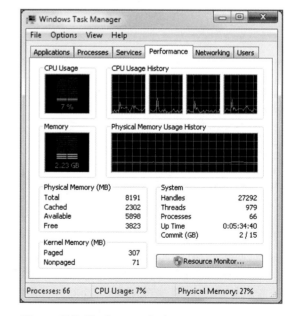

Figure 7-7: **Under most circumstances, on a personal computer, only a small fraction of the computer's resources are being used.**

NOTE

In Windows 7, you cannot turn off indexing—it is an integral part of the search facility. Windows Indexing has become quite efficient and seldom affects the performance of the computer. Also, you shouldn't index your full c: drive, as this includes program files that will slow down the search for your own data, music, and other personal files.

QUICKSTEPS

STOPPING PROGRAMS

You may choose to stop a program simply because you are done using it or in an attempt to keep a program from harming your data or other programs.

USE THE CLOSE BUTTON

One of the most common ways to close a program is to click the **Close** button on the upper-right corner of all windows.

USE THE EXIT COMMAND

Almost all programs have an Exit command in a menu on the far left of the menu bar; often, this is the File menu or tab. Open this menu and click **Exit**. The "Close" option on this menu generally means to close the current document but leave the program running so you can open another document. In a few instances, "Close" means the same as "Exit" when there is only "Close" and no "Exit."

Continued . . .

Control Windows Indexing

Windows 7 automatically indexes the files that are stored on a computer to substantially speed up your searches of files and folders.

1. Click **Start**, click **Control Panel**, select **Large Icons** view if it is not already selected, and click **Indexing Options** to open the Indexing Options dialog box.

2. If you want to change what is being indexed, click **Modify**, click the triangle icon to open the drives on your computer, and click the folders, as shown in Figure 7-8. Then click **OK**.

3. If you want to change the types of files being indexed, click **Advanced**. Choose if you want encrypted files indexed, or if you want similar words that have different marks (diacritics such as the accent, grave, and umlaut) that change the sound and meaning of the word indexed differently. Click the **File Types** tab, and select the types of files you want included. When you are done, click **OK**.

4. Close the Indexing Options dialog box.

STOPPING PROGRAMS *(Continued)*

CLOSE FROM THE TASKBAR

There are two ways to close a program from the taskbar.

Mouse over the icon, move the mouse to the red X in the upper-right corner of the thumbnail, and click.

–Or–

Right-click a task on the taskbar, and click **Close Window** (or **Close All Windows** if there are multiple instances).

CLOSE FROM THE KEYBOARD

With the program you want to close open and selected, press **ALT+F4**.

If none of these options work, see "Control Programs with the Task Manager."

NOTE

It could be that none of the options mentioned in the "Stopping Programs" QuickSteps will work if the program is performing a task or has some fault. In that case, if you want to force the program to stop, shut down Windows itself and click **Force Shut Down**.

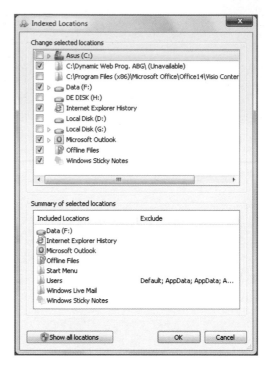

Figure 7-8: **Windows Indexing uses idle time to index your files and folders.**

Maintain Windows 7

Windows 7 maintenance consists of periodically updating fixes and new features, restoring Windows 7 when hardware or other software damages it, getting information about it, and installing new hardware and software.

Update Windows 7

Microsoft tries hard to encourage you to allow Windows 7 to update itself, from the point of installation, where you are asked to establish automatic updates, to periodically reminding you to do that. If you turn

on Automatic Updates, on a regular basis, Windows will automatically determine if any updates are available, download the updates (which come from Microsoft) over the Internet, and install them. If Automatic Updates was not turned on during installation, you can do that at any time and control the updating process once it is turned on.

TURN ON AUTOMATIC UPDATES

To turn on, off, and control Windows Update:

1. Click **Start** and click **Control Panel**. In Category view, click **System And Security**, and click **Windows Update**. In Large Icon view, click **Windows Update**.

2. Click **Change Settings**, determine the amount of automation you want, and click one of the following four choices after clicking the **Important Updates** down arrow (see Figure 7-9):

- The first and recommended choice, which is what I use, is the default. It automatically determines if updates are needed, downloads them, and then installs them on a frequency and at a time you specify.

- The second choice automatically determines if updates are needed and downloads them; it then asks you whether you want to install them.

- The third choice automatically determines if updates are needed, asks you before downloading them, and asks you again before installing them.

- The fourth choice, which is not recommended, never checks for updates.

Figure 7-9: **Automatic Updates** *determines which updates you need, and can automatically download and install them.*

3. Choose whether to include recommended updates when you are otherwise online with Microsoft, whether all users can install the updates, and whether to use Microsoft Update Service to receive updates for other Microsoft products you have installed, like Microsoft Office.

4. Click **OK** when you are finished, and close Windows Update.

APPLY UPDATES

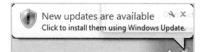

If you choose either the second or third option for handling updates, you will periodically see a notice that updates are ready to download and/or install.

When you see the notice:

1. Click the notice. The Windows Updates dialog box will appear and show you the updates that are available.

2. Click the individual updates to see detailed information about them.

3. Select the check box for the updates you want to download and/or install, and then click **OK**.

4. After you have selected all the updates you want, click **Install Updates**. You will see a notice that the updates are being installed.

5. When the updates have been downloaded and installed, Windows Update will reopen, inform you of this fact, and often ask to restart your computer.

6. Close any open programs, and click **Restart Now**.

Use the Action Center

The Windows Action Center contains messages that have been sent to you from Windows and other programs that, at least from the viewpoint of the program, you need to respond to. When a message is sent to you by a program, a flag with a red X appears in the notification area.

Click the notification area Action Center flag to open the Action Center jump list. Click any option on the jump list to go directly to the window or dialog box, where you can view the message and possibly take corrective actions.

–Or–

1. Click **Open Action Center** to review recent messages and resolve problems, as you can see in Figure 7-10.

2. Click the relevant item to address the issue, and when you are ready, close the Action Center.

CHANGE ACTION CENTER SETTINGS

You can change how the Action Center informs you of an alert message.

1. From the Action Center, click **Change Action Center Settings**.

2. Select the security and maintenance messages you want to see. Open any of the related settings that seem pertinent, returning to the Action Center when you are ready.

3. When your Action Center settings are the way you want them, click **OK** and close the Action Center.

Restore Windows 7

System Restore keeps track of the changes you make to your system, including the software you install and the settings you make. If a hardware change, a software installation, or something else causes the system not to load or not to run properly, you can use System Restore to return the system to the way it was at the last restore point.

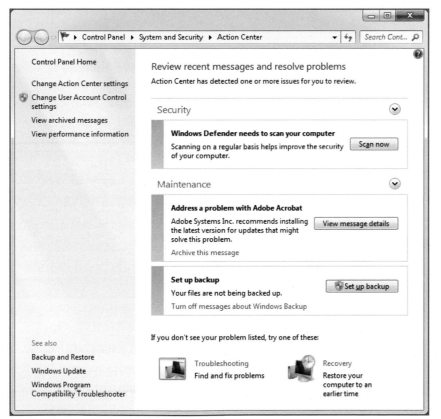

Figure 7-10: **The Action Center consolidates and maintains alert messages that are sent to you by the programs you run.**

SET UP SYSTEM RESTORE

In a default installation of Windows 7, System Restore is automatically installed. If you have at least 300MB of free disk space after installing Windows 7, System Restore will be turned on and the first restore point will be set. If System Restore is not enabled, you can turn it on and set a restore point.

1. Click **Start** and click **Control Panel**. In Category view, click **System And Security**, in any view click **System**, and finally click **System Protection** in the left pane. The System Properties dialog box will appear with the System Protection tab displayed, as you can see in Figure 7-11.

2. By default, the disk on which Windows 7 is installed should have system protection turned on, indicating that System Restore is operating automatically for that disk. Again by default, your other hard, USB, and memory card drives are not selected. If any drive does not have protection and you want it on, select the disk, click **Configure**, click **Restore System Settings And Previous Versions Of Files**, adjust the disk space usage as desired, and click **OK**.

3. When you have made the adjustments you want, click **OK**.

CREATE RESTORE POINTS

A *restore point* is an identifiable point in time when you know your system was working correctly. If your computer's settings are saved at that point, you can use those settings to restore your computer to that time. Normally, Windows 7 automatically creates restore points for the system drive on a periodic basis. But if you know at a given point in time that your

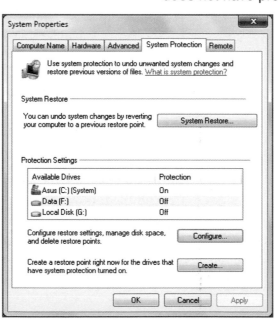

*Figure 7-11: **System Restore returns the system to a previous time when it was functioning normally.***

computer is operating exactly the way you want it to, you can create a restore point.

1. Click **Start** and click **Control Panel**. In Category view, click **System And Security**, in any view click **System**, and click **System Protection** in the left pane. The System Properties dialog box will appear with the System Protection tab displayed.

2. Click **Create** and type a name for the restore point. The date and time are automatically added, and you cannot change the name once you create it.

3. Click **Create** again. You will be told when the restore point is created. Click **OK** and click **Close** to close the System Properties dialog box.

RUN SYSTEM RESTORE FROM WINDOWS

If you can start and operate Windows 7 normally, try to execute the following steps. If you can't make it through these steps without Windows 7 crashing, go to the next section.

1. Click **Start** and click **Control Panel**. In Category view, click **System And Security**, in any view click **System**, and click **System Protection** in the left pane. The System Properties dialog box will appear with the System Protection tab displayed.

2. Click **System Restore**; a message explains the restore and, if you have a recent restore point, it is shown as the recommended restore point. If you want to use that restore point, click **Next** and go to step 4.

3. If you want to use another restore point, click **Choose A Different Restore Point**, and click **Next**. If you don't see a recommended restore point, also click **Next**. A list of restore points will open, as shown in Figure 7-12. Select the restore point you want to use, and click **Scan For Affected Programs**. This will tell you if any programs have been updated or had a driver installed after the restore point. If you go ahead with the restore, these programs will be restored to their state before the update. Click **Next**.

4. You are asked to confirm the restore point the system will be returned to and given information about that point. If you do not want to restore to that point, click **Back** and return to step 2 or 3.

5. System Restore will need to restart your computer, so make sure all other programs are closed. When you are ready to restore to the described point, click **Finish**.

6. A confirmation dialog box appears, telling you that the restore process cannot be interrupted or undone until it has completed. Click **Yes** to continue. Some time will be spent saving files and settings for a new restore point, and then the computer will be restarted.

7. When the restore is completed, you will be told that it was successful. Click **Close**.

TIP

You can restore from a system restore. Immediately before doing a system restore, a restore point is created and can be used to return to the point the system was at prior to performing this action. Simply re-run System Restore as described in either of the System Restore sections in this chapter, choose **Undo System Restore**, and follow the remaining instructions.

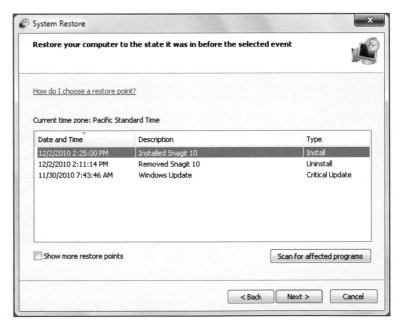

Figure 7-12: *You can do a system restore at any of the restore points on the computer and return all of the Windows 7 settings and registry to that point in time.*

RUN SYSTEM RESTORE FROM SYSTEM RECOVERY

Windows 7 has a System Recovery mode that allows you to start Windows in a minimal way and fix many problems. You can start System Restore in this mode.

1. If your computer is turned on, turn it off (use Shut Down and make sure the power is off) and let it sit for at least two full minutes. This allows all of the components to fully discharge and will give you a clean restart.

2. After your computer has sat for at least two minutes without power, remove any disks in the floppy, CD, or DVD drives, or any USB flash drives ("thumb drives") and turn the computer on. As soon as the memory check is complete, hold down the **F8** key. After a moment, the Advanced Boot Options menu will appear.

3. If necessary, use the **UP ARROW** key to go to the top choice, **Repair Your Computer**, and then press **ENTER**. Windows 7 will begin loading.

4. Select the type of keyboard you want to use, and click **Next**. Select and/or type your user name and password, and click **Next**.

5. Click **System Restore**. The System Restore window will open. Click **Next**. The list of restore points will be displayed, similar to what was shown in the previous section.

6. Follow the instructions in "Run System Restore from Windows" earlier in this chapter, from the second sentence of step 3 on.

7. The restoration process will begin and Windows 7 will restart. The System Restore dialog box will appear, telling you that the restoration was successful. Click **OK**.

Get System Information

When you are working on a computer problem, you, or possibly a technical support person working with you, will want some information about your computer. The two primary sources are basic computer information and advanced system information.

Figure 7-13: *Basic computer information provides an overview of the computer and its operating system.*

GET BASIC COMPUTER INFORMATION

Basic computer information provides general system information, such as the Windows edition, the processor and memory, and the computer name and workgroup (see Figure 7-13). To see the basic computer information:

Click **Start** and click **Control Panel**. In Category view, click **System And Security**, and in any view click **System**. The System window will open. After you have reviewed the information, click **Close**.

GET ADVANCED SYSTEM INFORMATION

Advanced system information provides detailed system information and lets you look at services that are running, Group Policy settings, and the error log. To see the advanced system information:

Click **Start** and click **All Programs**. Click **Accessories**, click **System Tools**, and click **System Information**. The System Information window will open. Click any of the topics in the left pane to display that information in the right pane. Figure 7-14 shows the summary-level information that is available. Click **Close** when you are done.

Add and Remove Software

Today, almost all application and utility software comes in one of two ways: on a CD or DVD, or downloaded over the Internet.

INSTALL SOFTWARE FROM A CD

If you get software on a CD or DVD disc, all you need to do is put the disc in the drive, wait for the AutoPlay dialog box to automatically appear, and follow the displayed instructions, of

Figure 7-14: ***Advanced system
information provides a great
depth of information useful in
troubleshooting.***

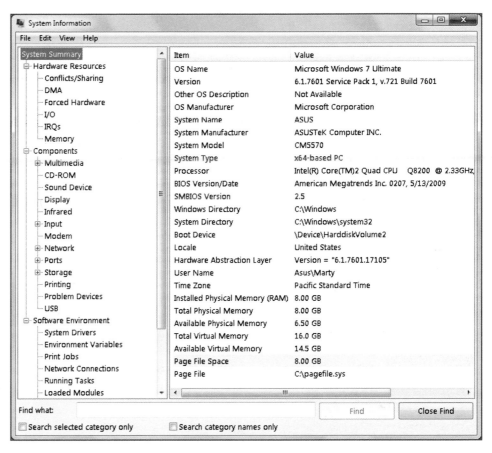

which there are usually only a few.
When the installation is complete,
you may need to acknowledge
that by clicking **OK** or **Finish** and
possibly restarting your computer.
Then remove the disc from its drive.
That is all there is to it.

TIP

If you are having trouble installing a program
for no discernable reason, make sure you are
logged on with administrative permissions. Some
programs or installation situations require these
permissions; without them, the program refuses
to install. See Chapter 6 to see how to establish
and work with administrative permissions.

QUICKSTEPS

SETTING POWER OPTIONS

Setting power options is important on laptop and notebook computers that run at least some of the time on batteries. It can also be useful on desktop computers to conserve power. The Windows 7 Power Options feature provides a number of settings that allow you to manage your computer's use of power.

1. Click **Start** and click **Control Panel**. In Category view, click **System And Security**, and click **Power Options**.

2. Choose one of the power plans, depending on whether you want to emphasize battery life (energy savings on desktops), performance, or a balance between the two (click **Show Additional Plans** to display the High Performance plan shown in Figure 7-15). You can also reduce the screen brightness on a laptop or notebook computer to reduce the power drain.

3. To see a more detailed setting, click **Choose When To Turn Off The Display**. If you are using a laptop or notebook computer, your power options will look like those in Figure 7-16. (A desktop computer won't have the battery settings.)

4. Click each of the drop-down lists, select the setting that is correct for you, and adjust the screen brightness. If you would like to control individual pieces of hardware (disk drives, USB ports, and so on), click

Continued . . .

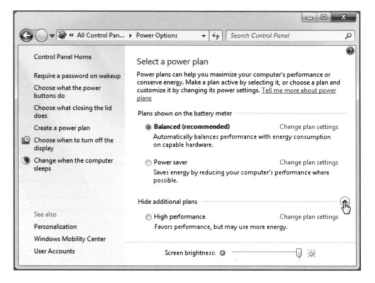

Figure 7-15: *Windows 7 has three preferred power plans that let you emphasize performance, energy consumption, or a balance between the two.*

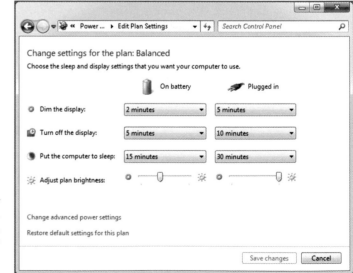

Figure 7-16: *You can set the amount of idle time before the display and/or the computer are turned off or put to sleep, respectively.*

UICKSTEPS

SETTING POWER OPTIONS (Continued)

Change Advanced Power Settings, click the plus signs to open the lists, click the action you want to change, and click the spinners to adjust the values. Click **OK** when you are finished.

5. When you are ready, click **Save Changes** to accept the changes you have made to your power options settings.

NOTE

See Chapter 1 for a discussion of the differences between shutting down a computer and putting it to sleep.

INSTALL SOFTWARE FROM THE INTERNET

To download and install a program from the Internet:

1. Click the **Internet Explorer** icon on the taskbar. In the address bar, type the URL (uniform resource locator or Internet address) for the source of the download, and press **ENTER**. (For this example, I'm downloading the Firefox web browser whose URL is http://www .mozilla.com, but you don't need to type the "http://www"—just type "mozilla.com.")

2. Locate the link for the download, and click it, as shown in Figure 7-17. You may need to approve the downloading in Internet Explorer by clicking the bar at the top of the window and clicking **Download File**.

Figure 7-17: **Mozilla's Firefox is a good alternative browser to Internet Explorer.**

3. A message box will appear, asking if you want to run or save the program. Click **Save**.

4. When you are told the download is complete, click **Run** to start the installation. Follow the instructions that are displayed.

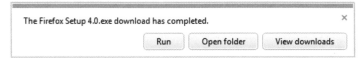

5. If the program does not have a valid digital signature (many do not), a message will appear telling you this and asking if you want to continue. Decide that and, if so, click **Run** again; otherwise, click **Don't Run**. User Account Control will also ask if you are sure you want to go ahead. Click **Yes** if you do, or click **No** if you don't.

6. Follow the program's installation instructions, making the choices that are offered to you.

7. When the installation is complete, you may be notified, the program may be started, Windows Explorer may be opened to show where the program is installed, and/or one or more shortcuts may be left on the desktop.

8. Close the Windows Explorer window and any other windows and dialog boxes that were opened by this process.

REMOVE SOFTWARE

There are at least two ways to get rid of a program you have installed and one way not to do it. You do not want to just delete the program files in Windows Explorer. That leaves files in other

TIP

Unless you are specifically told otherwise, always save a downloaded file to your hard disk and then, if a program-specific dialog box doesn't automatically appear, allowing you to start the program, start it by double-clicking the file on your hard disk. That way, if there is a problem, you can restart the program without having to download it a second time.

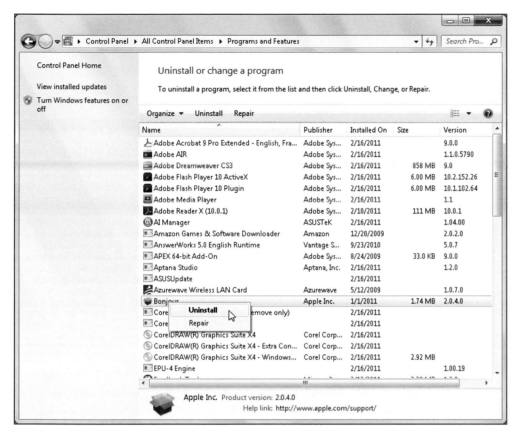

locations and all the settings in the registry. To correctly remove a program, you need to use either the uninstall program that comes with many programs or Windows 7's Uninstall Or Change A Program feature. To do the latter:

1. Click **Start** and click **Control Panel**. In Category view, click **Programs** and in any view click **Programs And Features**. The Uninstall Or Change A Program window will open, as you can see in Figure 7-18.

2. Click the program you want to uninstall, and click **Uninstall** on the toolbar. Follow the instructions as they are presented, which vary from program to program.

3. When the uninstall has successfully completed, close the Uninstall Or Change A Program window.

Figure 7-18: **Programs are removed through the Uninstall Or Change A Program feature.**

NOTE

The "change" part of the Uninstall Or Change A Program window is used to install updates and patches to programs. It requires that you have either a CD with the changes or have downloaded them. With some programs you will get a third option: Repair.

Add Hardware

Most hardware today is *Plug and Play*. That means that when you plug it in, Windows recognizes it and installs the necessary driver software automatically and you can immediately begin using it. Often, when you first turn on the computer after installing the hardware, you see a message telling you that you have new hardware or that Windows is installing the device driver. Frequently, you need do nothing more; the installation will complete by itself.

With other equipment, you must click the message for the installation to proceed. In either case, you are told when it has successfully completed.

Problems may occur when you have older hardware and the programs that run it, called *drivers*, are not included with Windows 7. In that case, you will see a dialog box saying you must locate the drivers. Here are some options for locating drivers:

- Let **Windows 7** see what it can do by itself by clicking **Locate And Install Driver Software** in the Found New Hardware dialog box. Windows 7 will scan your computer and look on the Microsoft site to see what can be found.

- **Microsoft** has drivers for the many popular devices and, as a part of Windows Update (discussed earlier in this chapter), the ability to scan your system and see if it has any drivers to help you. The first step is to look at Windows Update by clicking **Start**, clicking **All Programs**, and clicking **Windows Update**. Click **Check For Updates** in the upper-left area, and see if a driver for your device is found.

- The **manufacturer of the device** is generally a good source, but as hardware gets older, manufacturers stop writing new drivers for more recent operating systems. The easiest way to look for manufacturer support is on the Internet. If you know the manufacturer's website, you can enter it; or you may have to search for it. If you must search, start out by typing the manufacturer's name in the Internet Explorer address bar. This uses Bing search and gives you a list of sites.

- **Third-party sources** can be found using search engines like Google (google.com) and searching for "device drivers." You should find a number of sources, as you can see in Figure 7-19. Some of these sources charge you for the driver; others are free. Make sure the driver will work with Windows 7.

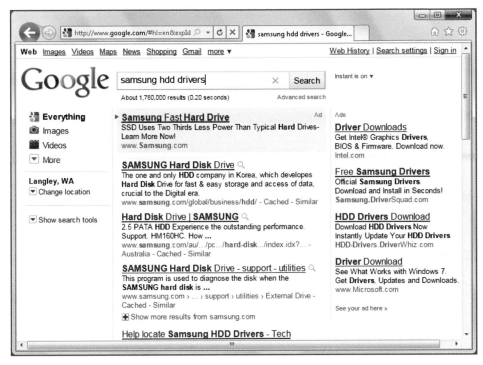

Figure 7-19: *Many device drivers can be found by searching the Internet, although you may have to pay for them.*

NOTE

If you are using Windows 7 and want to use Remote Assistance with someone using Windows XP or Windows Server 2003, you must be on the receiving end of the assistance and you cannot use Windows 7's Pause feature. Also, the person using Windows XP/Server 2003 cannot use Start Talk for voice capability.

TIP

Remote assistance is the perfect way to let your children or grandchildren help you with your computer. You will surprise them when you tell them you want to use Remote Assistance!

Use Remote Assistance

Remote Assistance allows you to invite someone to remotely look at your computer and control it for purposes of assisting you. The other person must be using Windows 7, Windows Vista, Windows XP, or Windows Server 2003 or 2008; and it will be helpful if both of you have an email account. To use Remote Assistance, you must set it up, and then you can be either the requester or the helper.

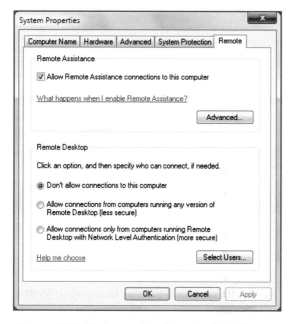

Figure 7-20: *Before using Remote Assistance, it must be turned on.*

SET UP REMOTE ASSISTANCE

Although Remote Assistance is installed with Windows 7, you must turn it on and set your firewall so that Windows 7 will allow it through. Both of these tasks are done in Control Panel.

1. Click **Start** and click **Control Panel**. In Category view, click **System And Security**, in any view click **System**, and click **Remote Settings** in the left pane. The System Properties dialog box will appear with the Remote tab displayed (see Figure 7-20).

2. Select **Allow Remote Assistance Connections To This Computer**, if it isn't already, and click **Advanced**.

3. Determine if you want a person to control your computer, and select the check box under **Remote Control** accordingly. Set the time an invitation for Remote Assistance is to remain open.

4. Click **OK** twice to close the two open dialog boxes. In Control Panel, click **Control Panel** in the address bar, click **System And Security**, and click **Windows Firewall**.

5. Click **Allow A Program Or Feature Through Windows Firewall**. The Allow Programs To Communicate Through Windows Firewall window will open and show the programs and features that are allowed through the firewall.

6. Click **Change Settings** toward the top of the window, then scroll through the list until you see **Remote Assistance**, and click it, if it isn't already selected (see Figure 7-21).

7. Click **OK** to close the dialog box, close the Windows Firewall window, and then close Control Panel.

REQUEST REMOTE ASSISTANCE

To use Remote Assistance, first find someone willing to provide it and request the assistance. Besides the obvious invitation text, the request for assistance message will include a password to access your computer and the code to allow the encryption of information

Remote Desktop is different from Remote Assistance, even though it is on the same Remote tab of the System Properties dialog box. Remote Desktop lets you sit at home and log on and use your computer at work as though you were sitting in front of it.

Figure 7-21: *Before you can use Remote Assistance, you must make sure that your firewall will let it through.*

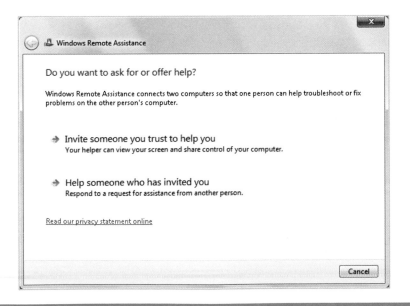

to be sent back and forth. All this is provided for you with Windows Remote Assistance. To begin a Remote Assistance session:

1. Click **Start**, click **All Programs**, click **Maintenance**, and click **Windows Remote Assistance** to open the Windows Remote Assistance dialog box.

2. Click **Invite Someone You Trust To Help You**, and then click one of the following methods:

   - **Save This Invitation As A File** that you can transfer as an attachment to an email message using any email program or web-based email such as Google's Gmail, or via a CD or USB flash drive.

Figure 7-22: *You need to send an invitation that asks a person for assistance and gives him or her the means to communicate in an encrypted manner.*

- **Use Email To Send An Invitation** if you are using Windows Live Mail or Microsoft Office Outlook or another compatible email package.

- **Use Easy Connect** if the other computer is using Windows 7.

3. If you choose **Use Email To Send An Invitation**, your email program will open and display a message to your helper and contain the invitation as an attachment, as shown in Figure 7-22. Address the email and click **Send**. Skip to step 6.

4. If you choose **Save This Invitation As A File**, select the drive and folder where you want to store the invitation—it may be across a network on your helper's computer. Click **Save**.

5. Attach the saved file to an email message or store it on a CD or flash drive, and send or deliver it to your helper.

6. If you choose **Easy Connect**, and in either of the other two cases, a Windows Remote Assistance window will open, providing you with the password you must also communicate to your helper, say, via phone. This window will wait for your helper to answer.

7. When your helper answers, you will be asked if you want to allow the person to see your computer. Click **Yes** if you do. Your computer screen will appear on your helper's computer.

8. Click **Chat**, click in the text box at the bottom, and type a message to the other person, who can see everything on your computer (see "Provide Remote Assistance," next). Click **Send**.

9. If the other person requests control of your computer, you'll see a message asking if that is what you want to do. If you do, select the check box, and then click **Yes**. If you become uncomfortable, you can click **Stop Sharing** or press **ALT+T** at any time.

10. To end the session, send a message to that effect and close the Remote Assistance window.

PROVIDE REMOTE ASSISTANCE

If you want to provide remote assistance:

1. Upon receiving an invitation as a file, drag it to the desktop and double-click it.

2. If you are using Easy Connect, click **Start**, click **All Programs**, click **Maintenance**, and click **Windows Remote Assistance**. Click **Help Someone Who Has Invited You**. It may take a couple of minutes to connect.

NOTE

You are protected from misuse of Remote Assistance in five ways: Without an invitation, the person giving assistance cannot access your computer; you can limit both the time the invitation remains open and the time the person can be on your computer; you can determine whether the person can control your computer or just look at it; you can click **Stop Sharing** or press **ALT+T** at any time to immediately terminate the other person's control; and you can click **Close** to instantly disconnect the other person.

3. Enter the password you have been given, click **OK**, and, if the other person approves, you are shown his or her screen and can request control of the other person's computer. You can view the screen in its actual size or scale it to fit your screen, as shown in Figure 7-23.

4. To request control of the other computer, click **Request Control**. Click **Stop Sharing** to give up control.

5. Click **Close** to end the session and close the Remote Assistance window.

Figure 7-23: **The remote screen is shown on the assistance provider's screen.**

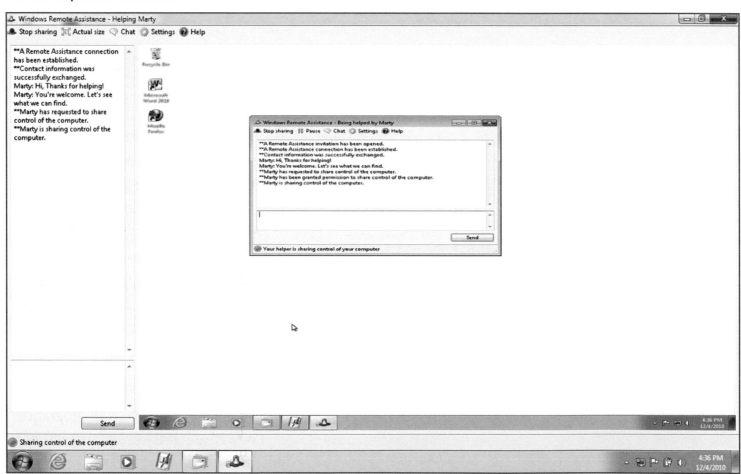

Chapter 8
Creating Documents and Pictures

After using the Internet, the next most popular function of a computer is to create and work with documents and pictures. Whether it is writing, financial planning, working with photos, or scanning your old pictures, all create and require that you work with documents on your computer, where documents are stored as files. In this chapter you will discover many aspects of creating documents and pictures, including installing and using digital cameras and scanners, and installing and using printers and fonts.

Create Documents and Pictures

Creating documents and pictures is primarily done with programs outside of Windows 7, although Windows has simple programs to do this, as described in Chapter 9. Windows 7 also has facilities to

NOTE

As in other chapters, in the steps here, you may be interrupted and asked by User Account Control (UAC) if you want to allow system changes. So long as it is something you started, click **Yes** or enter a password. To simplify the instructions in this chapter, the UAC instructions have been left out. Chapter 6 discusses UAC in more detail.

bring documents and pictures in from other computers, from the Internet, and from scanners and cameras.

As you begin to acquire documents, it is important to set up a filing system that is logical to you and diverse enough to spread out your documents so they are easy to find. When I started out using Microsoft Word many years ago, I kept all the files I created with Word in a single folder called "docs." When you start out, you often don't envision the number of documents you will quickly have. After no more than a year I had over a hundred files in that folder and it was becoming difficult to find the file I wanted, so I started adding folders for books I was writing, and then dividing the book folders into folders for chapters. You can easily grow your file system after you get started, but it doesn't hurt to give it a little thought as you are starting out.

Acquire a Document

The documents in your computer got there because they were created with a program on your computer, or they were brought to the computer on a disk, transferred over a local area network (LAN), or downloaded from the Internet.

CREATE A DOCUMENT WITH A PROGRAM

To create a document with a program:

1. Start the program. For example, start Microsoft Word by clicking **Start**, clicking **All Programs**, scrolling down and clicking **Microsoft Office**, and clicking **Microsoft Office Word**.

2. Create the document using the facilities in the program. In Word, for example, type the document and format it using Word's formatting tools (see Chapter 9 for more on Microsoft Word and other programs).

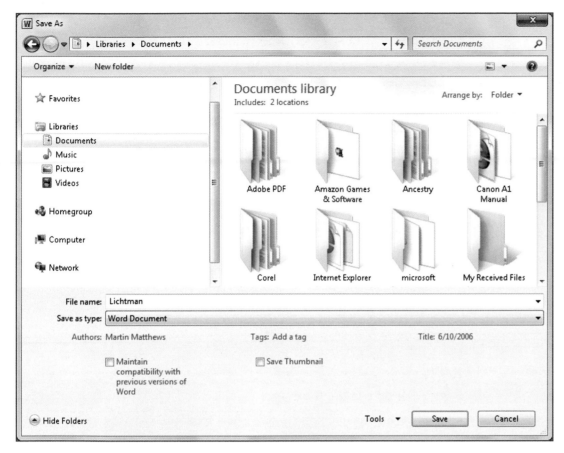

Figure 8-1: **Most document-creation programs let you choose where you want to save the files you create.**

3. Save the document (in Word 2010) by clicking the **File** button. Then click **Save As**, if needed, click **Browse Folders**, and select the disk drive and folder in which to store the document. Enter a filename, and click **Save**, as shown in Figure 8-1.

4. Close the program used to create the file.

OPEN A DOCUMENT ON A LOCAL DISK

Use Windows Explorer to locate and open a document on a disk on your computer.

1. Click **Start** and click **Computer**.

2. Double-click the drive from which you want to retrieve a document (this could be your primary or another hard drive in your computer or an external drive), and double-click to open any necessary folders to locate the document file and display it in the subject pane, the middle one if your Windows Explorer window is displaying a three-pane view: navigation, subject, and preview; or the right pane otherwise.

3. In the navigation pane, display (but do not select or open) the drive and folder(s) in which you want to store the file by clicking their respective triangles on the left.

4. Drag the document file to the displayed folder. When you are done, close Windows Explorer.

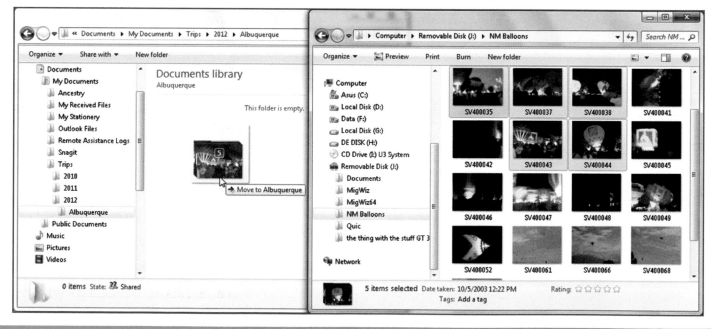

AutoPlay

PKBACK# 001 (M:)

General options

Open folder to view files
using Windows Explorer

Speed up my system
using Windows ReadyBoost

View more AutoPlay options in Control Panel

BRING IN A DOCUMENT FROM A REMOVABLE DRIVE

Use Windows Explorer to bring in a document from a removable drive such as a USB flash drive or a memory card as you might use in a camera.

1. Plug the removable drive or memory card into your computer. The AutoPlay dialog box will open.

2. Click **Open Folder To View Files**. Double-click to open any necessary folders to locate the document file and display it in the subject (middle or right) pane.

3. Click **Start** and click **Computer**.

4. Double-click to open any necessary drives, folders, and subfolders to locate and open the folder in which you want to store the file by clicking their respective triangles on the left.

5. Select (hold down **CTRL** to select multiple files) and drag the document file(s) to the displayed folder, as shown in Figure 8-2. When you are done, close Windows Explorer.

Figure 8-2: **You can drag a document file from either a disk on your computer or from another computer on your network.**

DOWNLOAD A DOCUMENT FROM THE INTERNET

Use Internet Explorer to bring in a document from a site on the Internet.

1. Click the **Internet Explorer** icon on the taskbar to open it.
2. Type an address, search, or browse to a site and page from which you can download the document file.
3. Use the links and tools on the website to select and begin the file download. For example, right-click a picture and click **Save Picture As**.
4. In the Save Picture dialog box, select the disk and open the folder(s) in which you want to store the file on your computer.
5. Type or edit the filename, and press **ENTER** to complete the download. When you are done, close your browser.

Create a Picture

Pictures are really just documents that contain an image. They can be created or brought into your computer in the same way as any other document (see "Acquire a Document"). For example, to create and save a picture in Microsoft Paint:

1. Click **Start**, click **All Programs**, click **Accessories**, and click **Paint**.
2. Create a picture using the tools in Paint. For example, click the **Pencil** tool, choose a color, and create the drawing.
3. Save the document by clicking the **Paint** or **File** menu (next to the Home tab). Then click **Save As**, select the disk drive and folder in which to store the document, enter a filename, select a Save As Type, and click **Save**. Close Paint.

Install Cameras and Scanners

Installing cameras and scanners depends a lot on the device—whether it is Plug and Play (you plug it in and it starts to function), what type of connection it has, and so on. Most recent cameras and scanners are Plug and Play devices. To use them:

1. Plug the device into the computer, and turn it on. If it is Plug and Play, the first time you plug it in, you will see a message that a device driver is being installed and then that it is ready to use. Finally an AutoPlay dialog box may appear, as shown in "Acquire a Document" in this chapter, and allow you to choose what you want to do. If this happens for you and you plugged in a scanner, skip to "Scan Pictures" later in this chapter. If you plugged in a camera, skip to "Import Camera Images," also later in this chapter. Otherwise, continue to step 2.

2. Click **Start** and click **Devices And Printers**. If you see your device, installation is complete, as shown in Figure 8-3, and you can skip the remainder of these steps.

3. Click **Add A Device**. The Add A Device Wizard starts. Click the device you want to install, and click **Next**. Scroll through the manufacturer and model lists, and see if your device is there. If so, select it and click **Next**. Confirm the name you want to use, click **Next**, and then click **Finish** to complete the installation.

4. If you don't see your device on the lists and you have a disk that came with it, place the disk in the drive, and click **Have Disk**. If a driver appears, complete the installation and close the Add A Device Wizard. If you cannot find the driver, close the Add A Device Wizard and the Devices And Printers window, and use the manufacturer's installation program on the disk.

Figure 8-3: **Most recent Plug and Play cameras and scanners are automatically detected and installed.**

Scan Pictures

Scanners allow you to take printed images and convert them to digital images on your computer. The scanner must first be installed, as described in "Install Cameras and Scanners" earlier in this chapter. If you ended up using the manufacturer's software to install the scanner,

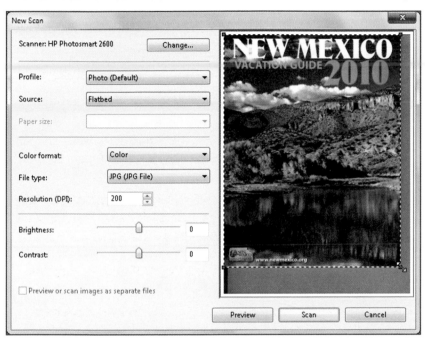

*Figure 8-4: **In the Windows 7 scanning software, you can change several of the parameters, including the margins of what to include, and see the results in the preview pane.***

you might need to use it to scan images, too. If you used Windows to install the scanner, use the following steps to scan an image:

1. Turn on your scanner, and place what you want to scan onto the scanning surface.

2. Click **Start**, click **All Programs**, and click **Windows Fax And Scan**. The Windows Fax And Scan window opens.

3. Click **New Scan** on the toolbar. The New Scan dialog box appears. The scanner you installed should be displayed in the upper-left area. Change the scanner if you wish.

4. Choose the color, file type, and resolution you want to use, and click **Preview**. The image in the scanner will appear in the dialog box.

5. Adjust the margins around the page by dragging the dashed lines on the four sides, as shown in Figure 8-4. When you are ready, click **Scan**.

6. The scanned image will appear in the Windows Fax And Scan window (see Figure 8-5). Select the image in the list at the top of the window and, using the toolbar, choose to:

- **Forward As Fax** using the Windows fax capability described later in this chapter

- **Forward As Email** using your default email application

- **Save As** using Windows Explorer to save the image as a file on one of the storage devices available to you

- **Print** using a printer available to you

- **Delete** the image

7. Work through the related dialog box(es) that appear to complete the scanning process. When you are ready, close the Windows Fax And Scan window.

Windows Fax and Scan

File   Edit   View   Tools   Document   Help

New Scan   New Fax   Forward as Fax   Forward as E-mail   Save as...

Scan	Dat... /	File Name		File Type	Size	Source
Documents	12/9/201...	Welcome Scan		.jpg	504.3 KB	Windows Fax and Scan Team
	12/9/201...	Image		.jpg	846.2 KB	HP Photosmart 2600

NEW MEXICO VACATION GUIDE 2010

Fax

Scan

For Help, press F1

Figure 8-5: Images that you scan can be faxed, emailed, saved, and printed.

NOTE

If the AutoPlay dialog box didn't appear, click **Start**, click **Computer**, click **Removable Disk** (if you have more than one of them, it would be the most recently accessed one), and open the necessary folders to see images of the pictures in your camera.

Removable Disk (P:)
▷ .Trashes
◢ DCIM
  100SSCAM
MISC

Import Camera Images

When most digital cameras are plugged into the computer, turned on, and installed (see "Install Cameras and Scanners" earlier in this chapter), the AutoPlay dialog box should automatically appear, calling the camera a removable disk and asking if you want to:

- **Import Pictures And Videos**, in essence, copying them to your hard disk
- **View Pictures** in your camera using Windows Photo Viewer
- **Import Pictures And Videos** from your camera using Windows Live Photo Gallery
- **View Pictures** in your camera using Windows Live Photo Gallery
- **Open Folder To View Files** to look at your camera as if it were a disk and the pictures as files using Windows Explorer

1. Click **Import Pictures And Videos Using Windows Live Photo Gallery**. The Import Photos And Videos dialog box should appear.

2. Choose if you want to review and organize your photos first or import them all immediately.

3. If you choose to review and organize, click **Next**. A window opens that allows you to select the photos you want imported. You can group photos by date, add names to groups, and add tags to groups that will form the basis of photo names (the date is already a part of the name). When you are ready, click **Import**.

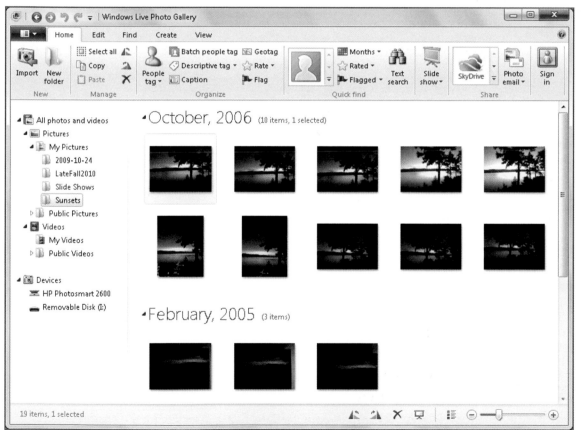

4. If you choose to import all items at once, select that option, enter a name, if desired click **Add Tags** and type a tag to add to the filename of all the pictures, and click **Import**.The first time you do this, you will see a message box asking if you want to use Windows Live Photo Gallery to open picture file types instead of the default Windows viewer. Click **Yes**.

5. In either case, you will see each of the pictures as they are imported. When the process is completed, the Windows Live Photo Gallery will open and show thumbnails of the pictures, as you can see in Figure 8-6.

Figure 8-6: **The Windows Live Photo Gallery gives you a quick way to organize and work with your pictures.**

Work with Photo Gallery Pictures

Once you have brought pictures into your computer from a camera, a scanner, an Internet download, or a removable disk, you can look at them on your computer screen. Assuming that you brought your pictures into Photo Gallery as discussed in "Import Camera Images" or "Scan Pictures" earlier in this chapter:

1. Click **Start**, click **All Programs**, and click **Windows Live Photo Gallery** (you may be asked to sign in to Windows Live, but you don't have to do that—click **Cancel**). The Windows Live Photo Gallery should open.

2. Select the name you assigned or date your pictures were taken to open the category that contains them, as was shown in Figure 8-6.

3. Hover your mouse over a picture to see an enlarged image.

4. To see an even larger image, double-click its thumbnail. The image will expand to fit the Photo Gallery window, similar to what is shown in Figure 8-7. The controls in the upper left and bottom right of the window allow you to cycle through a number of pictures and then, with the ribbon at the top, work with them.

5. If you have several pictures you want to view, click the **Previous** and **Next** controls at the top or on the bottom of the window to go through them sequentially. You can also use the other controls at the bottom of the window or in the ribbon at the top to perform their stated functions.

6. When you are done, click **Close File** on the far right of the ribbon to return to the gallery and view the photo thumbnails, or click **Close** in the upper right to leave the Windows Live Photo Gallery.

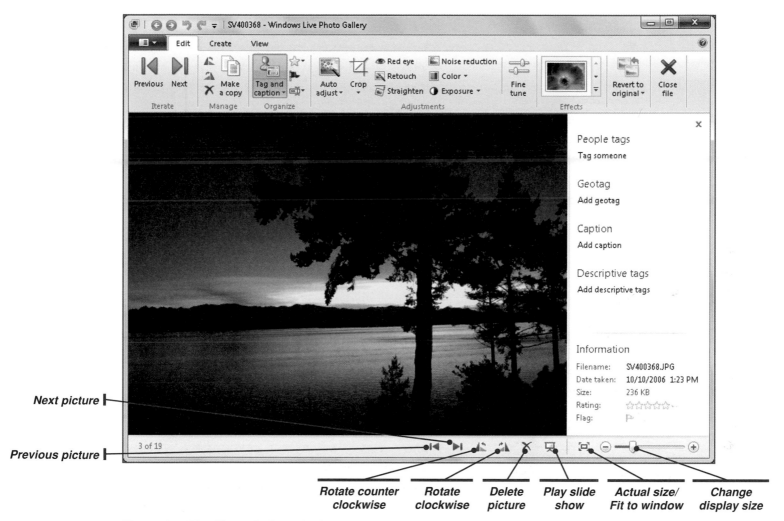

Next picture ⊢

Previous picture ⊢

Rotate counter | Rotate | Delete | Play slide | Actual size/ | Change
clockwise | clockwise | picture | show | Fit to window | display size

Figure 8-7: **The Photo Gallery single-image window offers a great way to view individually each picture in a set on your computer.**

QUICKSTEPS

VIEWING OTHER PICTURES

If your pictures are not in the Photo Gallery, to locate and view them:

1. Click **Start**, click **Computer**, and open the drive and folders necessary to locate your pictures.

2. Click the **Change Your View** menu down arrow, and click **Extra Large Icons** so that you can adequately see the thumbnail images.

3. Double-click the picture you want to view in a larger size. Either the Windows Photo Viewer or the Windows Live Photo Gallery (depending on which you have selected as your default) will open and display the picture. From here, you can work with the picture.

Capture Snips

Windows 7 includes the Snipping Tool to capture images of the screen, called "screen shots" or "snips." This can capture four areas of the screen:

- **Full screen** captures the entire screen.
- **Window** captures a complete window.
- **Rectangular area** captures a rectangle you draw around objects.
- **Free-form area** captures any area you draw around objects.

Snips can be very handy in helping to remember something that is only temporarily on the screen by capturing it in a screen shot, such as a phone number, a serial number, or a set of instructions or directions. While the information is displayed on the screen, use the instructions here and then save the results to a file. The key is to remember where you saved it. Having a folder called "Snips" is one answer, but maybe not the best one.

Once you have captured an area, it is temporarily stored on the Clipboard and displayed in the mark-up window, where you can write and draw on the snip to annotate it and, when you are ready, save the snip where you want it. To do all of that:

1. Display the windows or other objects on the screen whose images you want to capture (see the Tip on capturing a menu).

2. Click **Start**, click **All Programs**, click **Accessories**, and click **Snipping Tool**. The screen will be dimmed and the Snipping Tool dialog box will appear, along with a cross-hair to use to outline the area to be captured—by default, you will see a rectangle (see Figure 8-8).

Figure 8-8: **The Snipping Tool allows you to capture an image of an area of the screen for future reference or use.**

3. If you want to capture a rectangular area, drag the cross-hair from one corner of the rectangle to its opposite. To capture a different type of area, click the **New** down arrow, and click one of the other three types of areas. Then, with:

- **Free-Form Snip**, drag the cross-hair around the area to be captured

- **Window Snip**, click the window to be captured

- **Full Screen Snip**, the screen is automatically captured

TIP

To capture a snip of a menu, open the Snipping Tool, press **ESC**, display the menu to be captured, press **CTRL+PRINT SCREEN**, click **New**, select the type of area to be captured (Free-Form, Rectangle, and so forth), and delineate that area as you would otherwise.

Figure 8-9: *The Snipping Tool mark-up window allows you to annotate, email, and save a snip.*

4. In all cases, the mark-up window opens, showing you the area that was captured, as you can see in Figure 8-9, and allowing you to use the pen, highlighter, and eraser to annotate the snip.

5. From the mark-up window, you can also directly email the snip to someone by clicking **Send Snip**, which opens an email message with the snip in it, or you can send the snip as an attachment to an email by clicking the **Send Snip** down arrow and clicking **Email Recipient (As Attachment)**; save the snip by clicking **Save Snip**, select a folder, enter a name, select a file type, and click **Save**.

Print Documents and Pictures

It is important to be able to install and fully use printers so that you can transfer your digital documents to paper.

Install a Printer

All printers are either automatically installed or done so using the Devices And Printers window. Because there are differences in how the installation is done, look at the following sections in this chapter on installing Plug and Play printers, installing other printers, and selecting a default printer. Also, if you are installing a local printer, first consider the following checklist.

USE A PRINTER INSTALLATION CHECKLIST

A local printer is one that is attached to your computer with a cable or wireless connection. Make sure that your printer meets the following conditions *before* you begin the install:

NOTE

Some laptop computer-and-printer combinations are connected through a wireless connection. In this case, "plugging the printer into the computer" means to establish that wireless connection.

UICKSTEPS

USING STICKY NOTES

Sticky Notes are exactly what the name implies: little notes to yourself that you can place anywhere on your screen. You can type messages on these notes; change their color; cut, copy, and paste the text on them with the Clipboard to and from other programs; create additional notes; and delete the note. Here's how:

WICA 6:30 PM,
Friday 12/10/10,
Ric and Lisbeth

1. Click **Start**, click **All Programs**, click **Accessories**, and click **Sticky Notes**. If you don't already have a note on your desktop, one will appear.

2. If you already have one or more notes on the desktop, the most recent one will be selected. If you want a new note, click **New Note** (the plus sign in the upper-left corner).

3. On the new note, type the message you want it to contain, or, having copied some text from another source, right-click the note and click **Paste**.

4. Right-click the note, click the color you want it to be, and then drag the note to where you want it.

5. When you no longer want the note on the desktop, click **Delete Note** (the X in the upper-right corner), and click **Yes**.

- It is plugged into the correct port on your computer (see manufacturer's instructions).
- It is plugged into an electrical outlet.
- It has fresh ink, toner, or ribbon, which, along with the print heads, is properly installed.
- It has adequate paper.
- It is turned on.

INSTALL A LOCAL PLUG AND PLAY PRINTER

Installing Plug and Play printers is supposed to be fairly automatic, and, for the most part, it is.

1. With your computer and printer turned off, connect the devices to each other. Then make sure the other points in the previous checklist are satisfied (hold off turning the printer on until step 2).

2. Turn on your computer, let it fully boot, and then turn on your printer. Your computer should find and automatically install the new printer and briefly give you messages to that effect.

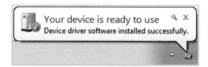

3. Click **Start** and click **Devices And Printers**. The Devices And Printers window will open, and you should see your new printer. Hover the mouse pointer over that printer, and you should see "Status: Printer: Ready," as shown in Figure 8-10. (If you don't see your printer, it was not installed. Go to the next section.)

4. Right-click the new printer, click **Printer Properties**, and click **Print Test Page**. If the test page prints satisfactorily, click **Close**. Otherwise, click **Get Help With Printing**, follow the suggestions, and close the Help and printer windows when you are done. When you are ready, click **OK** to close the printer Properties dialog box.

TOM WORKS ON EXCEL AND PDF DOCUMENTS

Computers are not second-nature to me, but I find them extremely important in communicating in today's world. I am more productive and, in some ways, better able to grasp the implications of data than previously, when I was buried in the details of generating information myself on a manual spreadsheet.

I mainly use the Internet and email, but I use other programs as well. For instance, as a member of a nonprofit organization for seven years, I receive budgets and financial statements created in Excel from our treasurer. The treasurer attaches the information to an email, and I download it and look at it with Excel. Now I know only the basics about using Excel, but I can read an Excel worksheet just fine, and reading the worksheets allows me to concentrate on the financials of the organization rather than on the steps in creating them. I add comments to the email and return it to the treasurer. This has been an effective and worthwhile way to quickly communicate with other board members.

In a similar way, I can read a PDF document with Acrobat Reader—for free. I don't have to purchase Acrobat Pro or another program that might have been used to create that document.

Tom B., 79, Washington

Figure 8-10: **When you connect a Plug and Play printer, it should be recognized by the computer and automatically installed.**

5. If you want the new printer to be the default printer used by all applications on the computer, right-click the printer and click **Set As Default Printer**.

6. Close the Devices And Printers window.

I find that for printers made in the last five years (since 2006), and probably earlier, that all you have to do is plug them in to a power outlet, connect them to your computer, turn them on, and start printing.

In the majority of instances they are truly Plug and Play. You may have to click **OK** once or twice to acknowledge using the default installation, but little else.

INSTALL A LOCAL PRINTER MANUALLY

If a printer isn't automatically installed in the process of using steps 1 through 3 in the previous section, you must install it manually.

1. If a CD came with your printer, providing it says that it is for Windows 7, place that CD in the drive, and follow the on-screen instructions to install the printer. When this is complete, go to step 3 in "Install a Local Plug and Play Printer," and determine if the printer will print a test page. If so, skip to step 7.

2. If you don't have a manufacturer's CD, click **Start** and click **Devices And Printers**. The Devices And Printers window should open.

3. Click **Add A Printer** on the toolbar, and click **Add A Local Printer**.

4. Click **Use An Existing Port:**, open the drop-down list, and select the correct port (on newer printers, it is probably USB001; on the majority of other printers, it is LPT1), and click **Next**.

5. Select the manufacturer and model of the printer you want to install (see Figure 8-11). If you can't find your printer, click **Windows Update** to download the latest printer drivers. Then, once more, search for the manufacturer and model. When you find the correct printer, click **Next**.

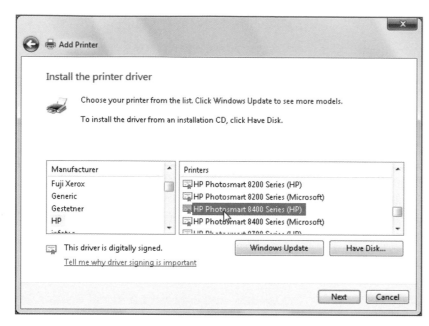

Figure 8-11: **Manually installing a printer requires that you know some facts about the printer.**

NOTE

You can print just the even or odd pages in a document by opening the Print window and then opening the first drop-down list under Settings and making the relevant selection.

6. Confirm or change the printer name, and click **Next**. Determine if you want to share this printer; if so, enter its share name, location, and comments. Click **Next**.

7. Choose whether you want this printer to be your default printer. Click **Print A Test Page**. If the test page prints satisfactorily, click **Close**. Otherwise, click **Get Help With Printing**, follow the suggestions, and close the Help and Printer windows when you are done. When you are ready, click **Finish** to close the Add Printer dialog box and close the Devices And Printers window.

IDENTIFY A DEFAULT PRINTER

If you have several printers available to you, one must be identified as your default printer—the one that will be used for printing whenever you don't select another one. To change your default printer:

1. Click **Start** and click **Devices And Printers**. The Devices And Printers window will open.

2. Right-click the printer you want to be the default, and click **Set As Default Printer**.

3. Close the Devices And Printers window when finished.

Print Pictures

Printing pictures from a program is exactly the same as described in the "Printing" QuickSteps. In addition, Windows has a Print Pictures dialog box used to print pictures from either Windows Explorer or the Photo Gallery.

1. Click **Start** and click **Pictures** to use Windows Explorer; or click **Start**, click **All Programs**, and click **Windows Live Photo Gallery** to use that program.

Figure 8-12: *The Microsoft Office Word 2010 Print window has many of the features available in other programs.*

QUICKSTEPS

PRINTING

Most printing is done from a program. The following sections use Microsoft Word 2010, whose Print window is shown in Figure 8-12, as an example.

PRINT DOCUMENTS

To print the document currently open in Word:

Click **Quick Print** on Word's Quick Access toolbar to immediately print using the default settings.

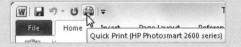

CHOOSE A PRINTER

To choose which printer you want to use:

Click the **File** button, and click **Print** to open Word's Print window shown in Figure 8-12. Open the **Printer** drop-down list, and choose the printer you want.

DETERMINE SPECIFIC PAGES TO PRINT

In the Print window, in the first drop-down list under Settings, you can select:

- **Print All Pages** to print all pages.
- **Print Selection** to print the text that has been selected.
- **Print Current Page** to print only the currently selected page.

Continued . . .

2. In either program, select the picture(s) you want to print. To select one, click it. To select a contiguous set of pictures, click the first one, hold down **SHIFT**, and click the last picture. To select noncontiguous pictures, hold down **CTRL** while clicking the pictures you want.

3. Click **Print** on the toolbar; or in the case of Windows Live Photo Gallery, click the **File** button, and then click **Print**. To print on a local or network printer, click **Print** again; alternately, you can order prints online. Using the selected printer, the Print Pictures dialog box will appear, as shown in Figure 8-13.

PRINTING *(Continued)*

- **Print Custom Range** to print a series of individual pages and/or a range of pages by specifying the individual pages separated by commas and specifying the range with a hyphen. For example, typing <u>4,6,8-10,12</u> will cause pages 4, 6, 8, 9, 10, and 12 to be printed.

TIP

If Quick Print isn't on your Quick Access toolbar, click the **Customize** down arrow to the right of the Quick Access toolbar, and click **Quick Print**.

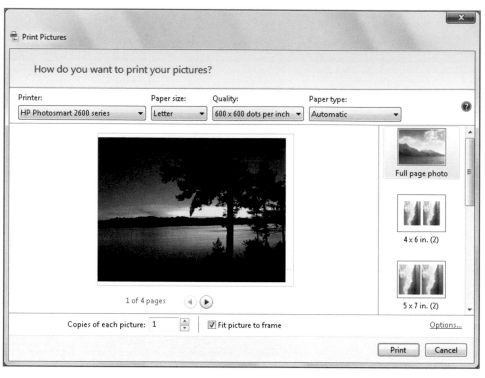

*Figure 8-13: **If you use high-quality photo paper and a newer color printer, you can get almost professional-grade pictures.***

4. Select the printer, paper size, quality, paper type, number to print on a page, number of copies, and whether to fit the picture to a frame. You can also click **Options** above the Cancel button to look at and possibly change several print settings. Click **OK** after looking at (and possibly selecting) the options.

5. When you are ready, click **Print**. The pictures will be printed. When you are done, close Windows Explorer or Windows Live Photo Gallery, whichever you have open.

Print to a File

There are two primary reasons to print to a file: to have a file you can take to a remote printer, and to get information out of one program and into another. The first requires formatting the information for a printer and then sending it to a file. The actual printer must be installed on your computer even though it is not physically connected to your computer. In the second case, you must create a "printer" to produce unformatted generic text. The following sections explain first how to create a text file printer and then how to print to a file.

CREATE A TEXT FILE PRINTER

1. Click **Start** and click **Devices And Printers**. The Devices And Printers window will open.

2. Click **Add A Printer** on the toolbar, and click **Add A Local Printer**. Click the **Use An Existing Port** down arrow, and click **File (Print To File)**.

3. Click **Next**. In the Install The Printer Driver dialog box, scroll down and click **Generic** as the manufacturer and **Generic/Text Only** as the printer.

4. Click **Next**. Enter a name for the printer, and click **Next**. Determine if you want to share this printer and, if so, enter a share name. Click **Next**.

File / Text Only

5. Click **Set As The Default** Printer (if you want to do that), skip printing a test page, and click **Finish**. A new icon will appear in your Devices And Printers window. Close the Devices And Printers window when you are done.

SELECT PRINT TO FILE

Whether you want to print to a file so that you can print on a remote printer or so that you can create a text file, the steps are the same once you have created a text file printer.

1. In the program in which you are printing, click the **File** menu (or button in Microsoft Office 2010 programs), and click **Print**.

2. Select the ultimate printer or the generic text file printer. Select the print range, number of copies, and other settings; and click **Print**. Select the folder, type the file name to use, and click **OK**.

Print Webpages

Printing webpages is little different from printing any other document.

1. Click the **Internet Explorer** icon on the taskbar to open your browser (assumed to be Internet Explorer 9).

2. Browse to the page you want to print, click the **Tools** icon, click **Print**, and then click **Print** again. The page will print with default options. (If you want to preview how the page will be printed, click **Preview** instead of the second Print. Use any of the options on the toolbar to change how the page will print, and then click the **Print Document** icon on the left of the toolbar.)

3. Close your Internet browser.

Configure a Printer

Configuring a printer is usually done for special purposes and often isn't required. Nevertheless, all configuring is done from the printer's Properties dialog box.

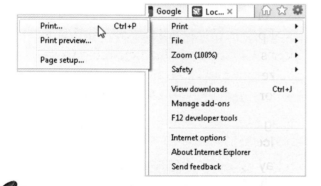

NOTE

When you right-click a printer in the Devices And Printers dialog box, there are three Properties options: Properties by itself, Printing Preferences, and Printer Properties. In the "Configure a Printer" section we are talking about *Printer Properties*.

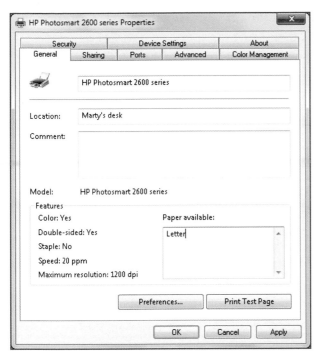

1. Click **Start** and click **Devices And Printers**. The Devices And Printers window will open.

2. Right-click the printer you want to configure, click **Printer Properties**, and click the printer you want to configure. The printer's Properties dialog box will appear.

In the General tab (shown in Figure 8-14), you can change the printer name, its location, and enter a comment. In the Sharing tab, you can determine whether to share the printer; in the Ports tab, you can specify the port used by the printer, configure ports, and set up printer pooling; and in the Security tab, you can determine who has what permissions to use and manage the printer. Though most printer configurations are self-explanatory, several items are worthy of further discussion and are explained in the following sections.

ASSIGN PAPER TRAYS

Some printers have more than one paper tray, and each tray can have different types or sizes of paper. If you assign types and sizes of paper to trays in the printer's Properties dialog box and a user requests a specific type and size of paper when printing, Windows 7 automatically designates the correct paper tray for the print job.

1. In the printer Properties dialog box for the printer whose trays you want to assign, click the **Device Settings** tab.

2. Click the type of paper in a tray, open the drop-down list, and select the type and size of paper in that tray, similar to what you see in Figure 8-15.

3. When you have set the paper type and size in each tray, click **OK**.

CONFIGURE SPOOL SETTINGS

The time it takes to print a document is normally longer than the time it takes to transfer the information to the printer. *Printer spooling* temporarily stores information to be printed on disk, allowing

Figure 8-14: **Printers, while having many settings, are often run without ever changing the default settings.**

Figure 8-15: *You can set the paper type and size in each paper tray.*

Windows to feed it to the printer as it can be handled. Under most circumstances, you want to use printer spooling and not tie up the program waiting for the printer. The printer's Properties Advanced tab lets you choose whether to spool, and gives you two options if you spool.

- **Spool Print Documents** and **Start Printing After Last Page Is Spooled** waits to print until the last page is spooled, allowing the program to finish faster and the user to get back to the program faster, but it takes longer to finish printing.

- **Spool Print Documents** and **Start Printing Immediately** allows printing to be done sooner, but the program will be tied up a little longer.

- **Print Directly To the Printer** does not spool information to be printed, so the program must wait on the printer to finish, but printing will be done the fastest.

The default, Spool Print Documents and Start Printing Immediately, provides a middle ground between getting the printing done and getting back to the program.

Control Printing

To control printing means to control the process as it is taking place, whether with one print job or with several in line. If several print jobs are spooled at close to the same time, they form a *print queue*, waiting for earlier jobs to finish. You may control printing in several

NOTE

The Print Spooled Documents First check box, located below the spool options, is selected by default. Normally, you want to keep it that way.

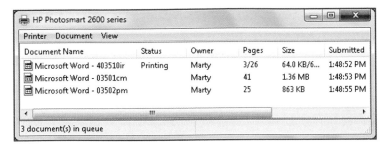

Document Name	Status	Owner	Pages	Size	Submitted
Microsoft Word - 403510ir	Printing	Marty	3/26	64.0 KB/6...	1:48:52 PM
Microsoft Word - 03501cm		Marty	41	1.36 MB	1:48:53 PM
Microsoft Word - 03502pm		Marty	25	863 KB	1:48:55 PM

3 document(s) in queue

Figure 8-16: ***Controlling printing takes place in the printer's window and allows you to pause, resume, restart, and cancel printing.***

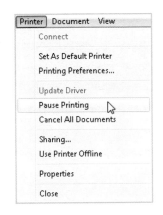

ways, as described next. These tasks are handled in the printer's window, which is similar to that shown in Figure 8-16, and is opened by right-clicking the printer you want to control in the Devices And Printers window and clicking **See What's Printing**, or by double-clicking the printer icon in the notification area of the taskbar 🖨 and then clicking **See What's Printing**.

PAUSE, RESUME, AND RESTART PRINTING

While printing, a situation may occur (such as needing to add toner) where you want to pause and then resume printing, either for one or all documents.

- **Pause all documents**   In the printer's window, click the **Printer** menu, and click **Pause Printing**. "Paused" will appear in the title bar, and, if you look in the Printer menu, you will see a check mark in front of Pause Printing.

- **Resume printing all documents**   In the printer's window, click **Printer** and click **Pause Printing**. "Paused" disappears from the title bar and the check mark disappears from the Pause Printing option in the Printer menu.

- **Pause a document**   In the printer's window, select the document or documents to pause, click **Document**, and click **Pause**. "Paused" will appear in the Status column of the document(s) you selected.

- **Resume printing a paused document where it left off**   In the printer's window, select the document, click **Document**, and click **Resume**. "Printing" will appear in the Status column of the document selected.

- **Restart printing at the beginning of a document**   In the printer's window, select the document, click **Document**, and click **Restart**. "Restarting" and then "Printing" will appear in the Status column.

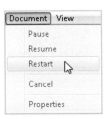

NOTE

You cannot change the order in which documents are being printed by pausing the current document that is printing. You must either complete printing the current document or cancel it. You can, however, use Pause to get around intermediate documents that are not currently printing. For example, suppose you want to immediately print the third document in the queue, but the first document is currently printing. You must either let the first document finish printing or cancel it. You can then pause the second document before it starts printing, and the third document will begin printing when the first document is out of the way.

CANCEL PRINTING

Canceling printing can be done either at the printer level for all the jobs in the printer queue or at the document level for selected documents. A canceled job is deleted from the print queue and must be restarted by the original program.

- **Cancel a job**   In the printer's window, select the job or jobs that you want canceled. Click **Document** and click **Cancel**. Click **Cancel** a second time to confirm the cancellation. The job or jobs will disappear from the window and the queue.
- **Cancel all the jobs in the queue**   In the printer's window, click **Printer** and click **Cancel All Documents**. You are asked whether you are sure you want to cancel all documents. Click **Yes**. All jobs will disappear from the queue and the printer window.

CHANGE A DOCUMENT'S PROPERTIES

A document in a print queue has a Properties dialog box, shown in Figure 8-17, which is opened by right-clicking the document and selecting **Properties**. The General tab allows you to change the following things:

- **Priority**   To change a document's default priority of 1, the lowest priority, so that the document can be printed before another that hasn't started printing yet, set the document's priority in the document's Properties dialog box to anything higher than the other document by dragging the **Priority** slider to the right.
- **Who to notify**   To change who is optionally notified of any special situations occurring during printing, as well as when a document has finished printing, put the name of another person (the individual's user name on a shared computer or network) in the **Notify** text box of the document's Properties dialog box.

Microsoft Word - 80504i Document Properties

General | Advanced | Printing Shortcuts | Paper/Quality | Effects | Finishing | Color

Microsoft Word - 80504i

Size:	931416 bytes
Pages:	23
Datatype:	NT EMF 1.008
Processor:	hpzppWN7
Owner:	Marty
Submitted:	2:55:41 PM 12/12/2010
Notify:	Marty

Priority:

Lowest ———————————————— Highest

Current priority: 50

Schedule:

○ No time restriction

○ Only from 12:00 AM To 12:00 AM

OK   Cancel   Apply

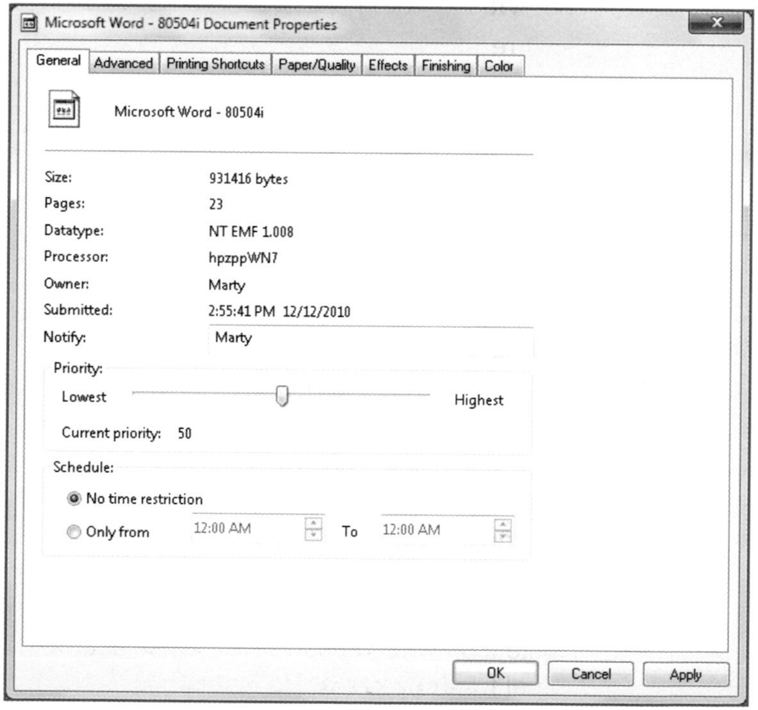

Figure 8-17: **Setting the properties of a document in the print queue can change its priority and when it prints.**

- **Set print time**   To change when a job is printed, open a document's Properties dialog box, click **Only From** at the bottom under Schedule, and then enter the time range within which you want the job printed. This allows you to print large jobs, which might otherwise clog the print queue, at a time when there is little or no load.

Figure 8-18: **Windows 7 comes with a large number of fonts, but you can add others.**

Handle Fonts

A *font* is a set of characters with the same design, size, weight, and style. A font is a member of a *typeface* family, all with the same design. The font 12-point Arial bold italic is a member of the Arial typeface with a 12-point size, bold weight, and italic style. Windows 7 comes with a large number of fonts, a few of which are shown in Figure 8-18.

Add Fonts

To add fonts to those that are installed by Windows 7:

1. Click **Start**, click **Control Panel**, click **Appearance And Personalization** in Category view, and in any view click **Fonts**. The Fonts window opens as shown in Figure 8-18.

2. Either use Windows Explorer to locate a font (or fonts) on your computer (this can be a flash drive, a CD/DVD, or a hard disk) or use Internet Explorer to download a font to your computer and then, with Windows Explorer, locate it so you can see and then select the actual font(s) you want to install.

To select several fonts, hold down **SHIFT** and click the first and last font (to select several contiguous fonts), or hold down **CTRL** and click each font (to select several noncontiguous fonts).

3. Right-click the selected fonts, and then click **Install**. A message will tell you the fonts are being installed. When you are done, the new fonts will appear in the Fonts window.

Delete Fonts

Remove fonts simply by selecting them in the Fonts window and pressing **DELETE** or by right-clicking the font(s) and clicking **Delete**. In either case, you are told you are deleting a font collection and asked whether you are sure you want to do that. Click **Yes** if you are. The fonts will be deleted *permanently* and *cannot* be retrieved from the Recycle Bin.

Use Fonts

Fonts are used or specified from within a program. In Microsoft Word, for example, you can select a line of text and then open the Font drop-down list on the Formatting toolbar (in versions prior to Office 2007) or in the Font group (in Office 2007/2010). Every program is a little different. One nice feature in recent versions of Word is that the list shows what the fonts look like.

Chapter 9
Using Applications

In our lifetimes, the computer has replaced the faithful typewriter, spiral notebooks of spreadsheets, manila folders filled with sheets of paper, and a pencil sharpener next to cups filled with freshly sharpened pencils. Even the smell of an office is different. The office, and therefore the home office, was clearly transformed with computers. Our productivity is also transformed with computers. We type and edit, with automatic spellcheckers and grammar checkers, and when our manuscript or letter is perfect, we print it or send it via email. Our computer calculates spreadsheet equations, graphing them for presentations and visual interpretations. Our backup files are stored on CDs in a small case or nearby shelf. Or maybe not. Today, our backups may be stored on an online server. When we need to find something, we search through files on our computer or on our online server, not in a file cabinet. The computer search programs do the work that our fingers used to do, in a fraction of the time.

In this chapter we will explore some of the most common applications seniors use, including Microsoft Office applications Word and Excel. We will see how we access these programs and store our files on an online server. Then we'll take a look at Windows built-in applications, such as Calculator, Notepad, and Paint. We will also take a look at another common application, Adobe Acrobat Reader.

Use Web Apps for Office Programs

With the appearance of *cloud computing*, or working with computer files and applications hosted on a remote server over the Internet and viewable in a browser rather than your own computer Office applications, Microsoft is moving Office to the Internet. This means that your files and programs are stored on an Internet server rather than on your stand-alone desktop computer, and that Office programs are accessed through a browser working on the Internet rather than from programs stored on your computer. This is a new world! Why this is even remotely a good idea really revolves around expanded ways of working with data files and other people and making them available any place, any time. The approach is much more about accessing and sharing data and collaboration than it is about an isolated person working alone. When you store data and have programs available from an Internet server (or "on the cloud"):

- You don't have to worry about whether you have the latest program updates.
- You don't have to worry about whether you have access to your computer at home, for instance, because you can access your files when you are traveling.

UNDERSTANDING WEB APPS

Microsoft Office Web Applications, called "Web Apps" for short, are a browser-based set of applications for viewing and lightweight editing in a familiar layout of your existing Word, Excel, and PowerPoint files over the Internet wherever there is a PC or Mac attached. Although these are the same programs you could purchase for a desktop computer, they do not have the sophistication and complexity that you have with the desktop programs. The Web Apps are "Office light." However, they are also free, and allow you to try out the software before paying money for more comprehensive desktop versions.

This book introduces you to Web Apps on the Internet using Microsoft SkyDrive, which can also store your data files. When you want to view or edit a Word file, for instance, you bring up a browser, sign on to skydrive.com, and scroll through your folders, just as you would with your own computer folders. When you find the document you want to open, click it, click **View** or **Edit**, and Microsoft Word Web App opens to do that.

NOTE

To set up your SkyDrive credentials and upload a file, you must first establish a Windows Live ID and account. Chapter 5 describes how to sign up for a Windows Live ID. When you have one, you can simply log in and get access to SkyDrive.

- You don't have to worry about someone else being able to read your documents when they don't own the program, or the same version.
- You don't have to pay for a generous amount of storage, until (or unless) you want to upgrade to higher-capacity storage.

Use SkyDrive

SkyDrive (skydrive.com), the Microsoft server hosting platform for its Web Apps, is where you can save your Office documents, enabling viewers not having Office applications or the latest version of them to view the document and do lightweight editing with a browser. If you have created a document on your own computer, saving your files to SkyDrive preserves the links, color schemes, and other design elements created with your local Office application. The file and all the supporting objects are saved to a private folder that you create on SkyDrive or to a public folder there at your choice.

ADD A FOLDER TO SKYDRIVE

SkyDrive starts out with one folder named My Documents to hold any files you want to store there, as you can see in Figure 9-1. You can add folders as you wish within My Documents, on the same level with it to hold documents, and for both Photos and Favorites. SkyDrive gives you immediate links to create folders for favorites and photos. (See the "Understanding SkyDrive Folders" QuickFacts.)

To log on to SkyDrive and create a new folder to hold your documents:

1. In your browser, type skydrive.com. If you don't have a Windows Live or Hotmail ID, click **Sign Up** and follow the instructions. If you do have an ID and it is displayed for you, move your mouse over your ID, click **Sign In**, type your password, and click **Sign In** again. If you do not see an ID, type yours, press **TAB**, type your password, and click **Sign In**. The SkyDrive page will display, as shown in Figure 9-1.

Figure 9-1: *You can save your documents to SkyDrive, where viewers can access them with a browser.*

2. Under your name on the upper-left area, click the **New** down arrow, and select **Folder** to add a new folder to the account. The Create A Folder view will appear.

3. Type the name for the folder.

ANN BENEFITS FROM BOD ONLINE DOCUMENTS

The way I see it, the Internet has enormously benefited organizations with boards of directors. I have served on nonprofit boards for over 30 years, and staff always seems to scramble getting board packets out. They hustle around to copy, deliver, or mail the information, while board members hope they will receive it before the meeting. During the last couple of years, some of my boards have taken a different approach to distributing board packets that works well—the board members log on to organizational websites to get the materials they need for the meeting. The staff does have to post the information, but this takes far less time than before. Costs to the organization are reduced in terms of time and materials. In addition, I have trouble filing things so I can find them when I want them. The material available to me online solves the problem; I can find the budget or minutes from a previous meeting without spending hours shuffling through the piles of paper or requesting yet another copy. I am convinced this use of the Internet is a great way for organizations and board members be more effective.

Ann K., 65, California

4. If you want to share the folder with others, click **Change** opposite Share With to choose those permitted to see the contents of the folder, as shown in Figure 9-2. Choose between Everyone (Public), My Friends And Their Friends, Friends, Some Friends, and Me. This sets the level of privacy you want for this folder, ranging from anyone to just you.

- Beneath Add Additional People, type the name or email addresses of those allowed to see your folder's contents.

- Click **Select From Your Contact List** to choose the permitted viewers from your email contact list.

5. Click **Next**. The Add Documents To *foldername* window is displayed. Continue at step 4 in "Add Files to SkyDrive" next.

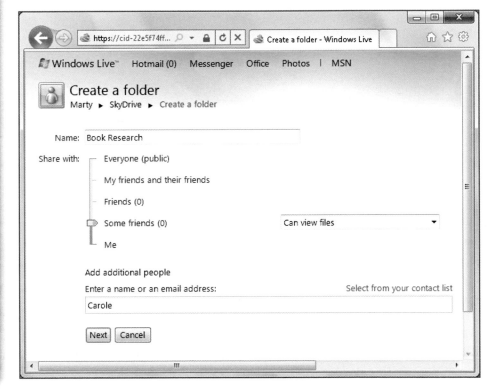

Figure 9-2: You can define how private you want the files in your folder to be.

QUICK**FACTS**

UNDERSTANDING SKYDRIVE FOLDERS

By default, your initial SkyDrive account will contain at least one folder: My Documents. You can add others. Examples of commonly used folders that you might create are Public, Favorites, and Shared Favorites. You can tell by the icons whether the folder is shared, private, or public.

- Indicates a public folder that is shared by the public or by people you select.

- Indicates a private folder, not shared with anyone else.

- Indicates a folder shared with your network of contacts.

When you add folders, you choose who can view their contents.

ADD FILES TO SKYDRIVE

You can add files directly to an existing folder or when the folder is created. You can either upload files to SkyDrive by dragging or selecting them from your computer to a designated folder, or save them when you create a file using Web Apps.

1. If you have added a folder, you will see the Add Documents To *foldername* page when you click **Next**. You can skip to step 4.

2. If you are adding a file to an existing folder, click **Add Files** on the SkyDrive home page. You will see a list of folders.

3. Click the folder you want to use. The Add Documents To *foldername* window appears.

4. You can upload files in two ways:

   - If you have Windows Explorer open, place that window next to your SkyDrive window, then drag your file in Explorer to the Add Documents To *Foldername* window, as is being done in Figure 9-3.

   - Click **Select Documents From Your Computer**, find and select your file, and click **Open** to place it into the SkyDrive window.

5. When all the files you want to be uploaded are displayed in the SkyDrive Add Files window, click **Continue**. You'll see a message informing you that the upload has been successful, along with icons of your uploaded files.

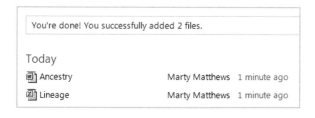

You're done! You successfully added 2 files.

Today

Ancestry	Marty Matthews	1 minute ago
Lineage	Marty Matthews	1 minute ago

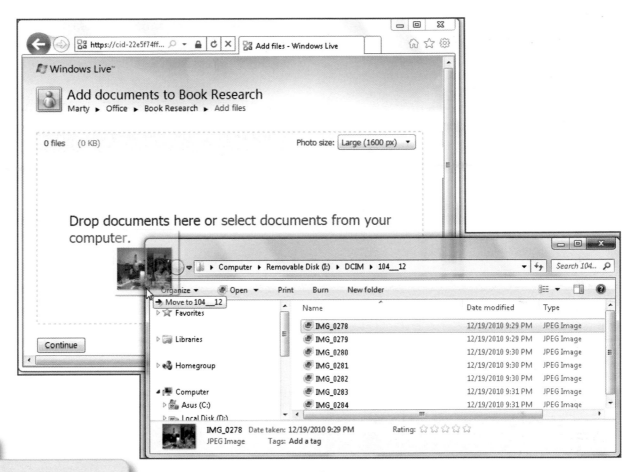

Figure 9-3: **Adding files to SkyDrive is as easy as dragging the files from your Windows Explorer, or using the browse function.**

TIP

To delete a SkyDrive folder with files within it, sign in and click the folder you want to delete. That folder's page will appear. Click **More** and click **Delete**. Click **OK** to verify that you want to delete the folder. Be warned that all files and photos will be deleted as well. To delete an *empty* SkyDrive folder, the Delete option is available on the toolbar next to More. It is not available under More.

Create or Edit Documents Using Web Apps

Earlier in this chapter, we described how, with a Windows Live ID and a SkyDrive account, you can upload files to Microsoft's SkyDrive location in order to keep them in the "cloud" so you, or others with your permission, can

UNDERSTANDING OFFICE STARTER EDITION

Beginning in the Fall of 2010, many computer manufacturers started including in their new computers the Microsoft Office 2010 Starter Edition of Word and Excel. This edition, while limited in some aspects, has more features that the online Web Apps versions of Word and Excel. If you are just getting started using Word and Excel and have a newer computer, click **Start**, click **All Programs**, and click **Microsoft Office 2010**. You will have the choice of buying either the *Home and Student* edition or the *Home and Business* edition (the primary difference is that *Home and Business* includes Outlook), or using the *Starter* edition. Select the latter and use it for as long as you like for free. When you find you want features not found in *Starter*, you can upgrade online. You just need to pay for it and download a key to unlock that edition.

Office   Photos | MSN
Recent documents
Your documents
Your groups
New Word document
New Excel workbook
New PowerPoint presentation
New OneNote notebook

access them at any time or place from a browser. Besides simply storing files there, you can also create new documents or view, edit, and download documents saved in the Word 2007 and Word 2010 default .docx file format, without having Word installed on your computer. (Documents saved in the earlier .doc file format can be directly viewed and will be converted to the .docx format to be edited with Web Apps.) The editing capabilities in the Word Web App are a subset of those in the desktop version of Word. However, if you are creating a simple document or primarily just editing your information and sharing it with others, SkyDrive and the Word Web App provide you a great opportunity to access your information from anywhere with only a browser and Internet connection.

Create a Document Using Web Apps

When you are signed in to Windows Live, you have some of the Microsoft Office applications available to you through the Office Web Apps. Simplified versions of Word, Excel, PowerPoint, and OneNote can be accessed online so that you don't need the desktop version of Office to work with these Office files. Here is how to create a new Word document with Web Apps:

1. In the Windows Live toolbar on the top of the window, click the **Office** menu, and click an application; in this case, **New Word Document**.
2. Type the name of the document. Click **Save**. The Word window will open, as shown in Figure 9-4.
3. Type your document, formatting it as needed. See the "Understanding the Ribbon" QuickFacts in Chapter 5 and "Edit Documents in the Word Web App" later in this chapter. Figure 9-5 displays an overview of the ribbon functions.
4. When you are finished, click **File** and then click **Save**.

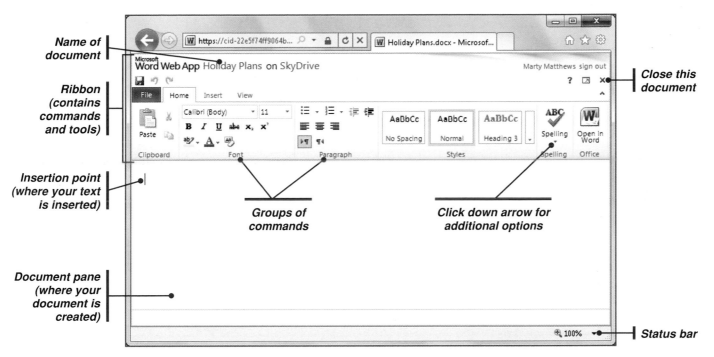

Figure 9-4: *The Word Web App is a simplified version of the desktop version of Word.*

Name of document — Name of document

Ribbon (contains commands and tools) — Ribbon (contains commands and tools)

Insertion point (where your text is inserted) — Insertion point

Document pane (where your document is created) — Document pane

Close this document — Close this document

Groups of commands — Groups of commands

Click down arrow for additional options — Click down arrow for additional options

Status bar — Status bar

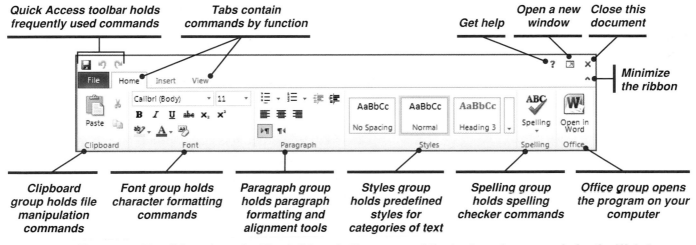

Quick Access toolbar holds frequently used commands

Tabs contain commands by function

Open a new window

Close this document

Get help

Minimize the ribbon

Clipboard group holds file manipulation commands

Font group holds character formatting commands

Paragraph group holds paragraph formatting and alignment tools

Styles group holds predefined styles for categories of text

Spelling group holds spelling checker commands

Office group opens the program on your computer

Figure 9-5: *The ribbon, here the Word ribbon, is the source of the tools and commands for the Web Apps.*

QUICKSTEPS

VIEWING YOUR EDITED DOCUMENT

On the Word Web App View tab are two commands that enable you to switch between seeing the document as it looks while being edited and how it will look in finished or reading mode. Figure 9-6 shows an example of the two views.

Click **View** and select an option:

- Click **Editing View** to edit the document with the ribbon but without all the formatting (this is the default view that appears when you open a document).

- Click **Reading View** to see how your formatting and edits appear in the finished document but without the editing ribbon. When you are reading, click **Edit In Browser** to return to the editing view, or click **Open In Word** to open the document with your desktop version of Word.

Edit Documents in the Word Web App

To read and edit a document in the Word Web App:

1. Click the SkyDrive folder that contains the document you want to view or edit.

2. Point your cursor at the file you want to edit. A menu opens up to the right allowing you to select from several tasks.

The Gettysburg Address for... Edit in browser Open in Word Share ▼ More ▼   ×

- **Edit In Browser** opens the document in the Word Web App.

- **Open In Word** opens the document in your desktop version of Word, assuming it is on your computer.

- **Share** allows you to change your sharing options.

- **More** opens a submenu with additional options.

- **Delete**, the X icon on the right, deletes the file from SkyDrive.

3. Click **Edit In Browser**. The document opens the Word Web App window, as displayed earlier in Figure 9-4. This window is similar to the desktop Word 2010 user interface, but if you're used to the desktop version, you'll notice the lack of several features, including the tools located on missing ribbon tabs and many of the options found on the desktop File tab. See "Work with Your Documents" to find more explanation of what you can do with your document.

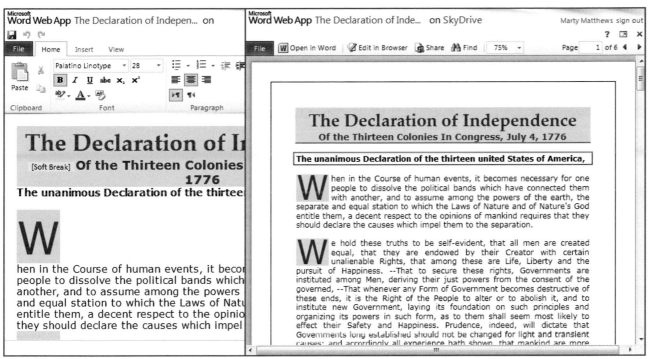

Figure 9-6: *You can use the View tab to switch between editing your document and seeing what it will look like when it is read or printed.*

TIP

For information on how to use the desktop versions of Office applications, please look for *Microsoft Word 2010 QuickSteps, Microsoft Excel 2010 QuickSteps, Microsoft PowerPoint 2010 QuickSteps,* or *Microsoft Office 2010 QuickSteps,* all published by McGraw-Hill.

4. After editing the document using the tools on the available ribbon tabs, click **File** and select whether you want to open the file in your desktop version of Word, save the changes you have made to the file on SkyDrive, print it, share it with others, review and change the file properties, or close the file.

5. When you are ready, click the **Close** icon on the upper right to return to your SkyDrive folders to work with other Web App documents in the same manner, navigate to other webpages, or simply close your browser.

Work with Your Documents

When you are creating or editing your documents, there are some simple guidelines about using the Web Apps that facilitate your experience and make it smoother.

USE TABS AND MENUS

Tabs are displayed at the top of the ribbon or a dialog box. Menus are displayed when you click a down arrow on a button on the ribbon, a dialog box, or a toolbar. Here are some of the ways to use tabs and menus:

- To open a tab or menu with the mouse, click the tab or menu.
- To select a tab or menu command, click the tab or menu to open it, and then click the option.

ENTER TEXT

To enter text in a document that you have newly created or opened, simply start typing. The characters you type will appear in the document pane at the insertion point and in the order that you type them.

INSERT LINE BREAKS

In Word, as in all word processing programs, simply keep typing and the text will automatically wrap around to the next line. Only when you want to break a line before it would otherwise end must you manually intervene. At the end of a paragraph, to skip to the next line or start a new paragraph, press ENTER.

SELECT TEXT

In order to copy, move, or delete text, you first need to select it. *Selecting text* means to identify it as a separate block from the remaining text in a document. You can select any amount of text, from a single character to an entire document. As text is selected, it is highlighted with a colored background, as seen in Figure 9-7. You can select text using either the mouse or the keyboard. See Table 9-1 for details of how to do this.

NOTE

If you want more sophisticated breaks, such as column breaks, section breaks, or even page breaks, edit the document in the desktop version of Word.

TYPE OF SELECTION	HOW TO DO IT
Select a single word	Double-click that word.
Select one or more characters in a word, or select two or more words by clicking:	1. Click to place the insertion point to the left of the first character. 2. Press and hold **SHIFT** while clicking to the right of the last character. The selected range of text will be highlighted.
Select one or more characters in a word, or to select two or more words by dragging:	1. Move the mouse pointer to the left of the first character. 2. Press and hold the mouse button while dragging the mouse pointer to the right or left. The selected text will be highlighted.
Select text with the keyboard	• To select text to the right or left as you move the arrow keys, press and hold **SHIFT** while using the arrow keys. • To select a line, place the pointer at the beginning of a line by pressing **HOME**. Press and hold **SHIFT**, and press **END**. • To select multiple words at a time, press **CTRL+SHIFT** and press the **RIGHT ARROW** or **LEFT ARROW** key. • To select a whole document, press **CTRL+A**.

Table 9-1: Ways to Select Text

Table 9-1 talks about clicking to the *left* of the first character you want to select by either clicking or dragging to the right. You can also do the reverse and click to the right of the last character and while clicking or dragging to the left. In other words, you can work in both directions.

After selecting one area using the keyboard, the mouse, or the two together, you can select further independent areas by pressing and holding **CTRL** while using any of the mouse selection techniques.

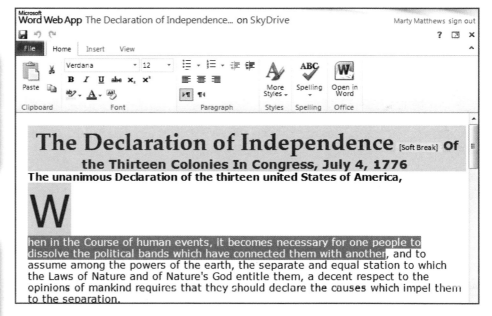

*Figure 9-7: **You will always know what you are moving, copying, or deleting because it is highlighted on the screen.***

TASK	WITH KEYBOARD	WITH RIBBON
Cut	Press **CTRL+X**.	Click **Home** and click **Cut** ✂ on the Clipboard group.
Copy	Press **CTRL+C**.	Click **Home** and click **Copy** 📋 on the Clipboard group.
Paste	Press **CTRL+V**.	Click **Home** and click **Paste** 📋 on the Clipboard group.
Undo	Press **CTRL+Z**.	Click **Undo** ↩ in the Quick Access toolbar.
Redo	Press **CTRL+Y**.	Click **Redo** ↪ in the Quick Access toolbar.

Table 9-2: ***Ways to Move and Copy Text***

> **NOTE**
>
> You can recover deleted text using Undo in the same way you can reverse a cut or a paste.

> **NOTE**
>
> You select a picture by clicking it. Once selected, a picture can be copied, moved, and deleted from a document in the same ways as text, using the Windows Clipboard.

COPY, MOVE, AND PASTE TEXT

Copying and moving text are similar. Think of copying text as moving it and leaving a copy behind. Both copying and moving are done in two steps.

1. Selected text is copied or cut from its current location to the Clipboard. See Table 9-2 for how to do it.

2. The contents of the Clipboard are pasted to a new location identified by the insertion point.

The *Clipboard* is a location in the computer's memory that is used to store information temporarily. The Windows Clipboard can store one object, either text or a picture, and pass that object within or among Windows programs. Once an object is cut or copied to the Windows Clipboard, it stays there until another object is cut or copied to the Clipboard, or until the computer is turned off. The Windows Clipboard is used by default.

DELETE TEXT

Deleting text removes it from its current location *without* putting it in the Clipboard, while ***cutting text*** removes it and *puts it on* the Clipboard. To delete or cut a selected piece of text:

- Press **DELETE**, or **DEL**.
- On the Home tab, click **Cut** in the Clipboard group.

Check Spelling and Grammar

By default, Word checks spelling and grammar as you type the document, so it might be that these functions have already been performed. You can tell if Word is checking the spelling and grammar by noticing if Word automatically places a wavy red line under words it thinks are misspelled or wavy green lines under words it thinks have a grammatical problem. You can also ask Word to perform a spelling check whenever you want—most importantly, when you are completing a document.

1. Click the **Spelling** down arrow, and click **Spelling**. If a misspelling is found, a menu with a suggested replacement will appear. You have these options:

   - Click the suggested word if it is correct, or select another word.
   - Click **Set Proofing Language** to change the language used, for example, French instead of English.
   - Click **Cut** to remove text, **Copy** to copy it, or **Paste** to replace the current word with a previously copied or cut word.

2. Click the document outside the menu to remove the spelling menu from the screen.

APPLY STYLES TO DOCUMENTS

A *style* applies a specific set of formatting characteristics to individual characters or to entire paragraphs within the theme. For example, you can apply styles to headings, titles, lists, and other text components. Consequently, styles determine how the overall design comes together in its look and feel. Styles are beneficial to document creation, because they provide a consistent look and feel to all text selected for formatting.

Word 2010 provides a gallery of styles that provides you with sets of canned formatting choices, such as font, size, bolding, and color, that you can apply to headings, titles, text, and lists. You use styles by identifying what kind of formatting a selected segment of text needs, such as for a header or title. Then you select the style of formatting you want to apply to the document.

1. Select the text to be formatted, for example, a title or heading.

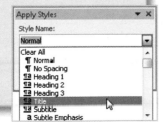

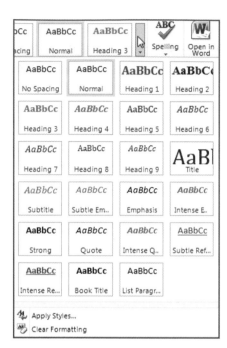

*Figure 9-8: **The Styles gallery shows you canned options for formatting headings, text, and paragraphs.***

2. In the Home tab click the **More Styles** down arrow in the Styles group. The Styles gallery is displayed, as shown in Figure 9-8.

3. Click the thumbnail of the style you want to apply.

APPLY CHARACTER FORMATTING

Character formatting can be applied using keyboard shortcuts or the Home tab on the ribbon. The Home tab, in the Font group, provides a visual selection of character formatting and spacing alternatives. See Figure 9-9 to identify which tools are available for character formatting. Keyboard shortcuts (summarized in Table 9-3) allow you to keep your hands on the keyboard while doing the same tasks.

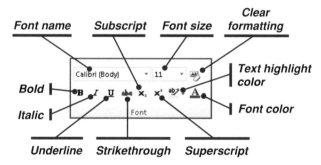

*Figure 9-9: **The Font group contains character formatting tools.***

APPLY FORMATTING	SHORTCUT KEYS
Bold	**CTRL+B**
Italic	**CTRL+I**
Underline continuous	**CTRL+U**
Align left	**CTRL+L**
Align right	**CTRL+R**
Center	**CTRL+E**

*Table 9-3: **Keyboard Character Editing and Paragraph Aligning***

FORMAT A PARAGRAPH

Paragraph formatting, which you can apply to any paragraph, is used to manage alignment, indentation, line spacing, and bullets or numbering. In Word, a paragraph consists of a paragraph mark (created by pressing **ENTER**) and any text or objects that appear between that paragraph mark and the previous paragraph mark. A paragraph can be empty, or it can contain anything from a single character to as many characters as you care to enter.

The Home tab Paragraph group contains the tools for formatting a paragraph. First you must click in the paragraph you want to align, and then click the command in the Paragraph group, as shown in Figure 9-10. The keyboard can also be used for some formatting. See Table 9-3.

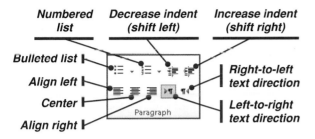

Figure 9-10: **The Paragraph group on the Home tab provides fast formatting for paragraphs.**

PRINT A DOCUMENT

To print a document using the Web App, you must first save the document.

1. Click **File** and then click **Print**. If you have not saved the document, you will be prompted to do so. Click **Save And Print**. The Print dialog box is displayed, as shown in Figure 9-11.

2. You have these options:

   - If your printer is not displayed, click the **Name** down arrow on the Printer Name list and click its name.

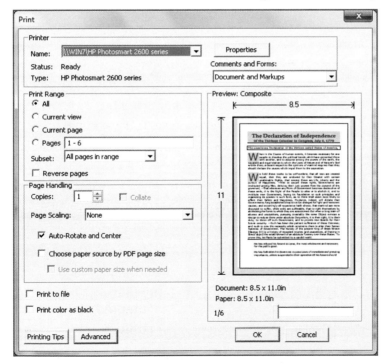

Figure 9-11: **The Print dialog box gives you options for printing your document.**

- In the Page Range area, click **All** to print all pages of the document; click **Current View** to print what is currently displayed; click **Current Page** to print only the current active page; click **Pages** and then type the page numbers you want (separate individual pages with a comma and page ranges with a hyphen, such as 3,4-9,12).

- Click the **Copies** arrows to indicate the number of copies you want printed, or type it in the text box.

- Click **Properties** to change printer and printing preferences, such as paper size and orientation of printing on the page, whether a border is printed, color considerations, and more.

3. Click **OK** to begin the print process.

Use Excel

An Excel worksheet is a matrix, or grid, of lettered *column headings* across the top and numbered *row headings* down the side. The first row of a typical worksheet is used for column *headers*. The column headers represent categories of similar data. The rows beneath a column header contain data that is further categorized either by a row header down the leftmost column or listed below the column header. Figure 9-12 shows an example of a common worksheet arrangement. Worksheets can also be used to set up *tables* of data, where columns are sometimes referred to as *fields* and each row represents a unique *record* of data. To understand Excel in all its capacity, refer to *Microsoft Excel 2010 QuickSteps* by John Cronan, published by McGraw-Hill.

Each intersection of a row and column is called a *cell*, and is referenced first by the column location and then by the row location. The combination of a column letter and row number assigns each cell an *address*. For example, the cell at the intersection of column D and row 8 is called D8. A cell is considered *active* when it is clicked or otherwise selected as the place in which to place new data.

Figure 9-13 shows the ribbon for the Excel Web App.

Column headers categorize data vertically

Data organized by column and row headers

Columns are identified by lettered headings across the top of the worksheet

Rows are identified by numbered headings along the left side of the worksheet

Row headers organize data horizontally

Active cell is ready to accept data

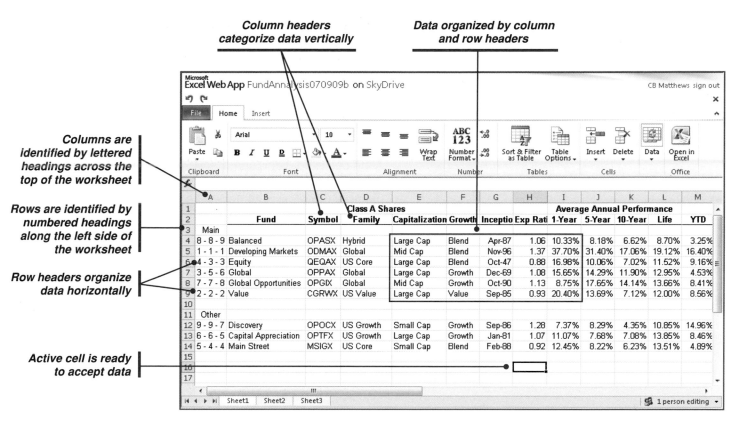

Figure 9-12: *The grid layout of Excel worksheets is defined by several components.*

Increase or decrease the number of decimal places

Insert a column, row, or cell

Delete a column, row, or cell

Format numbers according to the type of number

Open this worksheet in Office Excel

Figure 9-13: *The Excel ribbon offers specialized commands and tools for working with numeric data.*

Refresh the data or recalculate the equations in the workbook

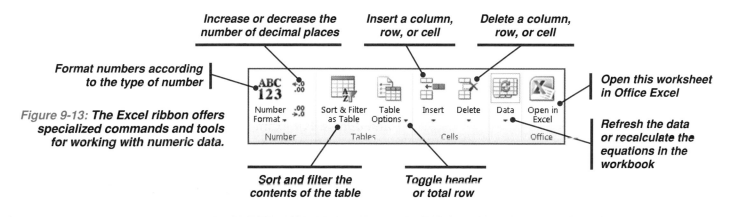

Sort and filter the contents of the table

Toggle header or total row

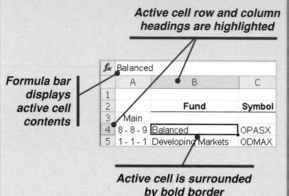
Enter and Format Text into a Worksheet

In an Excel worksheet, text is used to identify, explain, and emphasize numeric data. Textual data cannot be used in calculations.

- Enter text by typing, just as you would in a word processing program.
- Format text using the commands in the Font group for character formatting as shown earlier for Word in Figure 9-9.
- Align cell data using commands in the Alignment group, which is similar to the paragraph formatting illustrated in Figure 9-10, with the addition of top, middle, and bottom cell alignment.
- Wrap text within a cell by clicking **Wrap Text** in the Alignment group.

Enter and Format Numeric Data

Numbers are numerical data, from the simplest to the most complex. Excel provides several features to help you work more easily with numbers used to represent values in various categories, such as currency, accounting, and scientific.

1. Enter numbers by simply selecting a cell and typing the numbers.

2. To format the numbers, select them and click the **Number Format** menu in the Numbers group. You have these options:

   - **General** formats alphanumeric data—data composed of numbers and/or text. Only general formatted data that is purely numeric can be used in calculations.

   - **Number** formats the data as numeric data, which then can be used for calculations. Use **Increase Decimal** or **Decrease Decimal** in the Number group to add or remove decimal places.

   - **Currency** formats for dollars and cents. Click **Increase Decimal** or **Decrease Decimal** in the Number group to set the number of decimal places if it is not two places.

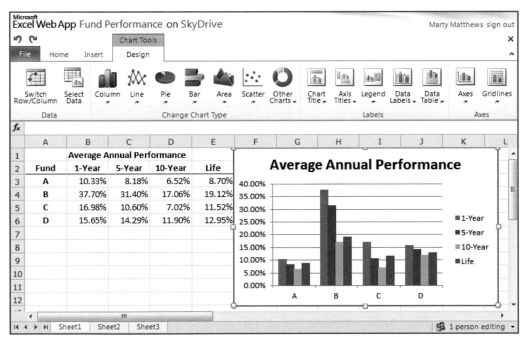
- **Accounting** formats data into numeric data that may or may not be currency and that may or may not have decimal places.
- **Short Date** formats the data with numeric dates, such as 1/06/2012.
- **Long Date** formats the data with alphanumeric dates, such as Friday January 6, 2012. Both types of dates can be used in calculations.
- **Time** formats data as time, which can be used in calculations. Enter the time format you want; that is, with or without A.M./P.M. or seconds.
- **Percentage** formats the data as a percentage, with the percent sign.

3. Press **ENTER** to accept the formatting and number.

Create Charts

One of the features of Excel is its charting capability. You can take numeric data and give it a visual twist. To create a chart from a worksheet:

1. Select the range of data you want included in the chart, including the headers.

2. Click the **Insert** tab, and click the type of chart you want. The chart will be displayed in the worksheet, as shown in Figure 9-14.

3. Using the design tools on the Chart Tools tab, change and edit your charts as you need, adding titles, legends, and data labels, for instance.

Figure 9-14: Using charts in worksheets is a way to display data in clearer and more quickly understood terms.

As with Word, you can upload Excel files to Microsoft's SkyDrive location in order to keep them in the "cloud" so you, or others, can access them at any time or place from a browser. Besides simply storing files there, using the integrated Microsoft Excel Web App, you can also create, view, edit, and download workbooks saved in the Excel 2007 and Excel 2010 default .xlsx file format without necessarily having a version of Excel installed on your computer. (You can view workbooks saved in the earlier .xls file format, but to edit them you must open them for viewing, click **Save A Copy** in the File tab, enter the new name, click **Save**, and finally open the copy for editing in the browser.) The editing capabilities in the Excel Web App are limited to the more basic features of Excel, such as those described in this chapter, as well as minor formatting actions and working with tables. In fact, if the workbook contains more advanced features such as shapes or a watch window, you cannot edit it (although you *may* be able to view and download it—you can't with a watch window). However, for those cases where your edits are predominately data-centric, SkyDrive and the Excel Web App provide you a great opportunity to access your information from anywhere with only a browser and Internet connection.

To use a workbook in the Excel Web App:

1. Open the SkyDrive folder that contains the workbook you want to view or edit.

Continued . . .

Choose a Chart Type

The Excel Web App organizes charts into eight types, categorized by the function they perform. Within each chart type are variations called *subtypes*. For example, the Line chart type has several ways to display trends. The main chart types are summarized in Table 9-4.

CHART TYPE	FUNCTION
Column, Bar, Line	Compare trends in multiple data series in various configurations, such as vertical or horizontal orientation, or trend lines
Pie and Doughnut	Display one data series (pie) or compare multiple data series (doughnut) as part of a whole or 100 percent
XY (Scatter)	Displays pairs of data to establish concentrations
Area	Shows the magnitude of change over time; useful when summing multiple values to see the contribution of each
Radar	Displays values relative to a center point; useful when categories are not directly comparable

Table 9-4: Eight Functional Types of Excel Web App Charts

Use Other Common Applications

Windows 7 comes equipped with several useful accessory programs. Among these are Notepad, a simple text editor; Paint, for drawing and modifying pictures; Character Map for selecting special characters; and Calculator. Here is a brief overview of them. In addition, Adobe Reader is a free third-party program commonly used to read PDF documents.

QUICKSTEPS

EDITING WORKBOOKS IN THE EXCEL WEB APP *(Continued)*

2. Point to the file you want, and in the pop-up menu, click **Edit In Browser**. The workbook opens in a screen that appears similar to the Excel 2010 user interface (see Figure 9-12) but lacks certain features, including the tools located on missing ribbon tabs and many of the options found on a standard File menu.

3. After performing editing using the tools on the available ribbon tabs, click the **File** tab and select whether you want to open the file in your device's version of Excel, save it under a different filename (you don't need to save the workbook, as Excel Web App does that automatically), share it with others, or download it to your device as a standard workbook.

4. When finished, return to your SkyDrive folders to work with other Office documents in the same manner, navigate to other webpages, or simply close your browser.

Run Accessory Programs

You can open the accessory programs by clicking **Start**, clicking **All Programs**, and choosing the **Accessories** folder. Calculator, Character Map, Notepad, and Paint are part of these accessories.

USE CALCULATOR

The Calculator, started from Accessories, has four alternative calculators, each with its own view:

- Standard desktop calculator, shown in Figure 9-15
- Scientific calculator
- Programmer calculator
- Statistics calculator

*Figure 9-15: **The Standard view of the Calculator provides a number of standard mathematical functions, including addition, subtraction, division, and multiplication.***

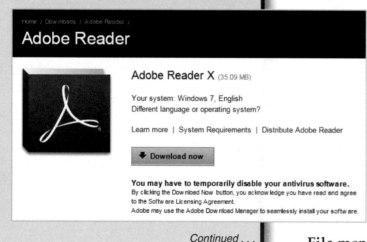
In addition, there are a unit converter; a date calculator; and four worksheets for calculating a mortgage, a vehicle lease, and fuel economy in both mpg and L/100 km that are extensions to the current view. To switch from one view to the other, click **View** and click the other view. To use a calculator, click the numbers and arithmetic functions on the screen or type them on the keyboard.

USE CHARACTER MAP

The Character Map, found in the System Tools subfolder in Accessories, allows the selection of special characters that are not available on a standard keyboard.

1. Click the **Font** down arrow, and click the font you want for the special character.

2. Scroll until you find the character, and then double-click it; or click it and click **Select** to copy it to the Clipboard.

3. In the program where you want the character, right-click an open area, and click **Paste** or press **CTRL+V**.

USE NOTEPAD

Notepad can be used to view and create unformatted text (.txt) files. If you double-click a text file in Windows Explorer, Notepad will likely open and display the file. If a line of text is too long to display without scrolling, click **Format** and click **Word Wrap**. To create a file, simply start typing in the Notepad window, click the **File** menu, and click **Save**. Before printing a file, click **File**; click **Page Setup**; and select the paper orientation, margins, header, and footer.

QUICKSTEPS

USING ACROBAT READER *(Continued)*

2. Click **Download Now**.

3. Click **Run** and then click **Yes** to allow Adobe to continue to download the program onto your computer. Next, click **Install** to complete the installation. You will see a display of the progress.

4. Finally, when you are told the installation has been successful, click **Finish**. You'll find a shortcut to Adobe Reader on your desktop.

5. To open a PDF file, either double-click the Acrobat Reader shortcut or double-click the PDF file. When you first bring Acrobat Reader up, you'll have to accept the reader's license agreement. Click **Accept**. A computer restart is required to finalize the installation.

6. Point your cursor at the icons on the toolbar. You'll see how you can navigate through the document, share it with others, change the magnification, change the display of the page, or use the search feature to find specific words or phrases. Figure 9-17 shows how the reader displays a PDF file.

USE PAINT

Paint lets you view, create, and edit bitmap image files in .bmp, .dib, .gif, .jpg, .png, and .tif formats. Several drawing tools and many colors are available to create simple drawings and illustrations (see Figure 9-16).

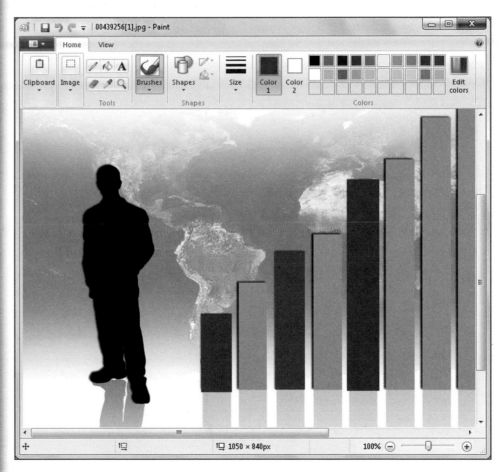

Figure 9-16: *Paint allows you to make simple line drawings or touch up other images.*

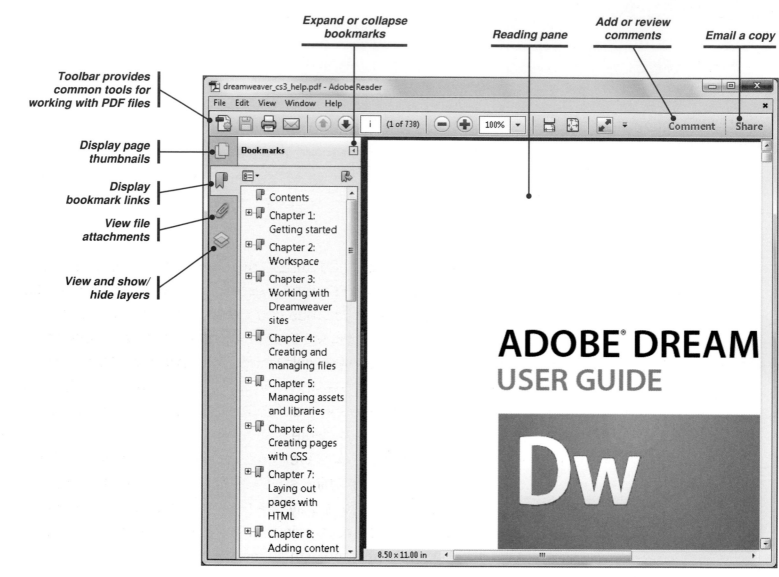

Expand or collapse bookmarks

Reading pane

Add or review comments

Email a copy

Toolbar provides common tools for working with PDF files

Display page thumbnails

Display bookmark links

View file attachments

View and show/hide layers

dreamweaver_cs3_help.pdf - Adobe Reader

File   Edit   View   Window   Help

i   (1 of 738)   100%

Comment   Share

Bookmarks

Contents

Chapter 1: Getting started

Chapter 2: Workspace

Chapter 3: Working with Dreamweaver sites

Chapter 4: Creating and managing files

Chapter 5: Managing assets and libraries

Chapter 6: Creating pages with CSS

Chapter 7: Laying out pages with HTML

Chapter 8: Adding content

ADOBE® DREAM

USER GUIDE

Dw

8.50 × 11.00 in

Figure 9-17: **Acrobat Reader allows you to read PDF files, a common file format.**

Chapter 10
Enjoying Multimedia

Multimedia is the combination of audio and video, with the term *media* referring to either audio or video. As an operating system, Windows 7 has to be able to handle audio and video files and accept their input from a number of different devices. It has four major programs—Windows Media Player, Windows DVD Maker, Windows Media Center, and Windows Live Movie Maker—that enable you to work with multimedia files and read and write them onto CDs, DVDs, flash drives, and music players, as well as *stream* them to other computers (streaming sends audio or video files to another computer in such a way that the other computer can display the files as they are being sent). We'll look first at sound by itself, then at video with sound.

Work with Audio

Audio is sound. Windows 7 works with and uses sound in several ways, the simplest being to alert you of various events, like an incoming email message or closing down the system. Chapter 2 shows you how to customize the use of sounds for these purposes.

The other use of sound is to entertain or inform you—be it listening to music or lectures from CDs, Internet radio, or another Internet site. It is this use of sound that is the subject of this section.

Figure 10-1: Windows Media Player Now Playing view shows you its controls when you move the mouse over it.

Play CDs

Playing a CD is as easy as inserting a disc in the drive. When you do that, by default, Windows Media Player opens and starts playing the CD. The other alternative is that you will be asked if you want Windows Media Player to play the disc. In that case, if you click **Play Audio CD Using Windows Media Player**, Media Player will open and begin playing the disc. Initially, the on-screen view, called "Now Playing," is a small window, as shown in Figure 10-1. If you click **Switch To Library** in the upper-right corner under the Close button **⊞**, a larger, more comprehensive window will open, as you can see in Figure 10-2. The Media Player library window has a variety of controls that enable you to determine how it functions and looks. These controls are located either in the functional controls and option menus at the top of the window or in the playback controls at the bottom.

- **Menu options** includes facilities to:
  - **Organize** the Media Player window
  - **Stream** media from your computer
  - **Create a playlist** of selected tracks

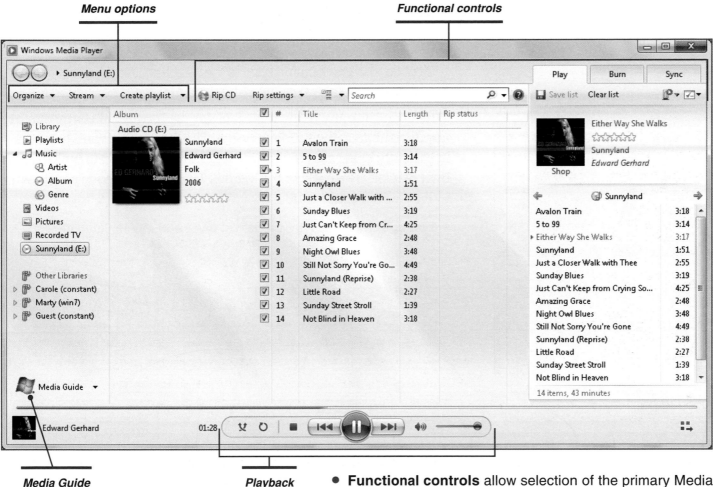

Media Guide

Playback controls

Figure 10-2: Windows Media Player Library view gives you access to a wide range of audio and video entertainment.

- **Functional controls** allow selection of the primary Media Player functions:

  - **Rip CD** copies audio CDs to the Media Library.

  - **Rip settings** apply to audio being copied from a CD.

  - **Play** plays selected tracks and creates a playlist.

  - **Burn** copies playlists from the library to writable CDs and DVDs.

  - **Sync** synchronizes content between portable music devices and your PC.

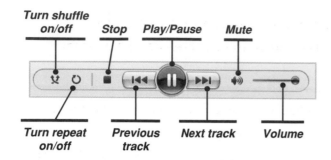

Turn shuffle on/off **Stop** **Play/Pause** **Mute**

Turn repeat on/off **Previous track** **Next track** **Volume**

- **Media Guide** opens the Windows Media Guide, an online media source for music, movies, TV, and radio.

- **Playback controls** provides CD player–like controls to play/pause, stop, go to a previous track, go to the next track, and adjust volume, as well as randomly play tracks (shuffle) and repeat a specific track.

When you click any of the three tabs for the functional controls in the upper-right area, the list pane opens. The Play tab initially lists what is currently being played, but can be cleared and used to build your own playlist. The parts of the Media Player in Play mode are shown in Figure 10-3, and include:

- **List options** hides (closes) the list pane and manipulates the list.

Navigation pane **Details pane** **List pane**

List options

Play to

Shop for CD/DVD

Previous/ Next playlist

Switch to Now Playing

Figure 10-3: The list pane shows what is currently playing and is where playlists are created.

- **Play to** starts an audio or video stream to a media device.
- **Clear list** stops what is being played and prepares the pane for creating a playlist.
- **Save list** saves the current playlist to your Media Library.
- **Shop CD/DVD** enables you to buy the item you are listening to or watching.
- **Previous** and **Next** let you cycle through the playlists in your library.
- **Switch to Now Playing** collapses the window to just the small window shown in Figure 10-1.

Control the Volume

You can control your computer's audio volume from several places, including the physical volume control on your speakers or on your laptop computer, the volume control on the bottom-right area of the playback controls of the Media Player, and the volume icon in the notification area on the right of the taskbar .

Clicking the **Volume** icon in the notification area opens a small Volume slider that you can drag for louder or softer sound, or you can click **Mute** (the blue speaker at the bottom of the slider) to do just that. Click anywhere on the desktop to close the Volume slider.

Access Online Media

If you have a broadband Internet connection (as described in Chapter 4) of at least 512 Kbps (more will improve your experience) and sound capability, you can find a large amount of media, including music, movies, and TV. Windows Media Player gives you access to this media through the Media Guide, whose icon is in the lower-left corner of the Media Player and opens into the window shown in Figure 10-4.

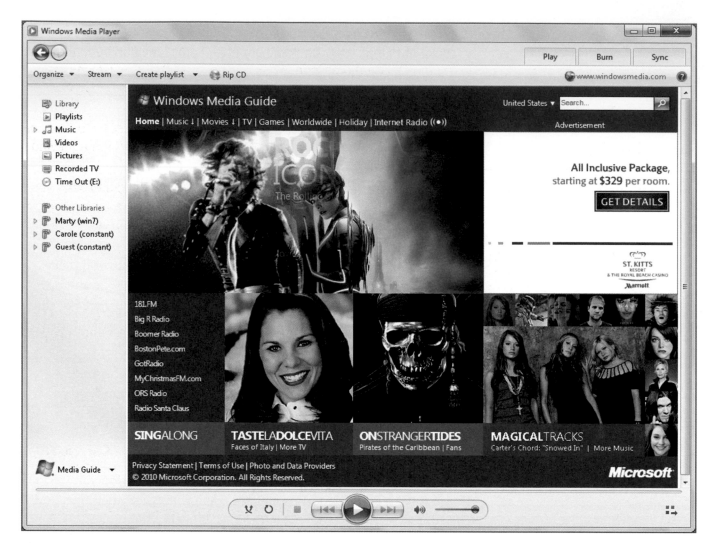

Figure 10-4: The Media Guide facilitates locating music, movies, and TV.

To use the Media Guide to locate media from a closed Media Player:

1. Click the **Windows Media Player** icon ▣ on the taskbar (it is pinned there by default). If you don't have a Media Player icon on the taskbar, click **Start**, click **All Programs**, and click **Windows Media Player**.

TIP

Doing direct searches from your Internet browser may help you find what you want.

QUICKSTEPS

FINDING YOUR MUSIC ONLINE

Having spent my adolescent youth in the 1950s, many of my favorite songs from that era are by The Platters and include *Unchained Melody*, *Smoke Gets in Your Eyes*, *Twilight Time*, and *Only You*. You can easily find and listen to this music and most other popular songs by simply typing a song's name into either the Google or Bing search text box. For example, I might type Platters – Unchained Melody. This produces a list of links to sites where you can listen to the song, as you can see on the left of Figure 10-5. Many of the links that are found are on YouTube. Clicking one of these links opens YouTube and begins playing the song. On the page that opens there are links to either other songs by the same artist or other artists performing the same song, as you can see on the right of Figure 10-5.

2. Click the **Media Guide** icon in the lower-left corner of the Media Player. It may be that the Media Guide icon has been replaced by the Online Stores icon because that is what was last used. In that case, click the **Online Stores** down arrow, and click **Media Guide**.

3. Click in the **Search** text box; type the name of the piece, the performer, or the genre; and either press **ENTER** or click the **Search** magnifying glass. The search results list will appear.

4. Select your choice within the results list, or if you don't find what you want, try a different search. From the results, you often are able to listen to or view a segment and find out where you can buy the entire piece.

5. Close the Media Player when you are ready.

Buy Media Online

There are many sources of media on the Internet. Two paths to buying media are through the Online Stores in the Media Player and through the popular iTunes.

USE MEDIA PLAYER

The Online Stores in the Media Player provides links to several stores—links that you can follow to locate and buy media.

1. Click the **Windows Media Player** icon on the taskbar. If you don't have a Media Player icon on the taskbar, click **Start**, click **All Programs**, and click **Windows Media Player**.

2. Click the **Online Stores** icon if it is displayed; otherwise, click the **Media Guide** down arrow, and click **Browse All Online Stores**. The Online Stores page will open and display several stores that sell music, videos, and audio books, all of which can be downloaded.

3. Click a store that looks promising and follow the instructions to use that store and download the media to your computer and into your music or video library.

4. Close Media Player when you are ready.

Figure 10-5: Finding music online is simply a
matter of typing the name of the performer and/or
the song in a search text box and then selecting
the one you want to hear, as shown on the left.
You can then go on to related songs as you see
on the right.

USE ITUNES

iTunes is an online media store operated by Apple, Inc. They claim
to be the world's number one music store. They also have the iTunes
Player, which you can download for free and is a competitor to the
Windows Media Player.

1. Click the **Internet Explorer** icon on your taskbar to open it. Click in
   the address bar, and type itunes.com.

2. Click the **What Is iTunes**, **What's On iTunes**, and **How To** links to
   learn more about iTunes. If needed, download QuickTime, a video
   player, to view the video on installing iTunes. Follow the online
   instructions, clicking the various QuickTime and Windows controls
   as needed.

CAUTION

iTunes and many other online stores make it *very easy to buy from them*, and you can quickly run up a sizable bill. You need to create an account with the store and provide your name, address, email, and credit card info. Once you do this, it is almost too easy to buy in the future!

Figure 10-6: iTunes is both a media player and a popular site for downloading media.

3. When you are ready, download and install iTunes, following the instructions and clicking the appropriate controls as needed.

4. After the installer has restarted your computer, double-click the **iTunes** icon on your desktop. iTunes will start, ask you a series of setup questions, and then open.

5. If it isn't already selected, click **iTunes Store** to open the window shown in Figure 10-6. Use the various links and the search box to select and possibly download the media you want.

6. Close iTunes when you are finished.

Figure 10-7: Media Player can be used to build a music library from your CDs.

Copy (Rip) CDs to Your Computer

Media Player gives you the ability to copy (or "rip") CD tracks that you like to your hard disk so that you can build and manage a library of your favorite music and copy this material to a recordable CD or DVD. To copy from a CD (see Figure 10-7):

1. Insert the CD from which you want to copy tracks. If it doesn't automatically start playing, click **Play Audio CD Using Windows Media Player** to open Windows Media Player.

2. Click **Switch To Library** in the upper-right corner. In the details pane, select the tracks you want to copy to your hard disk by clicking the check boxes to the left of each track. Click **Play** in the playback controls to listen to the tracks and to make sure your choices are correct.

3. If you wish, click **Rip Settings** and review the settings that are available to you. For the most part, the default settings provide the best middle ground between high quality and file size.

4. When you are satisfied that you have selected the correct tracks and settings, click **Rip CD**. The selected tracks will be copied to your hard disk. When you are done, remove the CD and close Media Player.

NOTE

Copying a music track from a CD to a digital file on your hard disk is time-consuming, even on a relatively fast computer. It also produces large files. To see the copying progress, look at the Rip Status column of the Media Player window, as well as the message in the bottom-right corner (see Figure 10-7).

NOTE

The material on most CDs and DVDs is owned and copyrighted by some combination of the composer, the artist, the producer, and/or the publisher. Copyright law prohibits using the copyrighted material in ways that are not beneficial to the owners, including giving or selling the content without giving or selling the original CD or DVD itself. To enforce this, most CDs and DVDs are protected to make copying difficult. Media Player provides the ability to copy copyrighted material to your hard disk and then to a recordable CD or a USB flash drive with the understanding that the copy is solely for your own personal use and you will not sell or give away copies. This is both a great gift and a responsibility. As one who makes his living on copyrighted material, I urge you not to abuse it.

NOTE

You cannot add music to playlists directly from a CD in your drive even though it appears in Media Player. You must first add the music to your library and then select it from there.

Organize Music

Once you have copied several CDs and have downloaded other music to your hard disk, you will likely want them organized. When music and videos are copied to the library, the contents are automatically indexed alphabetically by album, artist, and genre. You may want to combine selected tracks into a *playlist* that allows you to play pieces from several albums. To build a new playlist:

1. Open Media Player and click **Create Playlist** in the menu options area. Type the name you want for the new playlist, and press **ENTER**. A new playlist will appear in the list of playlists in the navigation pane.

2. Open an album, artist, or genre; and select a piece or the pieces (by holding down **CTRL** as you click multiple pieces) that you want in the new playlist. Drag the piece(s) to the playlist title in the navigation pane.

3. Select additional pieces you want to add, and drag them to the playlist title in the navigation pane. Click the playlist to display the contents of the playlist in the detail pane, or double-click the playlist to display it in the Play tab in the list pane and begin to play it.

–Or–

1. Open Media Player and click the **Play** tab to open it in the list pane. Select and display in the details pane the music you want in the playlist. Drag the piece(s) you want to the list pane, as you can see in Figure 10-8.

2. When you have added all the pieces that you initially want (you can always add more later), click **Save List**, type a name, and press **ENTER**.

Figure 10-8: Media Player provides a way to manage the media you store on your computer, including building playlists.

3. Listen to the playlist by clicking the play button in the playback controls. When you are done, click **Clear List**, click the **Play** tab to close the list pane, and close Media Player.

Make (Burn) a Music CD

Once you have created a playlist (see "Organize Music" earlier in this chapter), you can write (or "burn") it to a writable CD using Media Player's Burn feature. This creates an "audio" CD that works in a portable or car CD player. This is not the same as simply making a copy of the digital files.

JIM FINDS LOTS OF INFORMATION

I use my computer for a lot of things, including email, banking, and working with my photos, which includes organizing them, putting them on CDs, and printing them. Probably most valuable, though, is the access to the Internet, which I use quite often. Although I'm now retired, I often go on Web MD to look up drug interactions and other information. I also find the Internet very useful in looking up random information. For example, we had a house guest from France and got to talking about bridges. I mentioned a bridge in France I knew about that he did not. We looked it up on the Internet and, sure enough, found the bridge I had remembered. I think this capability is truly amazing to have in your home. Before the Internet, you might have been able to go to a library and find it, but even there, it would have been much more difficult.

Jim T., DDS, 76, Missouri

1. Put a blank recordable disc in the CD recording drive. The AutoPlay dialog box will appear and ask what you want to do. Click **Burn An Audio CD** to open Windows Media Player with the Burn functional area displayed.

2. Open your playlists in the navigation pane, and drag a playlist (or individual songs from an open playlist) that you want on the CD to the Burn List on the right. Do this in the order you want the songs played. You can see how much of the CD is being used and the amount of time remaining just above the Burn List, as shown in Figure 10-9.

3. You can make corrections to the Burn List by dragging additional songs there until you use up the remaining time, or by right-clicking a song on the Burn List and clicking **Remove From List** in the context menu that opens. You can also clear the Burn List and start over.

4. When you are sure you have the list of pieces you want to burn, click **Start Burn**. The digital files will first be converted to analog music files and then written to a CD or DVD. You can see the progress in the thermometer bar near the top of the list pane (it is not very fast!). When the burn is complete and if no one has changed the default settings, the disc will be ejected from the drive. Write the title on the disc with a soft felt-tip marker, or use a LightScribe drive to burn a label on the special discs you use for this purpose.

The resulting CD should be playable in most CD players.

Figure 10-9: Burning a playlist to a writable CD allows you to create a disc that has just your favorite songs.

Copy to (Sync with) Music Players

Windows Media Player allows you to plug in a digital music device, such as an iPod, and transfer music to and from (sync with) the device.

1. Start Windows Media Player, and click **Sync** in the Windows Media Player functional controls. You will be told to connect your device.

2. Start your device and then plug it into your computer. The first time you do that, Windows will install a driver for it, and then the AutoPlay dialog box will appear.

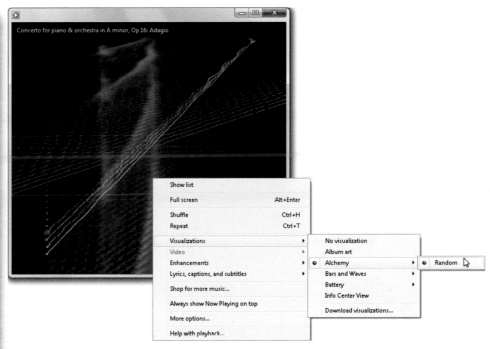

DISPLAYING VISUALIZATIONS IN WINDOWS MEDIA PLAYER

The Media Player's Now Playing window, shown in Figure 10-1, can, as an alternative to the cover art, display a graphic visualization of the music that is playing. Several visualizations come with Media Player, and you can download more. To display a visualization:

- Right-click the **Now Playing** window, click **Visualizations**, select one of the three types of visualizations (Album Art and Info Center View are static displays), and then click the visualization you want to use, as shown in Figure 10-10.

- If you want to download additional visualizations, right-click the **Now Playing** window, click **Visualizations**, and click **Download Visualizations**. Then follow the instructions on the websites you will visit.

Figure 10-10: You can have the Now Playing window display a visualization of music that is being played.

NOTE

If you choose to sync your entire library, consider the Shuffle Music option. With this option selected, Windows will put the music on the device in such a way that songs will randomly play. Each time you plug your device into your computer, a new random order will be established and copied to the device.

You can manually select playlists and songs that you want copied to the device, as shown in Figure 10-11.

3. In the Devices Setup dialog box, click **Finish** or **Cancel**, depending on your situation. If you click **Cancel**, drag the playlists and/or songs you want on the device to the Sync Lists on the right. If you wish, you can play the Sync List by double-clicking the first playlist or song.

4. When you are certain that you have all the music in the Sync List that you want on your device, click **Start Sync**. The music will be copied to the device.

Figure 10-11: *A digital music device can mirror your Media Player library if it has enough room and that is what you want.*

Work with Video

Windows 7 lets you watch videos from a DVD, from live or recorded TV, or downloaded from the Internet using Windows Media Player or Windows Media Center. It also allows you to capture videos and still images from a digital camcorder or digital camera using Windows Live Photo Gallery and then edit those into your own movie using Windows Live Movie Maker.

NOTE

After the first time you play a movie, the AutoPlay may not pop up; the movie may just start playing.

Play DVDs

Playing DVDs is as easy as playing CDs: Simply insert a DVD into its drive. When you do that, the AutoPlay dialog box will appear, and you will be asked if you want to play the DVD using Windows Live Media Player. We'll discuss Media Center later in this chapter, but if you click **Play DVD Movie** using Windows Media Player, the player will open and play the disc. The Media Player controls are virtually the same for DVDs as they are for CDs, as you can see in Figure 10-12, except the View Full Screen option enlarges the movie or video you are watching to fit the full screen, and the DVD menu has options for viewing menus and special features on the DVD.

NOTE

You can determine if your system supports making movies by running a diagnostic that is included in Windows 7. Click **Start**, type dxdiag in the Search text box, and then, under Programs, click **dxdiag**. Click **No** on checking for digital signing. The DirectX Diagnostic Tool dialog box will appear. In the System tab, you can see your CPU speed, the amount of memory you have, and your DirectX version. On the Display tab, you can see the amount of display memory you have. Click **Exit** when finished.

TIP

If you are using Movie Maker to record an analog signal coming from a video capture card and are having problems—which is common—don't fight it. Use the software that comes with the video capture card to create a file on your hard disk, and then import that file into Movie Maker.

Figure 10-12: *Watching movies, or in this case a concert, is increasingly popular, especially with a laptop on a trip.*

NOTE

There can be some copyright issues when using music from professionally recorded CDs, DVDs, and tapes. If you are making a movie solely for your own use and are not going to put it on the Internet, sell it, or otherwise distribute it, then there are no issues. If you are going to use your movie in any of the prohibited ways and it contains someone else's copyrighted material (either audio or video), you need to get permission from the copyright holder.

QUICKSTEPS

PREPARING TO MAKE A MOVIE

Making a movie with a computer takes more hardware than any other task. The faster your CPU, the more memory it has, the better your video display adapter, and the larger your disk, the more smoothly the task will go. The beauty is that most recent computers have what you need by default.

REQUIREMENTS CHECKLIST

The recommended hardware requirements for making movies are as follows:

COMPONENT	RECOMMENDED HARDWARE
CPU	2.4 GHz dual core
RAM memory	2GB
Hard drive free space	60GB
Optical drive	DVD±R

Continued . . .

Import Video from a Camcorder

Importing video directly from your camcorder to your hard disk is done using the Windows Live Photo Gallery.

1. Click **Start**, click **All Programs**, and click **Windows Live Photo Gallery**. In the Home tab, click **Import**.

2. Plug your camcorder into an OHCI-compliant FireWire port on your computer, and turn it on. Windows 7 will detect it, install the necessary driver software, and open the AutoPlay dialog box. Click **Close** in the AutoPlay dialog box.

3. In the Import Photos And Videos dialog box, click **Refresh**. Select your digital video camera, and click **Import**. The Import Video dialog box will appear. Type the name you want for the video, click either **Import The Entire Video** or **Choose Parts Of The Video**, and click **Next** (you can also burn the entire video to a DVD, but here we want to make a movie from the video).

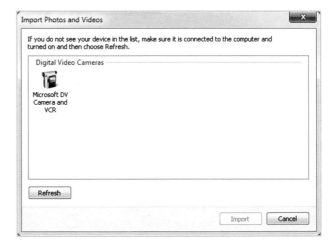

PREPARING TO MAKE A MOVIE

(Continued)

COMPONENT	RECOMMENDED HARDWARE
Video display card	Supports DirectX 9.0c, WDDM driver, Windows Aero, Pixel Shader 2.0, 32 bits/pixel, 128MB dedicated video memory or more
Video recording from DV camcorders	IEEE 1394 FireWire card, OHCI-compliant
Video capture from analog VCR/camera/TV	Windows 7–compatible video capture card
Audio capture from microphone, tape	Windows 7–compatible audio card and microphone

NOTES ON REQUIREMENTS

- Memory is most important. The more, the better.

- CPU capability is a close second in importance. To work with full-motion video, you need a lot of it. The minimum is really 2.4 MHz dual core.

- The initial capture of video from a camcorder to your computer can use approximately 12GB per hour captured in disk space.

- The video display card has become quite important to Windows Live Movie Maker. It will not work without the minimum shown in the table. See the Note on how to check this.

Continued . . .

- If you chose to import the entire video and your camcorder uses tape, it will be rewound, and then the capture will begin playing and importing the video without controls to pause, rewind, or fast-forward it. When the end of the video is reached, the importation will stop, the Import Video dialog box will close, and you will see a message telling you it is finished. Click **OK**.

–Or–

- If you chose to import portions of the video, the camcorder will not be rewound and you can use its controls to position the video. Also, you are given controls in the Import Video dialog box. Position the video in your camcorder to a little before where you want to start recording using either its controls or those in the Import Video dialog box, and click the **Stop** icon. Then, in the dialog box, click the **Play** icon. When you are at the spot you want to start importing, click **Import**. You can import some, stop it, reposition the video, and again click **Play** and **Import**. When you are done with the importation, click **Finish** to close the Import Video dialog box.

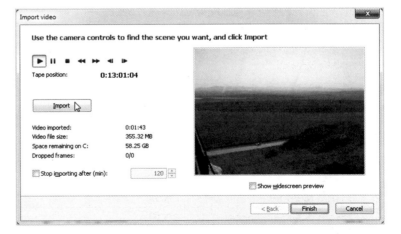

QUICKSTEPS

PREPARING TO MAKE A MOVIE

(Continued)

- With a digital video (DV) camcorder and an IEEE 1394 FireWire interface, get an Open Host Controller Interface (OHCI)–compliant FireWire card for your computer, if one isn't built in.

- A video capture card can bring in a video signal from a TV, a VCR, an analog camcorder, and (in most cases) a DV camcorder; however, the result is not as good as a digital recording.

TIP

It is better to import a longer video in smaller chunks or clips that you can then blend together into a movie.

NOTE

In Chapter 5, when I suggested you install Windows Live, Movie Maker was not selected by default so you may not have installed it at that time. Therefore, it may not be in your Windows Live list and you will need to go back to the Windows Live site and install it. See Chapter 5 for more information.

Windows Live Photo Gallery will show you where your video is stored. From either Photo Gallery or Windows Media Player, you can play the captured video by locating and double-clicking it.

Make a Movie

Making a movie out of the imported camcorder video and other material involves selecting and editing the available material; assembling it into the order in which you want it; adding narration, titles, and special effects; and finally publishing the finished product. Windows Live Movie Maker provides the means to do that. While working in Movie Maker, you are working on what Movie Maker calls a "project," which is a fluid collection of video clips, still pictures, titles, audio clips, narration, and special effects that you have added and laid out along a timeline. So long as you are in the project and have not published the movie, you can change almost anything. Projects can be saved and reopened for as long as you like.

To begin making a movie using the imported camcorder video and other material:

1. Click **Start**, click **All Programs**, and click **Windows Live Movie Maker**. Movie Maker opens with a new project tentatively named "My Movie." Start the project by adding content.

2. Click **Add Videos And Photos** in the Home tab Add group. In the Add Videos And Photos dialog box that appears, locate and select the video footage you want to work with, and click **Open**.

3. Repeat step 2, as shown in Figure 10-13, adding video footage, still pictures, and music (clicking **Add Music** in the Add group) that you want to use. Most audio, video, and picture file types are supported. When you have all the material you want, drag it around the content (right) pane until it is in the order that you want.

Figure 10-13: The process of making a movie entails selecting and editing video, audio, and still images.

You can continue to add, remove (right-click and click **Remove**), and rearrange elements in your project throughout its creation. You can also:

- **Trim** video clips
- **Add transitions** between pictures
- **Adjust the duration** for which a still image is shown
- **Add titles** to the video
- **Adjust the mix** between the sound on a video and the added music

TRIM VIDEO CLIPS

You can remove unwanted frames by *trimming*, or deleting, frames from the beginning or end of a video clip.

1. Select the video clip you want to trim.
2. Click the **Video Tools Edit** tab, and click **Trim Tool** in the Editing group. Trim Tool will appear superimposed upon the progress slider below the preview window.
3. If you want to trim the beginning of the clip, play the clip to the point at which you want to trim, and then drag the left trim handle to that point, dragging it back and forth until it is correctly placed.

4. To trim the right end of the clip, drag the right trim handle to the left until you get to the point where you want to trim off the rest of the clip.
5. When the trim handles are positioned at both ends where you want them, click **Save Trim** in the Trim tab's Trim group to save the trim positions and close the Trim operation.

ADD TRANSITIONS

When you bring in or drag a clip or a still image to the workspace, it simply abuts the preceding clip. The last frame of the preceding clip plays or a still image is displayed, and then the first frame of the new clip plays or the next still image is displayed. Movie Maker provides several transitions that you can add to smooth out the progression from one element to the next.

1. Click the rightmost clip or image of a pair where you want a transition.
2. Click the **Animations** tab, and click the transition you want to use. The focus will shift back to the left member of the pair so you can click the **Play** icon to see the transition.

TIP

While you are still working with a project and have not published the movie, you can think of trimming as simply "hiding" the ends of the clips. You can recover what you have trimmed until you publish the movie. Do this by selecting **Trim** and dragging the trim handles out to include more material.

ADJUST DURATION OF STILL IMAGES

By default, still images that are used in a movie are displayed for seven seconds. You can adjust this to anything from 1 to 30 seconds.

1. Select the still image whose duration you want to change.

2. Click the **Video Tools Edit** tab, click the **Duration** down arrow in the Adjust group, and click the duration (in seconds) you want to use.

ADD TEXT

Windows Live Movie Maker provides the means to add titles and text to movies you create. You have three choices of text that can be added from the Home tab Add group:

- **Title**, which is text in its own set of frames before the currently selected frame

- **Caption**, which is text that is displayed on the current set of frames or on a still photo

- **Credits**, which are added at the end of either a selected set of frames or still picture(s) and can have headings of "Credits," "Director," "Starring," and "Location," by clicking the down arrow

To add, for example, a caption:

1. Select the video or still image where you want the text, and in the Home tab Add group, click **Caption**. A text box with eight sizing handles will appear on the selected image with "[Enter text here]" selected, as you can see in Figure 10-14.

2. In the Text Tools Format tab, select the font, its size, whether it is bold and/or italic, and its color in the Font group, as well as the transparency and alignment within the text box in the Paragraph group.

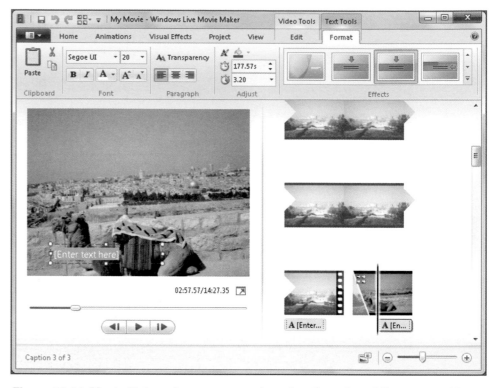

Figure 10-14: Movie Maker gives you a number of options for adding text and how that text is handled.

You can come back and edit the text later by reselecting the frames or still photos and double-clicking the text beneath it.

3. Type the text you want in the title. When you are finished, use the sizing handles to size the box to position the text. Press **SHIFT+ENTER** to create a line break.

4. Point on an edge of the text box to get a four-headed arrow, and then drag the text box to where you want it in the image.

5. Try out the various effects to see if you want to use any of them (too much can be annoying).

6. When you are ready, click another image to close the text box and leave the text.

ADD MUSIC

You can add background music to your video by including an existing music track.

1. In the Home tab Add group, click the **Add Music** icon (not the down arrow).

2. In the Windows Explorer window that opens, navigate to and double-click the music track you want to include. The Music Tools Options tab will appear and you'll see the music track appear above the frames over which it plays.

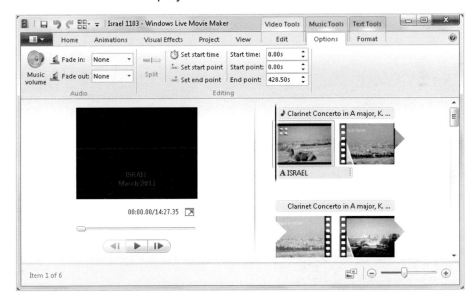

3. Click **Music Volume** and then drag the slider to adjust the volume. Click the **Fade In** or **Fade Out** down arrows, and select how you want the music to fade in and out. Similarly, set the **Start Time**, **Start Point**, and **End Point** by either entering the number in seconds or by clicking the **Set** commands and dragging the positioning bar in the clips.

MIX SOUND

After adding a music track, you have two soundtracks—one that was on the original video and one that you have added. By default, the volume level of both tracks is the same. You can adjust the relative level between the two soundtracks in the Project tab by clicking **Audio Mix**. The Mix slider will appear. Dragging the slider to the left increases the relative level of the video soundtrack; dragging it to the right increases the relative level of the music you have added. In both cases, the change is for the entire project. When you complete a change, close the slider by clicking anywhere below the slider.

Complete a Movie

The final step in making a movie is to create a movie file that you can upload to the Internet or output, either for a DVD or a portable device.

SAVE A MOVIE FILE

If you want to save your movie to replay on your computer or put it on a DVD:

1. In the Home tab, click the **Save Movie** down arrow, and review the choices for saving this movie, as shown in Table 10-1.

SETTING	DISPLAY	FILE SIZE/MINUTE
Recommended	640 × 480 pixels	50.98MB
High Definition	1440 × 1080 pixels	173.03MB
Burn A DVD	720 × 480 pixels	21.39MB
For Computer	640 × 480 pixels	40.71MB
For Email	320 × 240 pixels	11.97MB

Table 10-1: Settings for Saving a Movie

2. Click how you want to save the movie (the Recommended Setting is a good middle ground).

3. In the Save Movie dialog box that appears, select the drive and folder in which you want to save your movie, enter a name for it, and click **Save** (this will take several minutes).

   • With the DVD choice, Movie Maker will save the project, which may take a considerable amount of time if your video is of any length, and you will be told when it is complete.

4. Click **Open Folder** to open the folder in Windows Explorer that contains your new video. Leave this window open; you will be using it again in a minute.

SAVE A MOVIE TO DVD

With your new movie file, you can burn it onto a DVD, which you could also have done in the previous set of steps.

1. Click **Start**, click **All Programs**, and click **Windows DVD Maker**. If this is the first time you have used Windows DVD Maker, click **Choose Photos And Videos**.

2. Position the Windows DVD Maker window and the Windows Explorer window with your video so you can see them both.

EXPLORING WINDOWS MEDIA CENTER

With the right equipment, Windows Media Center allows you to view, record, and play back live TV. It also provides an enhanced playback and viewing experience with DVDs, CDs, and the music and photographic libraries you have on your computer. It connects you to web services from Microsoft and other vendors. Windows Media Center is available in Windows 7 Home Premium, Professional, Enterprise, and Ultimate editions.

To effectively use and get the full benefit from Windows Media, you need all the recommended computer components discussed in the "Preparing to Make a Movie" QuickSteps, and, if you want live TV, a TV tuner card in your computer and a connection to TV media. The tuner cards are available for moderate amounts from several companies. Look for compatibility with Windows Media Center.

To use Media Center:

1. Click **Start**, click **All Programs**, and click **Windows Media Center**. The first time you do that, you will go through an initial setup.

2. Click **Continue** and then click the **Express** arrow. Windows will look at the hardware that is available on your computer. If you have a TV tuner card, you will then need to click **Live TV Set Up**, and Media Center will be configured for the type of TV signal you have (antenna, cable, or satellite).

Continued . . .

3. Drag your video from Windows Explorer to DVD Maker. Type a name for the DVD title, and click **Next**.

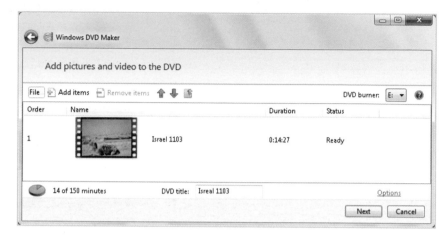

4. If you wish to see your video, click **Preview**, use the player controls, and when you are done, click **OK**. Review the text, customization, and style alternatives to add a menu to your DVD, including being able to select among multiple videos.

5. When you are ready, click **Burn**. Put a blank DVD in your drive, and the process will begin. It will take a bit of time, depending on how long your movie is and the speed of your computer and DVD drive.

6. When the DVD is created, it will be ejected from the drive and you'll be asked if you want to make another. Remove and label the disc using a soft felt-tip marker.

7. If you want to make another copy, click that option and insert another blank disc; otherwise, click **Close** and click **Close** again to close Windows DVD Maker. Click **Yes** to save your DVD project, enter a name, and click **Save**.

SHARE ON THE INTERNET

If you want, you can save your movie on the Internet.

1. In the Home tab Share group, click one of the Internet sites on which you want to save your video.

EXPLORING WINDOWS
MEDIA CENTER *(Continued)*

3. Then you will be asked questions about your ZIP code so that you can receive an online TV guide tailored to your local area. When you are done with the setup, you will see the main Media Center window shown in Figure 10-15.

At this point, you can use your mouse, the keyboard, or the TV remote control that came with your TV tuner card to navigate (move your mouse to see its controls) and watch TV, either in a window on your screen or in the default full screen. If you don't have a tuner card, you can play recorded TV. The possibilities of what you can do are significant.

TIP

Saving a movie is equivalent to printing a document: You still have the original content to rebuild the movie, but the movie itself can't be edited.

NOTE

Opening a *project* opens the media in Movie Maker, where it can be edited. Opening a *movie* sets it up for playback in Media Player or other video display programs and devices.

2. Depending on the site you select, you may have to register and enter an ID and password.

3. Follow the instructions to enter such things as a title, description, and other information. Movie Maker will then make the movie (a slow process), and it will be uploaded to the Internet. You will see a message when the process is complete.

Figure 10-15: The Windows Media Center brings live as well as recorded TV to your computer.

files. *See also* downloaded files (*cont.*)
   moving, 71
   recovering in Explorer, 68
   renaming in Explorer, 67
   searching for, 71–73
   selecting in Explorer, 67
   unzipping, 75
   writing to CD or DVD, 77–80
   zipping, 74
Filter Keys option, described, 50
Firefox browser, 181
firewall, setting up, 145–146
flash memory, explained, 5. *See also* memory
floating windows. *See also* windows
   left-aligning, 23
   right-aligning, 23
   vertically maximizing, 22
floppy drives, recognizing, 63
fly.com, comparison fares on, 105–106
folder sharing, setting, 144–149
folders
   adding in Favorites list, 91–92
   adding to SkyDrive, 221–223
   copying, 71
   creating in Explorer, 66–67
   deleting from SkyDrive, 225
   deleting in Explorer, 67
   filtering search results, 72
   listing in Explorer, 66
   moving, 71
   in navigation pane, 65
   opening, 11–13
   putting Favorites in, 92
   recovering in Explorer, 68
   renaming in Explorer, 67
   searching for, 71–73
   selecting in Explorer, 67
   sharing in SkyDrive, 223
   unzipping, 75

using for navigation, 65–66
writing to CD or DVD, 77–80
zipping, 74
Font group, character formats in, 234
fonts
   adding, 217–218
   defined, 217
   deleting, 218
Force Shut Down option, 170. *See also*
   Shut Down button
fragments, defined, 79

G

Gadgets feature, using, 55–56
Google Directions, using, 101–102
Google search, doing, 87, 97
government agencies, contacting, 98–100
grammar, checking in Word, 232–233

H

hard disk
   explained, 4–5
   exploring, 60
hardware, Plug and Play, 183
Help And Support, 13, 27
hidden icons, showing, 9. *See also* desktop icons
High Contrast option, described, 50
highlighting objects, 8
historical figures, searching, 94–96
history, deleting and setting, 91. *See also*
   Web History feature
History feature
   accessing, 88
   using, 90
home page
   changing, 88–90
   opening in tab, 88

HomeGroup folder sharing, using, 147–149
Hotmail account, establishing, 109. *See also*
   Windows Live Hotmail
HTML formatting, using with email, 119

I

icons. *See also* desktop icons; system icons
   adding to desktop, 37
   altering appearance of, 34
   displaying on desktop, 7, 9
   pinning to taskbar, 42–43, 45
IE (Internet Explorer). *See* Internet Explorer (IE)
images. *See* camera images; pictures
indexing, controlling, 169–170
InPrivate feature, opening, 160
integrated computers, 3
Internet. *See also* World Wide Web
   browsing, 85–86
   copying pictures from, 92
   copying text from, 92
   copying webpages from, 92–93
   getting information from, 94–96
   getting news from, 96–98
   searching historical figures, 94–96
Internet connections. *See also* connection types
   checking, 83–84
   setting up, 82–84
Internet Explorer (IE), 83–84
   controlling content, 160
   InPrivate feature, 160
   Internet Options, 160
   menus, 91
   searching Internet from, 86
Internet mail, requirement for, 83. *See also*
   email messages
Internet searches
   historical figures, 94–96
   from Internet Explorer, 86

mouse operations, performing, 8–9
mouse pointer, 7
    changing, 36
    using, 9
movie files, saving, 270–271
Movie Maker, using, 261, 264–270
movie making, preparing for, 262–263
movies. *See also* camcorder; video files
    adding captions, 267–268
    adding music to, 269
    adding text, 267
    adding transitions, 266
    adjusting duration of stills, 267
    making, 264–265
    mixing sound, 270
    saving display settings, 270
    sharing on Internet, 272–273
    trimming video clips, 266
    verifying support for, 261
Mozilla's Firefox browser, 181
multimedia, defined, 245
music
    adding to movies, 269
    copying, 255
    creating playlists, 255–256
    finding online, 251–252
    organizing in Media Player, 255–256
    Shuffle Music option, 259

N

Narrator option, described, 50
navigating Windows 7, 18
Navigation pane, 14
navigation pane, folders in, 65
Network and Sharing Center
    described, 144
    icon, 10
    using, 146–147

New Technology File System (NTFS),
    140–141
newsgroups
    account setup, 124–125
    initiating threads, 126–127
    posting messages in, 126–127
    reading messages in, 126–127
    responding to threads, 126–127
    subscribing to, 125
    unsubscribing from, 125
newsletters, reading, 97–98
newspapers, reading online, 97
Norton Internet Security, 158
Notepad program, using, 242
notification area, 7–8
    displaying system icons, 46
    features of, 9–10
    icons in, 10
notification icons, customizing, 46
NTFS (New Technology File System),
    140–141
numeric data
    entering in Excel, 238–239
    formatting in Excel, 238–239

O

object size, increasing, 33–34
objects
    altering appearance of, 34
    highlighting, 8
    moving, 9
    selecting, 8, 68
    in Windows Explorer, 58
On Screen Keyboard option, described, 50
operating system, explained, 6
optical disc, explained, 4
optical drives, inserting discs in, 5–6
option buttons, explained, 18

P

pages. *See* webpages
Paint program
    creating pictures in, 195
    using, 243
panes, turning on and off, 15
paragraphs, formatting, 235
Parental Controls, setting up, 142–143
password-protection, using, 156
passwords
    changing, 138, 140–141
    creating, 139–140
    removing, 141
    reset disks, 138–139
    strong type of, 141
    using, 138
Paste command, using, 73
Paste task, performing in Web Apps, 232
PCs (personal computers). *See also* computers
    desktop type of, 3
    integrated type of, 3
    portable type of, 2
PDF files, reading, 242–244
performance, monitoring, 168
Personalization window, displaying, 30
Personalize option, accessing, 18
Photo Gallery, 200–201. *See also* camera images
    importing video from camcorder, 262–264
    printing pictures, 208–210
    using, 199
Photos screensaver option, 36
pictures. *See also* camera images; Photo Gallery
    changing in Start menu, 41
    choosing for desktop, 30–31
    copying from Internet, 92
    creating, 195
    printing, 208–210
    saving, 195
    scanning, 196–197